Popular Music in Contemporary France

Berg French Studies

General Editor: John E. Flower

ISSN: 1345-3636

Popular Music in Contemporary France

Authenticity, Politics, Debate

David L. Looseley

Oxford • New York

First published in 2003 by
Berg
Editorial offices:
1st Floor, Angel Court, 81 St Clements Street, Oxford, OX4 1AW, UK
838 Broadway, Third Floor, New York, NY 10003–4812, USA

Berg is the imprint of Oxford International Publishers Ltd.

Library of Congress Cataloguing-in-Publication Data
A catalogue record for this book is available from the Library of Congress.

British Library Cataloguing-in-Publication Data
A catalogue record for this book is available from the British Library.

ISBN 1 85973 631 9 (Cloth)
       1 85973 636 X (Paper)

Typeset by JS Typesetting Ltd, Wellingborough, Northants
Printed in the United Kingdom by Biddles Ltd, Guildford and King's Lynn

To Avril, Rhiannon, my parents May and Len, and my sister
Jennifer Humble, amongst whose records I first encountered
French popular music in the 1960s

Contents

Acknowledgements

I am pleased to acknowledge the help of the Arts and Humanities Research Board and the University of Leeds in funding a year's research leave for this project, and the assistance of a wide range of people in its preparation and completion. I am indebted to the following French academics and others involved in music or policy, who have variously provided documentation, information or interviews: Jean-Rémy Abélard, Marie-Agnès Beau (French Music Bureau, UK), Olivier Donnat, Antoine Hennion, Fred Hidalgo (*Chorus*), Didier Martin (Martin Musique, La Flèche), Monique Massé, Frédérique Mauduit (Ministry of Culture), Pierre Mayol (Ministry of Culture), André Ménage, Xavier Migeot, Philippe Poirrier, Jacques Rigaud, Anna-Michèle Schneider (Ministry of Culture), and particularly Patrick Mignon and Philippe Teillet for their time and patience. Special thanks go to my friends Guy Groulay, Jocelyn Termeau, Nelly Termeau and Michel Varache, for the multiple benefits of their personal knowledge, record collections, linguistic advice and hospitality.

I would also like to say thanks to friends and colleagues in the French Department at the University of Leeds, where since 1994 I have found a remarkably congenial and supportive working environment. I am especially grateful to David Roe and Christopher Todd, who year after year have taken the time to look out for and supply press and audiovisual sources. Susan Dolamore and Jim House have also been a great help in this regard and Nigel Armstrong, Marie-Anne Hintze and Kamal Salhi have provided some valuable linguistic advice. Thanks to David Platten and Max Silverman, whose generosity in sharing courses and ideas of a cultural nature has made an important intellectual contribution to the book, while David's other life as guitarist and recording artist has proved useful. Both have also kindly read parts of the book in draft, as has Kim Harrison. Susan Miller, musician with Charanga del Norte, and Angela Griffith of Greenhead College Huddersfield have advised me on music terminology. I also much appreciated the help of French studies colleagues Jeremy Ahearne (Warwick), Peter Hawkins (Bristol) and Chris Tinker (Heriot-Watt); and am indebted to the following students, undergraduate and postgraduate, for their ideas, documentary help and enthusiasm: Abbie Boak, Helen Charles-Edwards, Sharon Dickinson, Helen Easter, Eleanor Edwards, Kim Harrison, Evan Hughes, Zebi Jackson, Rachel Jenkins, Eleanor Moore, Jonathan Sewell and all the members of my special-subject groups over the years.

Lastly, thanks to my daughter Rhiannon, who has helped me keep one foot in contemporary music, the other in contemporary France and, with her dry humour and sharp intelligence, both feet firmly on the ground; and to my wife Avril, for reading, discussing and everything.

The epigraph to Part I is taken from Bernard Lavilliers's song 'Noir et blanc', published by Big Brother Company and released by Barclay on the singer's 1980 album *Voleur de feu* (CD no. 029 042 2). Thanks to the French Music Bureau (UK) for assistance regarding permission to reproduce.

French Abbreviations

BIPE   Bureau d'information et de prévisions économiques (Bureau for Economic Information and Forecasting)

CENAM   Centre national d'animation musicale (National Centre for Music Animation)

CIR   Centre d'information du rock (Rock Information Centre; now part of IRMA)

CNC   Centre national de la cinématographie (National Cinema Centre, Ministry of Culture)

CNCL   Commission nationale de la communication et des libertés (National Commission for Communication and Liberties; forerunner of CSA)

CSA   Conseil supérieur de l'audiovisuel (Higher Audiovisual Council; the national regulatory body for broadcasting since 1989)

DDC   Direction du développement culturel (Directorate for Cultural Development, Ministry of Culture)

DDF   Délégation au développement et aux formations (Delegation for Development and Training; successor to the DDC)

DEP   Département des études et de la prospective (Department for Studies and Forecasting, Ministry of Culture; formerly the SER)

DMD   Direction de la musique et de la danse (Directorate for Music and Dance, Ministry of Culture)

FAIR   Fonds d'action et d'initiative rock (Action and Initiative Fund for Rock)

FLIP   Force de libération et d'intervention pop (Pop Liberation and Intervention Force)

FLJ   Front de libération de la jeunesse (Youth Liberation Front)

FN   Front national (National Front)

FNAC   Fédération nationale d'achat des cadres (Executives' National Purchasing Federation; nation-wide chain selling books, records and photographic materials)

HEC   École des hautes études commerciales (School of Advanced Business Studies)

IFCIC   Institut pour le financement du cinéma et des industries culturelles (Institute for the Financing of Cinema and the Cultural Industries)

IRCAM   Institut de recherche et coordination acoustique/musique (Institute for Music/Acoustic Research and Coordination)

IRMA   Centre d'information et de ressources pour les musiques actuelles (Information and Resource Centre for Present-Day Musics)

MIDEM   Marché international du disque, de l'édition musicale, de l'équipement et de la vidéo-musique (International Market for Records, Music Publishing, Equipment and Music-Video; annual trade fair)

MJC   Maisons des jeunes et de la culture (Houses of Youth and Culture; a national network of youth centres begun after the Liberation)

ORTF   Office de la radiodiffusion-télévision française (French Radio and Television Office; French broadcasting body, broken up in 1974)

PCF   Parti communiste français (French Communist Party)

PS   Parti socialiste français (French Socialist Party)

RMC   Radio Monte-Carlo

RTF   Radio-Télévision française (forerunner of ORTF)

SACEM   Société des auteurs, compositeurs et éditeurs de musique (Society of Music Authors, Composers and Publishers; copyright and royalties organisation)

SER   Service des études et de la recherche (Studies and Research Service; now the DEP)

SMAC   Scènes de musiques actuelles (Present-Day Music Stages)

TNP   Théâtre national populaire (the National People's Theatre; set up in Paris under Jean Vilar in 1951 to bring theatre to a wider audience)

TUC   Travaux d'utilité collective (Community Service Employment; for the young unemployed)

Introduction

In the European concert of musical nations, France remains absent: since at least Lully, it has been accepted that the French are not musical, or even music-loving [. . .]. It is true that the French language does not naturally encourage expression in the form of sound, that Cartesianism rejects arty vagueness but has not for all that created forms which are guaranteed to last. Furthermore, discourse on music easily exceeds the music itself, giving rise to more literature, debate, controversy and polemics than would seem reasonable. And yet, for the last twenty years or so, the situation has been evolving faster and more profoundly than in the preceding three centuries.

> Maurice Fleuret, Director of Music at the
> Ministry of Culture (1981–6), 1989[1]

At 1 a.m. on 19 February 2001, the French singer-songwriter Charles Trenet, who had started in show-business in the early 1930s, died in hospital at the age of eighty-seven. The media swiftly went into overdrive, with special editions, supplements, phone-ins and recollections. President Chirac spoke gravely to the nation and party leaders were solicited for a reaction or a snatch of song. The same panoply of remembrance was deployed for the tenth anniversary of Serge Gainsbourg's death less than a month later, for George Brassens's twentieth the following October, and when Gilbert Bécaud died in December. The frequency and intensity of such displays, harking back to the mourning of Piaf in 1963, seem to confirm the special place *la chanson française* reputedly has in French public life. Yet they do not entirely chime with the equally common depiction that Fleuret alludes to, of France as the permanent absentee at the 'concert' of Europe's 'musical nations'. This book is in part an attempt to make sense of this paradox.

Chanson itself, however, is not my primary concern, though it is certainly part of it. In my view, the recent change of attitude which Fleuret detects in France – its unexpected arrival at the concert – is inseparable from the naturalisation which has taken place there of Anglo-American styles of pop music. My purpose, then, is twofold. It is to trace the history of this naturalisation – its musical, industrial, social and political ramifications; and to analyse the discourses and debates it has generated, the different ways in which it has been written about and argued over in the public sphere since 1958, the start of the Fifth Republic. How, for example, has France reacted to pop's internationalism, or to its cheerful indifference to the supposedly universal standards of aesthetic excellence by which 'Culture' has traditionally been judged there? This is a multi-faceted saga, telling of the legitimation of an imported music perceived as alien, of the development of a modern domestic music industry and new social patterns of taste, of a remarkable U-turn in government thinking on the subject. And inevitably it is the tale of the relationship between this musical cuckoo and the native species I evoked above, epitomised by Trenet and the others and imprecisely known as *la chanson française*.

Problematic though this term is, I do not want at this juncture to linger on the nicer distinctions between '*chanson*', 'popular music' and 'pop music', particularly as, with such contemporary phenomena, meanings are seldom stable. Not only have they stretched or shifted over the years, in both French and English, but the sub-generic lexis in French, though borrowed from English – *le rock, le punk, le rap, la techno, le funky, le hard* – does not always carry the same connotations; nor is there even much consensus on what exactly those connotations are. For convenience, then, my strategy will be as follows. I shall use the term 'popular music' to embrace all the musical forms conventionally distinguished from 'classical' – pop, jazz, folk, *chanson*, and so on (the layered meanings of '*chanson*' being explored as the book progresses). I shall use the term 'pop music' (or just 'pop') more narrowly, as shorthand for all the commercially produced forms of popular music identified with Western youth from the mid-1950s. Pop in this loose generic sense was once called *le yéyé* in French, then *la pop* or *la pop-music*, and now – no more precisely or reliably – *le rock*. These names all refer to the types of mass-produced music deriving to some degree from that American fusion of black and white popular styles which gave birth to rock'n'roll in the mid-1950s, widely considered to have begun commercially with Elvis Presley, Chuck Berry, Sam Phillips of Sun Records, and a handful of others. Since then, constantly adapted, recycled and overwritten yet still deriving from the syncopated rhythm of rock'n'roll in some respect, these styles have spread throughout the world, affecting the musical, cultural and social lives of diverse communities and nations, particularly among the young.

On a more theoretical level, I am especially interested in this ongoing process of *naming* pop music in France. I share the political scientist Philippe Teillet's view that *le rock* is actually a discursive artefact, which 'only exists through a discourse (history, criticism, news) of which it is the object and which shapes it'.[2] Naming pop therefore becomes an important epistemological and even ideological matter, whose manifestations I shall examine as and when they occur, since I believe they indicate moments at which some form of discursive conflict has taken place. The difficulty of naming thus reveals that there is more at stake in debates about popular music than simply industrial, economic or even aesthetic issues. In some profound sense, they are also debates about national integrity.

In the rest of this introduction, I want to spell out my approach by addressing three questions that it raises. Why examine French popular music in the public sphere, as a social rather than an aesthetic phenomenon? Why pop rather than the more prestigious *chanson*? And why discourse and debate? I shall also give a brief explanation of the book's structure.

Why in the public sphere? Because I want to argue that since the 1960s popular music has become ever more implicated in French political life and civil society. The cultural kudos enjoyed by the Mitterrand regime (1981–95) derived in part from its engagement with the musical tastes of what became known as 'the Mitterrand generation'. When the President finally left the Elysée Palace in May 1995, a commemorative compilation of hits was released entitled *Les Années Mitterrand* (The Mitterrand Years), most of them related to anti-racism or multiculturalism. Its cover showed Mitterrand from the back, in his once-familiar wide-brimmed hat (an ephemeral homage to his Socialist predecessor Léon Blum), walking away with quiet dignity. Much of public radio's all-day coverage of his death the following January was devoted to singers and songs connected with his presidency. Such affective associations are not, of course, peculiar to France. In the UK after Diana's death in 1997, many who watched the funeral declared that its most moving moment had been Elton John's awkwardly rewritten 'Candle in the Wind'. As a counter-example, the attack on the World Trade Centre in September 2001 prompted Clear Channel, the world's largest radio network, to list over 150 records which it advised its stations not to play because of the potentially sensitive nature of their lyrics. So why France particularly?

As Fleuret intimates, France in the Fifth Republic has undergone a step-change in its relationship with music, after years of assuming it was not a musical but a literary nation, devoted to print. This change is a matter not just of a boom in listening, singing and playing, which has taken place in other Western countries, but of what has more dramatically been called a 'musical-isation' of French society.[3] New technologies and consumer capitalism have brought music into its homes, its towns and cities, its factories, shops, lifts and banks. Amateur music-making is flourishing as never before, and the government has even launched an annual 'Fête de la musique' (a street festival of music) to celebrate the change. 'The post-modern individual', writes Gilles Lipovetsky, 'is hooked up to music from morning until night, it is as if he [*sic*] needs always to be somewhere else, to be transported and enveloped in an ambiance of syncopation.'[4] The suddenness of this post-modernisation where France is concerned, which, as Lipovetsky's allusion to syncopation hints, mostly concerns popular rather than classical music, makes it a particularly revealing case study.

Yet although there has been a remarkable surge in popular-music studies in 'Anglo-Saxon' countries, this has not happened to the same extent in France, even though much of the theoretical apparatus which is used for the purpose originated there. French popular music, offering a complete spectrum from the most derivative pop to the poetic *chanson* and modern jazz, is arguably as rich a seam for academic study as French cinema, an art similarly born of the industrial age. The conflicts between art and industry which both film and popular music engender have also taken particularly intriguing forms in France, where the preservation of 'French' cultural values has long been a preoccupation. But while Anglophone and Francophone scholars have researched French cinema for decades in all its dimensions, relatively little work has been done on contemporary or recent popular music in France, in either English or French. I do not pretend to fill this void but I want at least to make a start.

This does not, however, tell us why French pop specifically is worth examining, especially when few in the English-speaking world would think of it as having distinguished itself in its forty-year history, whereas the mercurial talents of some *chanson* stars – Piaf, Aznavour, Brel (a Belgian who made his career in France) – have given them iconic status at home and abroad. Viewed from the outside, France's pop music over the last four decades, especially when televised, has often looked frivolous, sounded tacky and been steadfastly derided. As Philip Sweeney of *The Sunday Times* commented perfectly accurately in 1996, 'musical frog-bashing is a perennial pleasure among Anglo-Saxon commentators'; and he instanced the verdict of Brian Appleyard that 'one hundred per cent of French pop is awful'.[5] So why not study *chanson* instead? There are several reasons. First, French pop has been studied less than *chanson*, though neither has been studied very much.[6] Second, it has actually been transformed since 1960 and views like Appleyard's have been redundant for a number of years. Third and most important, my aim is precisely to study French pop in relation to *chanson* since they are ultimately inseparable. They are, however, quite plainly distinguished discursively, and not only by Anglophone writers like Appleyard.

This also helps explain my particular interest in discourse and debate. Part of the justification is provided by Fleuret's contention that public discourse on music plays a bigger role in French musical life than music itself. More specifically, Peter Hawkins speaks of 'the special status of *chanson* as a national institution, as almost a defining characteristic of French culture'. Nevertheless, he goes on, *chanson* has a 'paradoxical status: a cult form of expression, part of the national popular heritage, but barely recognised officially; a popular institution with typically French characteristics, but one which is not taken seriously by at least some of the nation's intelligentsia'.[7] These representations of *chanson*, which Hawkins rightly points up, tell only half the story, however. For while *chanson* is indeed low on the cultural state's agenda, pop has moved up considerably, having been recognised and supported by the Ministry of Culture since 1981, after years of neglect.

What exactly does this switch at government level mean? For some fundamentalists, who object violently to the whole idea, it means that officially the popular is now as much part of French culture as the classical. For others, it means that *chanson* is being undervalued. For a third group, it means that cultural policy is at last becoming democratic. These diverse interpretations have considerable bearing on national constructions of culture. As Paul Rutten writes of Dutch music policy: 'The meanings attached to cultural artefacts which circulate in society are in no way "naturally" connected to the cultural objects. They are the outcome of social and cultural battles over meaning. The music policy debate should be conceived of as an arena where a battle over the meaning of musical genres is fought.'[8] Exploring some of these 'battles' in the French context is a central purpose of this book.

To reflect these preoccupations, the book is divided into two parts. The first provides a history of French pop and its sub-genres since 1958 (Chapters 2 and 3), set against a briefer overview of popular music generally in France since the nineteenth century (Chapter 1) and an analysis of responses to pop from the French music world and the intelligentsia (Chapters 4 and 5). The second part is devoted to the responses of the state particularly, before 1981 (Chapter 6) and since (Chapters 7 and 8). I am especially interested here in the ways both pop and policy have been conceptualised and debated (Chapters 9 and 10).

I have separated the musical and political histories in this way for two reasons. On a practical level, I hope the research will be of interest to a varied readership, from those specialising in French studies, cultural studies and popular music, to those working on or in cultural policy and European politics. I have often been struck by how both French popular music and the French model of cultural policy illuminate many issues in cultural studies and policy analysis, and yet how sketchily they are known in much of the English-speaking world. With this in mind, I have tried to strike a balance in both parts between tracing a history (largely uncharted) and analysing a debate, though I make no attempt at an exhaustive survey of either the music industry or the music-policy process. I do, though, provide a little more explanatory detail than might normally be expected of a French studies series, for those less familiar with France and its history, and I translate all French terminology and quotations into English or use published translations where available.

The second reason is that pop's recognition by government has, I believe, been an extremely significant episode not only in the history of French cultural policy – 'the most visible and controversial of the sectors to which the Ministry of Culture extended official recognition after 1981', according to Kim Eling[9] – but also in the history of French popular music itself; even perhaps the *most* significant episode in the last quarter-century or so. The two parts of the book are in fact conjoined by a concern with the steady legitimation of pop, which, I suggest, has only achieved full citizenship with its recognition by the state, partial and problematic though this has been. The legitimation process also raises an important theoretical issue which runs through both parts of the book: the nature and definition of 'authenticity' in French popular music.

Notes

1. Quoted in Anne Veitl and Noémi Duchemin, *Maurice Fleuret: une politique démocratique de la musique 1981–1986* (Comité d'histoire du Ministère de la culture, 2000), p. 347. Complete references to all works cited are given in the Bibliography.
2. Philippe Teillet, 'Une Politique culturelle du rock?', in Patrick Mignon and Antoine Hennion (eds), *Rock: de l'histoire au mythe* (Anthropos, 1991), p. 218.
3. Marc Touché, 'Où suis-je? Qui suis-je? Dans quel état j'erre?', downloaded article extracted from Touché, *Mémoire vive* (Édition Association Musiques Amplifiées, 1998).
4. *L'Ere du vide: essais sur l'individualisme contemporain* (Gallimard/Folio, 1983), p. 33.
5. Philip Sweeney, 'Le Sound Barrier', *The Sunday Times*, 11 February 1996, 'The Culture' supplement, p. 14.
6. The dearth where *chanson* at least is concerned has recently been addressed by Peter Hawkins's excellent monograph: *Chanson: The French Singer-Songwriter from Aristide Bruant to the Present Day* (Ashgate, 2000).
7. Ibid., p. 6.
8. 'Popular Music Policy: A Contested Area – The Dutch Experience', in Tony Bennett, Simon Frith, Lawrence Grossberg, John Shepherd and Graeme Turner (eds), *Rock and Popular Music: Politics, Policies, Institutions* (Routledge, 1993), p. 40.
9. *The Politics of Cultural Policy in France* (Macmillan, 1999), p. 128.

PART I

Defining Authenticity

De n'importe quel pays, de n'importe quelle couleur
La musique est un cri qui vient de l'intérieur

(Bernard Lavilliers, 'Noir et blanc')

– 1 –

Popular Music before 1958

The history of popular music in France since 1958 is inseparable from the histories of youth culture and the cultural industries. All three raise issues about French conceptions of art and culture, behind which lies a further connoted issue: authenticity.

This is a slippery term whose meaning is constantly renegotiated and therefore, to borrow the word Richard Peterson uses in the context of country music, 'fabricated'. That is, as Peterson puts it, 'authenticity is not inherent in the object or event that is designated authentic but is a socially agreed-upon construct'. Nevertheless, authenticity is also, as Roy Shuker notes, a 'central concept in the discourses surrounding popular music, [. . .] with considerable symbolic value'. And this, in my view, is particularly true of France. In what Shuker calls 'its common-sense usage', authenticity in popular music (and in pop particularly) means artistic integrity. It 'assumes that the producers of music texts undertook the "creative" work themselves; that there is an element of originality or creativity present, along with connotations of seriousness, sincerity, and uniqueness'. Beyond this, Shuker goes on, authenticity is defined by a series of dichotomies: 'creativity' or 'self-expression' is supposedly more authentic than manufactured commercialism; the independent sector is more authentic than the majors; live performance more authentic than recorded, and so on. Further binaries are added if one looks at the uses to which popular music is put in specific communities or subcultures. Here, for example, community music is more authentic than globalised, mass music. In all of these dichotomies, there is an assumption that, as Shuker puts it, 'commerce dilutes, frustrates, and negates artistic aspects of the music'.[1] This assumption may be unexamined and questionable, but it is none the less fundamental to the culture and ideology of contemporary popular music. This is particularly true of French popular music, as I shall attempt to show, though here the assumption is overlaid with another, which is that authenticity also has to do with popular music's organic, historic connection with a people. In this additional sense, which one might describe as *national* authenticity, a music is genuinely 'popular' when it is born of, 'natural' to and expressive of a national community. Over the last half-century, the French cultural establishment has experienced considerable difficulty tolerating the industrialisation, commodification and globalisation of the arts in general and of music in particular, processes which pop is assumed to have introduced into France from abroad, or at the very least exacerbated. Artists, intellectuals and culture workers have often adopted an Adornian pessimism in this regard and in recent years have mounted a last-ditch resistance in the name of a 'French cultural exception', to which the notion of national authenticity is, I suggest, fundamental.

Succinctly summarised by the cultural economist Joëlle Farchy, French cultural exceptionalism is the conviction that 'books, films and musical works are not run-of-the-mill goods which can be abandoned to the laws of the free market'.[2] When unpacked with the help of economic theory, Farchy goes on, this conviction implies that the exchange value of a cultural good can only be measured by means of a 'convention of originality', that is, by what the market conventionally considers 'original'; and originality, in art markets generally, is gauged according to three criteria. The first is authenticity, which here means that a work of art must be produced by an artist alone, with as little division of labour as possible. The second is that the work must be unique so that reproductions of it are considered of lesser value. The third is newness (*nouveauté*), according to which a work of art's value is judged in relation to art history.[3]

To be effective, the convention of originality requires the sacralisation of the artist, who is distinguished from the artisan or engineer because he or she is driven to make a 'product' only by his or her inspiration, not by public demand or according to a set of pre-existing specifications resulting from market research.[4] This model of the artist as solitary, inspired and, therefore, exceptional goes back to the Renaissance but still underpins Adorno's critique of mass culture in the twentieth century. However, the rise of cultural technologies since the late nineteenth century – and especially of information technologies in the late twentieth – clearly challenges it, blurring the time-honoured line between art and industry. Huge advances in music reproduction, from the shellac 78 rpm record through vinyl, cassettes and CDs to MP3, mean that it is now impossible to make untroubled distinctions between an original and a copy, a work of art and its commodity value. New creative media have sprung up which are industrially reproducible by nature not adoption, like cinema and television, which have never had pre-industrial forms. Music may at first appear to be a different case since it existed before industrialisation, so that it is susceptible of being represented as disfigured by recording. But this representation is anachronistic. High-performance sound-reproduction technologies mean that the record, rather than being an intruder in the relationship between music and listener, is a participant, no less integral to the history and nature of popular music than the music hall or other live venue.

In recorded music as in film, then, the notion of the solitary artist is problematic. In the production of a master tape, the creative source is rarely singular. It includes the person or team who wrote the song, the singer or group who performs it, the arranger, producer and sound engineer. Even though Paul McCartney wrote 'Yesterday' alone, then sang and played guitar on the original studio session with none of the other Beatles present, it was still George Martin who suggested adding a string quartet and helped make it what it was. Then, once the master tape has left the studio, there are the packaging and image designers and, since the 1970s, those who produce the video. Of course, all of these interventions make for high production costs, which mean that profitability is crucial, in a market where all records cost roughly the same (however much is spent making them), where sales are unpredictable, and where outlay is often higher than return given that as many as 80 per cent of album releases may fail to break even.[5]

The cultural industries, then, wed art to industry. Alfred Hitchcock once described the creative paradox of the film director as that of a painter given canvas, brushes and palette worth 1.3 million dollars and allowed to paint anything at all as long as it brings in 2.3 million dollars.[6] It is this endemic contradiction which has placed popular music at the heart of cultural debate in France. This is true of other countries too, but in France it has taken a particularly intense and fascinating form because cultural values have for centuries been high on the national agenda. Throughout the twentieth century but particularly since the Second World War, the growth of a local music industry dependent on technologies and styles which have become global, with the USA at their core, has been seen as jeopardising the French cultural exception. It is the historical background to this conflict which I want to trace in this first chapter.

The Making of a Modern Music Industry

In the early 1950s, Pierre Delanoë, a civil servant, began writing songs with Gilbert Bécaud in his spare time. Indirectly, this was to lead to Delanoë's becoming a founder member of the radio station Europe 1 and eventually the administrator of the performing rights organisation, the SACEM. Looking back in the 1990s on the start of this second career, he observes that the music business he encountered then was much as it had been a century before when the SACEM had been created in 1851. Born in 1918, he remembers that street singers were still common in his childhood, particularly in the Montmartre area between Barbès and Clichy, at funfairs, and even in blocks of flats, where a singer would pass from one courtyard to another and coins would be thrown down wrapped in paper by appreciative tenants.[7] On street corners, sheet-music specially annotated for singing (known as '*petits formats*' since the nineteenth century) would be sold so the crowd could join in. Although by the start of the 1950s the street singers had mostly disappeared, sheet-music was still the core of the music economy, more so than the 78 rpm, which was expensive and fragile. The first song Delanoë wrote with Bécaud, 'Mes mains' (My Hands), was premiered by a pre-war singer, Lucienne Boyer, at her farewell concert. The public instantly began buying the sheet-music, published by Beuscher, and a million copies were sold. In the offices of the big music publishers like Beuscher – or Salabert, Semi, Raoul Breton – a fledgling lyricist could pair up with a fledgling composer and meet established stars like Piaf, Luis Mariano, Georges Guétary or Yves Montand on the look-out for new material. They could have a song accepted for publication, sign a contract and receive an advance of perhaps 10,000 old francs while the firm tried to place their work. A music publisher could also help launch the careers of new artists, as had been the case with Trenet and Charles Aznavour, who were both indebted to Raoul Breton for their success. Aznavour would eventually buy the company to prevent it falling into foreign hands.

In the early 1950s, then, the publishing house was a place of encounter, exchange and transaction, one of the key sites in which popular-musical culture functioned. Soon, however, all of this was swept away. 'Mes mains' proved to be Delanoë's last big-selling *petit format*, as the old publishing houses closed or were bought out, so that by the mid-1990s, only Beuscher and Raoul Breton remained fully French. The French music industry was in fact transformed from the late 1950s by the steady adoption of American commercial practices, at the root of which was vinyl.

French popular song grew out of an anonymous oral tradition going back to the troubadours of the Middle Ages. But the phenomenon of named individuals singing and writing songs, and of people coming together in specific places to hear them, is much more recent and brought dramatic change. As the *chanson* specialist Louis-Jean Calvet notes, the song form has always evolved in keeping with the places in which songs have been performed.[8] Calvet traces this process back to 1734 with the beginning of the *caveaux*, song clubs which met in back rooms of upmarket restaurants where members would eat, drink and sing topical satires set to familiar melodies. The *caveaux*'s working-class equivalents were the *goguettes*, which developed after the restoration of the monarchy in 1815 and of which there were several hundred in Paris by the mid-1800s. The *goguettes* too were clubs for amateur singers and songsmiths, who met regularly in wine shops, cafés and drinking houses to sing either their members' latest creations (again using existing melodies) or the songs of well-known singers like Béranger (1780–1857). Initially associated with popular opposition to the restoration of the monarchy in 1815, the *goguettes* were ideal sites for *agents provocateurs* to entrap dissident Bonapartists; some, like La Société des patriotes, were even started up by police informers for that purpose.[9] Later, under the July Monarchy of 1830, the politics of the *goguettes* became republican, though regular police harassment together with public demand for entertainment and a quiet life meant that many were involved in nothing more seditious than social drinking and bawdy singing. Nevertheless, the oppositional culture of the *goguette* was to produce two of the best-known political lyricists of the nineteenth century: Eugène Pottier (1816–87), who wrote the words of the 'Internationale', and Jean-Baptiste Clément (1836–1903), who in 1867 penned the lyric of the famous 'Le Temps des cerises' (The Time of Cherries), which was to become associated with the popular uprising of the Paris Commune of 1871, in which both writers took part. The *goguettes* in fact became cradles of class consciousness and socialism, where disaffected workers, artisans and traders 'learnt to suffer and hate together'.[10]

From these roots is derived the modern representation of the *chanson* as a viscerally oppositional form: left-wing or even anarchist, gritty and participative, 'authentic'. Authentic in what sense? Although Claude Duneton prefers the term 'popular', he implicitly answers this question in his monumental history of pre-twentieth-century *chanson*: 'The *goguettes* of the July Monarchy were the great source of the popular song, that is, of the song born among the people and sung by the entire nation; they encouraged in the French their habit of writing saucy verses counterbalancing the tendency to the easily maudlin, the clumsy outpourings of a bourgeoisie wallowing in Romanticism.'[11] *Chanson's* authenticity, then, stems from its being the voice of popular France, expressive of a national mindset of down-to-earth, irreverent, common sense rather than middle-class gush; the voice in fact of civil society.

Following the revolution of 1848, a decree passed under Napoleon III in 1852 banned public meetings which did not have police authorisation. This helped bring about the demise of both *caveaux* and *goguettes*, assisted by two further institutional turning points. One was the creation of the SACEM in 1851, which applied to musical performance the principle of copyright already applicable in the theatre. Once songwriters were remunerated for public renditions of their work, there was the prospect of regular earnings from writing and composing. This also encouraged lyricists to write their own melodies and double their money, or to team up with a composer as Delanoë did. The other turning point came in March 1867 with the lifting of a ban on performance with costumes and props in drinking establishments, originally imposed under pressure from theatre managers who feared competition. Had the ban remained in force, even the familiar cane and boater of Maurice Chevalier, who began his career in such establishments in 1899, would have been prohibited.[12]

These proved to be major changes, as popular song was steadily professionalised and commercialised. While wealthier Parisians listened to Offenbach on the *grands boulevards*, new 'cabarets' appeared, cheaper and less salubrious watering holes where it became customary to pay to hear specific singers, the best known of whom was Aristide Bruant (1851–1925) at Le Mirliton, formerly the famous Le Chat noir in Montmartre, who sang in naturalist vein about the excluded living in the slum belt of Paris known as the 'zone'.[13] More commercial were the *cafés-concerts*, or *caf'conc'*, which started during the Second Empire and became a celebrated feature of *belle époque* Paris. The *caf'conc'* marked the beginning of the process by which the singer would become a star, and the star a commodified icon marked out by extravagant clothing, demeanour and lifestyle; the beginning in fact of popular music as a mass culture.[14]

At the start of the twentieth century, there were some 150 *cafés-concerts* in Paris alone. However, they in turn had vanished by the end of the First World War, giving way to the more spectacular English-style music halls, which had reached Paris in the mid-to-late nineteenth century: legendary establishments like Les Folies-Bergère (1869), Le Casino de Paris (1890), Bobino (1880) and L'Olympia (1893). What distinguished the music halls was that they were entirely for professional performance. Whereas in cabarets and even *cafés-concerts*, customers came to drink and carouse, in the music halls there were no beverages and customers were physically demarcated as an audience by a stage. Another difference was that the show consisted of a range of variety acts as well as singers: jugglers, comics, dancers, and so on. Hence the use of the term *variétés* (as in *chanson de variétés*) to distinguish styles of music that in English might be described as easy listening, intended primarily as commercial entertainment. The rise of the *café-concert* and the music hall inspired the Hollywood myth of a supposedly authentic Parisian nightlife, of the Moulin rouge (1889), Pigalle and Montmartre. In reality, however, their rise marks the transformation of French popular song from craft into product. The more informal cabarets did not cease to exist, but the two types of venue purveyed two types of song.

Despite the imposition of swingeing taxes on box-office receipts after the Great War,[15] the 1920s were the apogee of the French music halls and the colourful 'revues' associated with them, like Mistinguett's *Paris qui danse* and *Ça, c'est Paris*. But they were laid low at the height of their success by the advent of radio, records and sound in movies. Audiences began to tail off and many halls closed or were converted into cinemas, as the Olympia was in 1928. Even so, French popular music had become a thriving business by the 1920s. The confluence of new measures with new media, from copyright and the *café-concert* to records, radio and films, created the hit song and the multi-talented singing star, epitomised in Maurice Chevalier, who combined stage, screen and recording careers at home and abroad. These were good times too for the successful songwriter, whose songs might now be performed on an industrial scale and bring previously unimaginable income. In the first decades of the twentieth century, Paris enjoyed a reputation as the European centre of international live music of all kinds. Stravinsky, Rakhmaninov and Bartók lived there for a time, Diaghilev's Russian Ballet made its mark there with Stravinsky's *Rite of Spring* in 1913, and popular venues like the Moulin rouge and the Folies-Bergère enjoyed world renown.

However, neither the cultural nor the economic benefits of sound technology were unequivocal. From the Great War, the country's international influence began to decline and it was forced into a defensive posture as America came to dominate both record and film industries. Although experiments with sound recording were taking place in the 1850s, the real history of the record industry begins in the mid-1890s with the marketing of Emile Berliner's gramophone.[16] Rapidly, the company set up in London to exploit the invention, the Gramophone Company and its US subsidiaries, developed a catalogue of music and comedy recorded on 78 rpm discs. International competition then set in as other record companies sprang up in Europe and North America which adopted the technology, including the Société Pathé Frères in France, initially involved in both cinema and recorded music. The international landscape of the record industry was transformed again in the 1930s when the Depression, coupled with competition from radio (which for a time could reproduce live music better than the record could), created its first slump. Concentration began, producing four dominant international players, known today as majors: EMI in the UK (1931) and Decca (1929), RCA Victor (1929) and CBS (1939) in the USA. Struggling financially, Pathé's record division was eliminated in the restructuring, bought out by EMI. By 1939, then, the balance of artistic and economic influence had shifted in favour of London and the USA. France's absence from the world stage then became irreversible in the post-war period. Those already on the scene in 1950 were better placed to benefit from the next, massive phase of record industry growth and secure their positions for the second half-century.

This next phase came with the invention of the microgroove 33 rpm vinyl disc in the late 1940s, a cheaper, less fragile and longer-playing product than the shellac 78 rpm. The twelve-inch 33 rpm disc was pioneered by CBS and a competing 45 rpm by RCA. After some initial rivalry, both formats were adopted and they revived the fortunes of the record market, leading to a period of 10–20 per cent growth which was to last until the late 1970s. Two new majors also emerged in the 1950s, shortly before the advent of rock'n'roll. In Europe, the Dutch group Philips created its own music subsidiary; and Warner Bros, the US film company which had bought up the Brunswick record label in 1934, now launched Warner Bros Records. This made six international majors in all. Meanwhile a number of independent French record companies were set up after the Liberation. Most notable among them was Barclay, named after its founder Eddie Barclay, who took the risk of importing the new microgroove record. By the early 1960s, the label had signed up the biggest names in *chanson* (Brel, Brassens, Ferré, Ferrat, Aznavour) and some from the burgeoning French pop scene. Also influential was Vogue, created around the same time. Together, the two labels came to dominate the French independents in the 1960s and were largely responsible for the growth of *chanson* and the introduction of French pop.

Writers, performers and labels were greatly assisted in the 1940s and 1950s by radio – both the state radio and the three major 'peripheral' stations (broadcasting from just outside France) – Radio Monte-Carlo (RMC), Radio Luxembourg and, from 1955, Europe 1. Programmes devoted to popular music in one form or another, like 'Ploum ploum tralala' or 'Chansons grises, chansons roses' (Blue Songs, Happy Songs), were abundant and allowed songs to reach a much wider audience than the music hall did. There were live music shows daily, providing work for bands and singers. Established stars like Trenet, Montand, Chevalier and Piaf appeared regularly and newcomers like Line Renaud or Luis Mariano could be launched, particularly after Radio Luxembourg brought back the pre-war formula of the talent contest in 1949. One programme, entitled 'Le Disque des auditeurs' (Listeners' Record Choice), also introduced the record request show, and another, 'La Chanson éternelle' (Eternal Songs), prefigured the hit parade by allowing listeners to vote for their favourite records. This was the beginning of a process that would see radio and records form a commercial synergy, as programming, on the peripheral stations particularly, became more and more dominated by record shows, as had happened in the USA in the first half of the 1950s with spectacular results: it had helped give birth to rock'n'roll.[17]

Music before 1958

The live music performed in the music halls of the 1920s was designed to liberate and distract, responding to a public thirst for modernity and forgetfulness after the Great War: from the vivacious numbers of Yvette Guilbert and Maurice Chevalier to the spectacular revues of Mistinguett and the Folies-Bergère. 'Typical revues presented forty-five or fifty tableaux in two acts –

bright kaleidoscopes of flamboyant dress and settings and comic and dramatic sketches. The music hall was a dream factory full of behind-the-scenes machinery and lighting systems, a technological complex producing the magical succession of scenes and bathing them in rainbow hues and bright whites.'[18]

More exotic styles also arrived, mostly from the Americas but of African origin: the tango (which had reached France before 1914), the samba and jazz-band music. By 1917, American soldiers were present on French soil in some numbers, bringing their own music with them and sometimes their own stars.[19] Such wartime encounters heralded the establishment of a significant number of African-Americans in France who believed they had found a more open racial attitude than their own country offered.[20] American performers and dance bands began appearing on music-hall bills, most famously perhaps Josephine Baker, an unknown nineteen-year-old dancer who arrived in 1925 with the 'Revue nègre' (Black Revue) and made a successful career in Europe. America was coming to France economically too by this time, thanks to the post-war Dawes Plan for European development. US goods thus flowed in, followed by the assembly-line methods which produced them.[21] Hollywood was enough of a threat to the indigenous film industry for the first quota of national production to be introduced in 1928. Some of the music which accompanied these migrations was band music linked to foreign dance crazes like the Charleston; suddenly the traditional French dance halls began looking old-fashioned and started calling themselves '*dancings*' in a semblance of English.[22]

Even so, audiences still listened to the recitals, recordings or broadcasts of home-grown sentimental singers like Fréhel, Damia or the rising Piaf, where they found stories of the street to weep to, populist melodramas with a cast of pimps, broken-hearted prostitutes and sun-tanned legionnaires, known misleadingly as the 'realist song'. Steadily, however, during the 1930s, the modernising wind of the 1920s began to blow through *chanson* too. It came partly from the assimilation of jazz rhythms and arrangements, and partly from a subject matter of more complex and wider-ranging emotions, expressed with greater lyrical sophistication. It was associated with the incremental rise of the singer-songwriter. Hawkins perceptively observes that French song has periodically become a popular art with literary ambitions at times when artists and intellectuals have taken an interest in it.[23] At such moments, *chanson* acquires a different form of legitimacy from that conferred simply by the market, and some creative individuals are encouraged to turn to it as a serious form capable of the expressive subtlety of literature. Montmartre's Le Chat noir in the late nineteenth century is one instance: Bruant sang there, Satie named his third 'Gymnopédie' after it, and its journal printed work by Verlaine and other poets.[24] Hawkins identifies two other such periods: the 1930s, with contacts between Cocteau, Max Jacob and Trenet, for example; and the 1940s, with the Existentialists, Raymond Queneau, Jacques Prévert and others, when Saint-Germain became a melting pot like Bruant's Montmartre.

While Piaf, who wrote only occasionally, chiefly contributed a singing style to the new sub-genre, a semiotics of emotional theatricality and sparse stage presence (the singer in black alone in the white light of a single projector),[25] the actor and singer Mireille (Hartuch), paired with Jean Nohain in a songwriting duo, helped modernise its form by combining jazz rhythms with a melodic and lyrical whimsy. Later, she was to influence *chanson* by a different means when in 1955 she formed her own school for singers and songwriters and gave them the chance to perform on radio. Mireille's own compositions also cleared the way for the sparkling poetry of Trenet, who was to exert an enormous influence on the post-war genre by breaking with the weepy sentimentalism of the 'realist song' and demonstrating the poetic and melodic possibilities of word-play. He introduced a ludic inventiveness into the song lyric which, in the absence of songs of note directly evoking the experience of the Popular Front period, somehow managed to capture its ephemeral mood of hope.[26] On closer inspection, however, Trenet's work exhibited an ironic duality in which, beneath his merry exuberance symbolised in the comic hat and popping eyes of his 'singing fool' persona on stage (*le fou chantant*), a private universe of sadness was intimated with a lightness of touch which the *chanson réaliste*, or 'realist song', was seldom capable of.

After the Occupation, these pre-war developments began to fructify. The Liberation saw the rise of an intimate Left-Bank cabaret scene as an alternative to the big commercial Right-Bank venues, and with it a taste for intellectual bohemianism and existential gloom. Saint-Germain-des-Prés became its prime site (Club Saint-Germain, Le Tabou), though Montmartre remained influential, particularly a cabaret called Les Trois Baudets opened by Jacques Canetti in 1947. Such venues were often too small for a singer-songwriter to have any accompaniment other than his (rarely her) own guitar or piano. But composing, singing and accompanying oneself actually gave the solo artist a freedom of movement and an artistic independence unknown to most commercial entertainers. So the Left-Bank club circuit became a laboratory for a galaxy of young singer-songwriters working in a new style, initially known as the Left-Bank song (*chanson rive-gauche*). As they became better known and crossed over to the bigger Right-Bank venues like the Olympia, which Bruno Coquatrix re-opened as a music hall in 1954, their work was acknowledged as popular poetry by a range of other suffixes: *chanson d'auteur* (author-song), *chanson à texte* (text-song) or *chanson poétique* (poetic song). Léo Ferré (1916–93), Georges Brassens (1921–81) and Jacques Brel (1929–78) are today perceived as the Olympians of French song around whom cluster lesser Gods like Aznavour, Barbara, Jean Ferrat, Gainsbourg, Francis Lemarque and Boris Vian. There were also important writers who did not sing, like the famous team of Jacques Prévert and Joseph Kosma (who wrote 'Autumn Leaves'), and singers who did not write but were sensitive enough interpreters of the text-song to be influential in their own right, notably Juliette Gréco and Yves Montand. Canetti too was a catalyst in its crystallisation as a style, since virtually all the text-song stars passed through Les Trois Baudets in their early careers, while some found their way on to the Polydor and Philips labels for which Canetti successively worked.

As these *chanson* careers blossomed, the 1950s and early 1960s became the heyday of the French singer-songwriter and the poetic text-song. Concurrently, vinyl records and record-based radio were beginning the long ascent that would nudge the live cabaret and in the end the reborn music hall from centre-stage, just as it would the culture of the music publisher nostalgically evoked by Delanoë. A radically different style of popular song was also reaching France from America, very much bound up with these interdependent media. Soon, it would threaten the survival of the *chanson, rive-gauche* or otherwise.

Notes

1. Richard A. Peterson, *Creating Country Music: Fabricating Authenticity* (University of Chicago Press, 1997), p. 5; Roy Shuker, *Key Concepts in Popular Music* (Routledge, 1998, pp. 20–1).
2. *La Fin de l'exception culturelle?* (CNRS Éditions, 1999), p. 7.
3. Ibid., pp. 10–11.
4. Ibid., p. 11.
5. Ibid., p. 13.
6. Ibid., epigraph [p. 60].
7. Pierre Delanoë, *La Chanson en colère: entretiens avec Alain-Gilles Minella* (Mame, 1993), p. 32.
8. Louis-Jean Calvet, *Chanson et société* (Payot, 1981), Chapter 5.
9. Claude Duneton, *Histoire de la chanson française: de 1780 à 1860* (Seuil, 1998), 2 vols, vol. II, pp. 408–12.
10. Serge Dillaz, *La Chanson française de contestation* (Seghers, 1973), pp. 11–12; quotation p. 14.
11. Duneton, *Histoire de la chanson française*, vol. II, p. 621.
12. Dillaz, *La Chanson française de contestation*, p. 24; Georges Coulonges, *La Chanson en son temps de Béranger au juke-box* (Les Éditeurs Français Réunis, 1969), p. 31.

13. Mario d'Angelo, *Socio-économie de la musique en France* (Documentation Française, 1997), p. 18.

14. Serge Dillaz, *La Chanson sous la Troisème République, 1870–1940* (Tallandier, 1991), p. 36.

15. Jeffrey H. Jackson, 'Making Enemies: Jazz in Inter-War Paris', *French Cultural Studies*, vol. 10, no. 29 (June 1999), pp. 179–99, pp. 182–4.

16. I am indebted in this paragraph to Farchy, *La Fin de l'exception culturelle?*, pp. 21–7, 40–1 and 55–6; and Catherine Chocron, 'Les Enjeux économiques du rock', in Anne-Marie Gourdon (ed.), *Le Rock: aspects esthétiques, culturels et sociaux* (CNRS Éditions, 1994), pp. 113–14.

17. On French radio, see Alain Poulanges, 'La Chanson à Saint-Germain et alentour', in Philippe Gumplowicz and Jean-Claude Klein (eds), *Paris 1944–1954. Artistes, intellectuels, publics* (Éditions Autrement, 1995), pp. 183–93 (pp. 187–8); on American radio's role in the rise of rock'n'roll, see Richard A. Peterson, 'Why 1955? Explaining the Advent of Rock Music', *Popular Music*, vol .9, no. 1 (January 1990), pp. 97–116.

18. Charles Rearick, *The French in Love and War: Popular Culture in the Era of the World Wars* (Yale University Press, 1997), p. 69.

19. Ibid., pp. 28–9.

20. Colin Nettlebeck, 'Jazz at the Théâtre Graslin: A Founding Story', *French Cultural Studies*, vol. 11, no. 32 (June 2000), p. 216.

21. Jackson, 'Making Enemies', pp. 181–2.

22. Rearick, *The French in Love and War*, p. 88.

23. Hawkins, *Chanson*, pp. 214–16.

24. D'Angelo, *Socio-économie de la musique*, p. 18.

25. Hawkins, *Chanson*, p. 79.

26. Dillaz, *La Chanson sous la Troisième République*, Part III, Chapter 7 ('Le Front populaire').

– 2 –

The 1960s: Authenticity and Barbarism

The birth of rock'n'roll in America is well documented and only needs to be briefly recalled here. Most historians agree that it was in 1954–5 that, in Richard Peterson's words, 'a rock aesthetic displaced the jazz-based aesthetic in American popular music'.[1] In the late 1940s and early 1950s, a number of sociological, technological and industrial changes revolutionised the American popular-music industry and therefore the music itself. Post-war adolescents (whose numbers were beginning to grow, though the oldest baby-boomers had not yet reached puberty) found little to appeal to them in the essentially young-adult content of early 1950s popular song. At the same time, new technologies were appearing. On top of the vinyl revolution, tape was now being used in recording, affording new opportunities for manipulating sound in the studio. Leo Fender's Broadcaster solid-body electric guitar was marketed from 1948 and his Precision bass from 1950. The lightweight portable transistor radio and the relatively cheap record-player also went on sale. These developments in turn helped produce changes in the American record industry and media: most critically, the emergence of independent record companies (Sun, Atlantic, Stax, Chess and others) ready to abandon the swing bands and crooners put out by the majors and cater for younger tastes. Local radio stations then began to segment and specialise accordingly round a range of music styles, increasing the public's exposure to them.

All these factors (and more) created the material conditions for the dissemination of a commercial style for teenagers fusing black rhythm'n'blues with white country music. At the time, rhythm'n'blues, developing from the folk traditions of America's black communities, was classed as 'race music' and kept off white radio stations and their Top 40s, even though some young white audiences were becoming enthusiastic about it. Combining it with a white idiom was thus a pragmatic way of opening up a mass market. Many Americans, however, particularly in the segregated southern states, were appalled by the spectacle of white adolescents assimilating black rhythms and dance styles. Worse, even in the reassuringly white hands of an Elvis or a Buddy Holly, rock'n'roll's beat, lyrics, choreography and dress codes – a very long way from the comfortable urbanity of the crooner – barely disguised its erotic charge and rebellious energy. In the UK, to which the music spread around 1956 before reaching continental Europe, it proved to have much the same potency for the young, though a quite different ethnic dimension. The same is true of France, though here it would be some years before the right sociological, industrial and technological conditions were assembled to give rise to a music of comparable authenticity.

Although pop's embarkation in France is sometimes made to sound like a surprise invasion, by the late 1950s it was virtually inevitable, built into the wider logic of economic Americanisation which France had been experiencing since the First World War with the Dawes Plan and since the Second with the Marshall Plan. Hollywood and Tin Pan Alley had been purveying their versions of the American way of life since the arrival of jazz and the talkies. During the Occupation, jazz was frowned upon by the authorities (German and French) and Hollywood films banned, with the result that, as US troops again set foot on French soil at the Liberation, there was a new surge of demand for American popular culture and products. As blocks of flats replaced slums on the outskirts of Paris and new domestic appliances reached the more affluent homes, along with nylon, formica and plastic, America became a signifier of consumer modernism and a cult of the new.[2] The world that had produced the pre-war *chanson* and from which its veracity derived was vanishing, the world of the 'zone', the Montmartre cabaret and the Moulin rouge, of an older, more parochial Paris. The French music business was also being modernised. In 1957, for example, the first record pressing plant in France, MPO, was set up, later to become a multinational leader, among the first to manufacture cassettes (1972), CDs (1984) and CD-Roms (1987).[3]

French showbiz was also Americanising fast. As well as Mireille and Trenet who had already absorbed jazz, Django Reinhardt, sometimes with Stéphane Grapelli, had been playing his own creative brand of jazz since his fabled days with the Quintet of the Hot-Club de France in the 1930s. Pre-war big bands, too, like Ray Ventura's 'College-Boys' (*Collégiens*) or Jacques Hélian's orchestra, were still performing, while the New Orleans saxophonist and clarinettist Sidney Bechet moved to France in 1949 and played with Claude Luter's band. Édouard Ruault, a jazz pianist who had opened France's first discothèque during the Occupation, adopted an American name, Eddie Barclay, to launch his own band and record label. Yves Montand started his singing career celebrating 'the plains of the far West' in a cowboy hat. Aznavour was adopting the style of the American crooner. Dance styles of non-French origin like the cha-cha and be-bop swept the country. Initially, rock'n'roll was just the latest of such crazes. Yet it announced a massive new growth-spurt in the Americanisation of the French music industry and French musical tastes.

This began a little earlier than is often thought. 'Rock Around the Clock' became a best-seller in France in 1956, as it did everywhere else, and that year Elvis Presley was already enough of a threat for the *chanson* magazine *Music-Hall* to write: 'Elvis Presley, the incredible new idol of the Yankee bobby-soxers, is coming over to devour the microphones of Europe. Fortunately, Paris isn't on his schedule: phew!'[4] French imitations soon followed. Delanoë adapted his first Elvis song in 1957, and at roughly the same time Boris Vian penned a number of rock'n'roll pieces, half-imitation, half-parody, including 'Rock and Rollmops' and 'Va te faire cuire un œuf, man!' (Go Fry an Egg, Man), recorded by Henri Salvador under the punning pseudonym of Henry Cording and his Original Rock and Roll Boys.

With somewhat more conviction, one of their songs, 'D'où viens-tu Billy Boy' (Where Do You Come From, Billy Boy), was released in 1958 by Danyel Gérard and became a hit. Although this too was originally a spoof, Gérard became known as the French Elvis Presley, before conscription swept him offstage. Another early exponent was Richard Anthony, who had moderate success with 'Nouvelle Vague' (New Wave) and 'J'ai une petite MG' (I've Got a Little MG). Anny Cordy, who had been recording French covers of US hits for some time, switched to the less aggressive kind of rock'n'roll song such as 'Witch Doctor' ('Docteur Miracle' in French). But all of these were anodyne derivatives that produced no social discontinuity, no sense of rock as a movement. It was not until 1960–1 that the story properly begins, in so far as rock'n'roll could by then no longer be dismissed as a fad but had to be recognised as the hub of a distinct youth culture.

For young people generally, in the USA and Europe, social and economic conditions were turning the period of adolescence into a prolonged interlude with its own properties. The post-war baby-boom, the raising of the French school-leaving age from fourteen to sixteen in 1959 and the expansion of higher education, industrial recovery and the transformation of the economy into one dependent on consumer goods, all helped create the late 1950s 'teenager'. The label was initially applied to a welcome new category of shopper with more disposable money and time to spend on clothes, records and entertainment than many adults. But by adopting rock'n'roll as a call sign, the teenager, particularly male, began to assume a sociological significance which had not been bargained for. In France specifically, a third of the population was under twenty by 1964.[5] It is true, as Arthur Marwick suggests, that 'a much more clearly articulated family framework, backed [. . .] by the still very relevant traditions of the Catholic Church', meant that 'French teenagers had less opportunity to develop their own specialist tastes and rituals' than American adolescents.[6] But this only postponed the inevitable until around 1960.

French young people's ecstatic response to the new music was an early warning sign, though youth hysteria and idolatry were not entirely unheard of before then. In the 1940s, dance musics like be-bop and boogie-woogie, available in the smoky cellars of Saint-Germain and elsewhere, had become associated with the young and were frowned upon by adult society. In a quite different mode, the Spanish-born crooner Luis Mariano had become a singing idol who made female fans swoon. Then there was the Bécaud phenomenon. Gilbert Bécaud became France's first youth idol, nicknamed 'Monsieur 100,000 volts' after his first major appearance in 1954. When Bruno Coquatrix converted the Olympia back into a music hall, he decided to let adolescents in free to the matinee of the opening show, which featured Bécaud. An unexpected 5,000 turned up and they were soon whipped into a frenzy by his wildly dramatic stage act as he pounded his piano and paced the stage with sexually charged songs. In the course of the concert, 500 seats were reportedly broken and twenty pairs of knickers thrown on stage.[7] But with rock'n'roll, such scenes were on a quite different scale.

Over a two-year period, rock was involved in disturbances in some 500 towns across three continents, making it easy for the public imagination to equate the savagery of the music with delinquency, as the energy it generated spilled over into mass hysteria and violence,[8] seemingly resonating with the disaffection of urban, working-class males: gang warfare in New York's west side, Teddy Boys in London. In France too, rock'n'roll began as a Paris phenomenon identified with the '*blousons noirs*' (black jackets), gangs of youths who had been causing concern since the late 1950s. Following the classic youth-cultural scenario, the gangs, clad in leather jackets copied from Marlon Brando in *The Wild One* (1953, *L'Équipée sauvage* in France) and James Dean in *Rebel Without a Cause* (1955, *La Fureur de vivre*), had territorialised the public squares of working-class Paris and begun stealing, fighting with chains and razors, and generally causing an affray. The Sacré-Cœur gang, for example, was known to be tougher than the neighbouring Square de la Trinité outfit, which had the young Jean-Philippe Smet among its members and his friends Jacques Dutronc and Christian Blondieau. All three were to become pop singers, Smet as Johnny Hallyday, Blondieau as Long Chris and Dutronc under his own name.[9] Some gangs formed bands, knocking out US hits on makeshift instruments. One of the rare indoor meeting-places at their disposal was a dance hall called Le Golf Drouot in the rue de Montmartre, where the manager, Henri Leproux, had acquired one of the first imported Selectmatic jukeboxes, which came pre-loaded with American hits. He had also set up a small area for performance, so customers could dance to both records and live music. It was here that Smet began performing as Hallyday.

The spread of rock'n'roll in France from this restricted milieu to a national teenage constituency has a number of specificities. In the USA, it was legal to drive at sixteen, two years sooner than in France; and America's consumer society was considerably more advanced. Consequently, the rapidly established rock myths of back-seat smooching, motorbikes and drive-in movies meant little in real terms to French youths growing up in an economy still recovering from wartime devastation.[10] To an extent, this cultural inappropriacy was true of post-war Britain too. After all, what Iain Chambers calls the 'explosive combination' of black and white cultures which had generated rock in the rural southern states of America, in a culturally specific atmosphere of racial tension, meant no more to white working-class boys from London like Tommy Steele or Cliff Richard than to their Parisian equivalents. For both, therefore, 'there existed few other possibilities than imitating a barely understood American style', or, as the French sociologist Paul Yonnet calls it, a 'culture of the mask'.[11] On British rock'n'rollers, the iconic menace of the greased hair, sneering mouth and black leather jacket looked theatrical and faintly laughable. But in France, where even the slicked-back sculptural quiff was limply known as a 'banana', the linguistic barrier coupled with a conservative education system and the other cultural differences outlined by Marwick made the sense of posturing more obvious still, as did the rarity and high price of appropriate musical instruments and the shortage of adequate concert venues, which meant that French fans' passion for the music was largely mediated through the music press in the very early days.[12] Meanwhile, like a constant reproach, there was *chanson*, pristine in its national authenticity. As Tony Dunn observes, continental pop groups 'sounded always muted and imitative. They had initially to compete against strong, indigenous systems of peasant- and folk-ballad on the one hand, and the pre-industrial musical forms of the artisanate and the urban poor on the other hand. Maurice Chevalier (who had his older following in England) is always threatening to drift across Euro-pop.'[13]

Before television had become widespread, the transistor played a key role in the formation of this culture, since it was an instrument of separation. The heavy radiogram in the 1950s living room brought the family together round a parental choice of music, on radio or record. But with the portable transistor and record-player (the Teppaz in France, the Dansette in the UK), adolescents could more easily listen when they liked to what they liked. By 1960, the peripheral radio stations like Europe 1, RMC and Radio Luxembourg (later RTL) were exposing French adolescents to Anglo-American rock'n'roll records daily; and French record companies, momentarily wrongfooted by the phenomenon after years of churning out *variétés*, began producing French equivalents as fast as they were able: Barclay signed Eddy Mitchell; Vogue snapped up Johnny Hallyday and Françoise Hardy, releasing Hallyday's first single, 'T'aimer follement' (Loving You Madly) in March 1960. One presenter on Europe 1, Lucien Morisse, so disliked it that he broke it on air, unwisely predicting that Hallyday would never be heard again.[14] Six months later,

'Johnny' appeared live at Paris's Alhambra as a support act, to a mixed reception. In 1961, he went on tour, which helped disseminate the genre across France. Other working-class young men followed suit, forming groups with suitably macho names like Les Chats sauvages (The Wildcats), Les Pirates or Les Vautours (The Vultures). Some solo artists followed Hallyday and took American stage names, among them Eddy Mitchell, vocalist with Les Chaussettes noires (The Black Socks), Dick Rivers, with Les Chats sauvages, or Frankie Jordan. Unlike *chanson* stars, these performers did not write their own material. French record companies realised that the best way of supplying them with songs was to obtain the rights on US hits and have them adapted into French. Hallyday's 'T'aimer follement' was a cover of 'Makin' Love', Eddy Mitchell's version of Chuck Berry's 'Johnny B. Goode' became 'Eddy sois bon' (Eddy, Be Good). Vince Taylor, however, was the genuine article: a rock'n'roll singer born in Britain and living in America, until a concert in Paris brought to him to the attention of Barclay.

This new wave of French rockers came to national prominence in February 1961 at France first's rock'n'roll 'festival', held at Paris's Palais des sports, where Hallyday, the Chaussettes noires, Richard Anthony, Frankie Jordan and a handful of acts from other countries were on the bill. A second event followed in June at the same venue, where crowd enthusiasm spilled over into violence and damage to property. Richard Anthony was attacked with a broken bottle, five policemen were hospitalised and twenty-five fans arrested.[15] This was how the media and parents first became fully aware of rock'n'roll as a social phenomenon. They found its volume and syncopation, the overtly sexual gyrations of its originators and imitators, and the hysteria of audiences bewildering and indecent. Vince Taylor, in leather from head to toe like Gene Vincent, was a particular pariah. He was the ultimate alien, his menacing attire and hyper-erotic stage act incarnating all that was other about American rock'n'roll.[16] His scheduled appearance at a third jamboree at the Palais des sports, in November 1961, had to be cancelled at the last minute because the 5,000 fans were out of control.[17]

That year, a number of deputies in the National Assembly called for rock concerts to be banned. In response, Frankie Jordan drew up a fifty-page report defending the music, which led to an hour-long live debate on Europe 1 with the deputies concerned.[18] In the end, no national ban materialised, though at local level, in the bigger cities with troubled suburbs, it was a different story. Screenings of Elvis films took place with an edgy police presence and numerous provincial rock concerts were vetoed. During Hallyday's 1961 tour, the mayors of Cannes, Strasbourg and Bayonne would not let him play, while in Montbéliard police used tear gas to control crowds. Similar scenes had been witnessed in other countries, of course, but this did not diminish the impact on a stunned France. The press began wringing its hands. 'What is rock'n'roll?', cried the weekly news magazine *L'Express* in evident distress, 'A good? An evil? A barbaric fashion, a beneficial release of tension?'; while in *Le Courrier du Parlement* one MP was filled with compassion for misunderstood youth, 'too often left to themselves, without morality, discipline, critical sense or ideals, and with nothing to hang on to, sickened by a society in which they cannot find their place'. More gruffly, de Gaulle commented that if the young were so full of energy, they should be building roads.[19]

Rock's crude aesthetic and its appeal to the irrational also generated cultural anxieties since it appeared antithetical to the more reflective emotion and even cerebration fostered by the Left-Bank *chanson*. As early as 1958, Vian mocked Elvis's primitivism, pointing out that even an illiterate could adapt an Elvis song, simply by staying true to the original.[20] Hugues Aufray, who had grown up with Trenet's songs and been a pupil at Mireille's school, had started a promising career in the Left-Bank clubs of the 1950s but had difficulty following it up once rock arrived because he could not adapt to its three-chord simplicity, its almost comic onomatopoeia and its lyrics 'expressing sentiments which bore no relation to mine'.[21] Frankie Jordan confessed that he would not even buy his own records, preferring jazz and 'true' rock'n'roll.[22] But rock's extremism could not go on indefinitely, especially once television began to take notice. To compete with Anglo-American product, French record companies were keen to clean up their protégés and avoid alienating parents. As had already happened in the USA and the UK, it was time for rock'n'roll to be brought to heel.

A number of factors contributed to the process. First, like Hallyday and Mitchell, the first French rock'n'roll fans were mainly boys aged between fifteen and twenty with conscription into the Algerian War hanging over them. Danyel Gérard, Hallyday and Mitchell were all called up just as Elvis had been, creating much the same photo opportunities for a new look of clean-cut solemnity before the flag. Second, adolescent girls were attracted to the music and female singers were duly launched, helping retrieve rock'n'roll from its associations of male delinquency. Sylvie Vartan, Sheila, France Gall, Françoise Hardy, the English singer Petula Clark and others were projected as skittish, fun-loving and wholesome. This in turn produced a wave of equally innocuous-looking boy singers, like Claude François, Adamo or Frank Alamo. Thus eviscerated, rock'n'roll could be safely transmitted to a wider youth constituency as a consumer style. French pop was born, known as *le yéyé*.[23] By the mid-1960s, pop impresarios like Eddie Barclay and Johnny Stark, formerly Hallyday's manager, were auditioning between 1,000 and 2,000 young hopefuls a year, of whom some twenty might cut a single, though probably only three of these would be successful enough even to recoup the cost.[24]

This proliferation transformed the French record industry. Whereas 78s had not sold in any great number, vinyl did, so that hits began to clock up sales of 100,000, which at the time earned the singer a gold disc. Much of the new output was still composed of Anglo-American chart toppers adapted into French and often mediocre, but it nevertheless managed to undercut the industry's staple commodities: the exotic variety singer (Gloria Lasso, Dario Moreno) at one extreme and the Left-Bank singer-songwriter (Maurice Fanon, Joël Holmès) at the other,[25] as cabarets closed and radio stations switched sides. The 'classics', however, the Brels and the Aznavours, survived, while the most successful youth stars soon began to aspire to classic status themselves. Having switched from Vogue to Philips, Hallyday performed at the Olympia in a dinner suit in September 1961. Only half his set consisted of rock'n'roll, the rest devoted to gentler numbers and the launch of the twist. This faintly ludicrous dance, manufactured in the States and disseminated by singers with innocuous names like Chubby Checker, was easily assimilated and respectable French personalities of all ages were soon photographed twisting delightedly. Hallyday won his first gold disc with Checker's 'Let's Twist Again'.[26]

More crucial than TV in the clean-up process was radio. In the summer of 1959, four years after its launch, Europe 1 was still searching for a house style and a niche audience. Hence the launch of a weekly music programme for teenagers broadcast just after school, called 'Salut les copains', a title taken from a 1957 song by Bécaud and Delanoë and roughly the equivalent of the 'Hi there guys and gals' which became the catch-phrase of Radio Luxembourg DJ Jimmy Savile. The show began that summer fronted by Daniel Filipacchi and Frank Ténot, two established jazz presenters (Ténot had been involved with Le Hot-Club de France) who crossed over into pop. It was an immediate success and became daily in October of the same year. Its effect was to give the new music an institutional identity, reinforced in June 1962 when a linked teen magazine was piloted with the same title. The trial run of 100,000 copies was cleared in days and within a year it was selling over a million, far ahead of France's first pop magazine, *Disco-Revue*, launched the previous year. In a formula soon to become standard, the *Salut les copains* magazine contained news, anecdotes and biographical information on stars, a hit parade based on readers' votes, and song lyrics. Unlike *Disco-Revue*, though, it also carried features on wider youth issues. This and the magazine's photography were its main editorial innovations, but of equal importance was its philosophy, the principle that pop fans were all *copains*, mates. The term spoke of wholesome friendships between boys and girls and an apolitical culture of classless youths passionate about a music that advocated nothing more harmful than vigorous fun. The stars themselves were also *copains*, referred to by their first names, as was the programme's presenter, 'Daniel' (Filippachi). Hallyday began writing a regular 'letter' of homespun teen advice for the magazine.

Thinly disguised imitations soon followed: *Bonjour les amis* (Hello Friends) and *Age tendre* (Tender Age), linked to France's first TV pop programme, launched by Albert Raisner in 1961, 'Age tendre et tête de bois' (Young and Headstrong, another title lifted from a Bécaud song). Magazines were even launched by the Communist Party (PCF) (*Nous les garçons et les filles*) and the Catholic Church (*J2 Jeunesse* for boys and *J2 Magazine* for girls). Unexpectedly, both organisations, already allied by their hostility to post-war American imports and determination to use mass-cultural forms to their advantage, played a key role in pop's implantation in France,[27] though they both remained uncomfortable with the new Americanised, eroticised youth culture and neither seriously threatened *Salut les copains*, which continued to corner the market until a new generation of more sophisticated periodicals appeared, notably *Rock & Folk* in 1966 and *Best* in 1968.

On the evening of 22 June 1963, Ténot and Filipacchi held a free open-air concert to mark the magazine's first birthday, at the Place de la Nation in Paris, featuring Hallyday, Vartan, Richard Anthony and many others. Around 30,000 fans were expected; 150,000 turned up. A contingent of *blousons noirs* from the tough neighbourhood of Belleville reputedly engaged in thuggery. The papers even told of rape, theft and vandalism, though the Prefect of Police, Maurice Papon, played all of these down. *Le Figaro's* Philippe Bouvard attempted to whip up further disapproval by equating the effect of the twist with Hitler's speeches at the Reichstag, while Pierre Charpy in a *Paris-Presse* article headed 'Salut les voyous' (Hi There Thugs) wrote menacingly: 'We cannot resist this tide by sermons. We have to strip its sorry heroes of their tawdry trappings: there are laws, a police force, courts. It is time to use them before the barbarians of the Place de la Nation wreck the future of the nation.'[28] But repressive indignation was not the only reaction to the event. Young people and even some parents wrote in to the magazine to protest in injured tones to 'Daniel' about such unfair accounts of an enjoyable evening spent among *copains*.[29] In retrospect, the reactions can be interpreted as a final reckoning between what were by now competing representations of pop, from which only pop walked away. What they also demonstrated was a public realisation that something of genuine sociocultural significance had happened to French youth which could no longer be ignored. A brilliant though partly misguided article by Edgar Morin, published in *Le Monde* shortly afterwards, made a serious attempt to articulate what that was. By 1963, pop culture was difficult to interpret in the standard categories of social class. The very first rock'n'rollers in the pre-*yéyé* 1950s were often from middle-class backgrounds, like Danyel Gérard, whose uncle was an MP, or Richard Anthony, grandson of an ambassador.[30] Then came 'the summer of the *blousons noirs*' in 1959, when rock'n'roll's aggression was seized upon by disaffected working-class males like Hallyday. Morin's argument (to which I shall return in Chapter 5) was that the phenomenon had now outgrown and reconfigured these categories, signifying the emergence of a new kind of class, which defied classification in standard sociological terms and homogenised young people nationally and internationally.[31]

It was with this triumph of *yéyé*, I suggest, that a particularly tenacious Anglo-Saxon representation of French pop was born: vacuous and embarrassingly inauthentic, a colonised music that eternally misses the point. To an extent, this is an ethnocentric view, especially if one bears in mind the mediocrity of much of the UK's output in the same period. At any event, Morin is certainly impressed by the quality of *yéyé* songwriting and there is perhaps a case for revisiting some of its Anglo-American adaptations and French originals, since they were often the work of distinguished *chanson* lyricists like Vian, Gainsbourg and Delanoë, who showed a degree of skill, wit and sensitivity in rendering the contemporary concerns of French adolescents.[32] Nevertheless, London became the focal point of professional music in Europe, and the coming of beat groups only worsened France's dependence. While less demanding adolescents remained with *yéyé* into the mid-1960s, others, in particular middle-class youths and students, were turning to new British and American youth icons. Two of these are of particular significance: the Beatles and Bob Dylan.

Once reports of Beatlemania reached France followed by the Beatles themselves, *yéyé* tried to adjust. Hallyday underwent one of his style transformations which were to become legendary; Beatles and other beat-group hits were adapted into French; and occasional French newcomers – Antoine, Jacques Dutronc – picked up the edge of ironic cool wafting in from the UK. This was taken further by the influence of Bob Dylan, adapted into French by Delanoë and others and disseminated by Hugues Aufray in particular, whose career was relaunched by the Dylan phenomenon. Dylan was an important conduit through which US counterculture reached France, reinforcing the myth of an international homogeneity in Western youth which Morin had mooted in 1963. The first signs of Dylan's cultural ascendency came in 1966 with what was anachronistically called a 'beatnik' movement. But later that year, news of the Californian hippies began reaching France via pop journalists like Henry Chapier in *Combat* and Alain Dister in *Rock & Folk*. *Crapouillot* did a controversial special issue on LSD in October 1966 and *Match* ran a feature on California the following April. In early 1968, the journalist Michel Lancelot devoted a book to the hippies, *Je veux regarder Dieu en face* (I Want to Look God in the Face).[33]

Lancelot contended that the movement was a deeply American phenomenon looking back to Emerson and Thoreau, which France had difficulty understanding properly other than as an amusing eccentricity: 'Of this phenomenon, we have retained only the flowers in the hair, the colourful clothes, a touch of Orientalism, a few Beatles tunes and one maxim: "Make love not war".' In crossing the Atlantic, the 'tragedy' of American youth has become 'a typically Parisian farce'.[34] Clearly, inauthenticity is once again the issue in this diagnosis: the tendency to ape the harmless trappings of Anglophone youth culture, only half-understood. Lancelot explains this tendency by three factors: the scarcity of reliable information on the hippie movement; the resulting tendency of some French journalists to write whatever they like; and the drugs question, which in France is deliberately eclipsed, distorting the entire picture since the movement cannot, he insists, be properly understood without reference to it. In Gaullist France, TV censorship was indeed prevalent, as Lancelot could personally attest since his comments on drugs in three separate programmes had all been cut. On this issue, he maintains, the censorship derives from France's pride in its own entrenched rationalism: 'where will it lead us, this head-in-the-sand policy which we so readily adopt whenever some intellectual spoilsport (*empêcheur de penser en rond*) comes along and upsets our Cartesianism, which once appeared hereditary but today looks almost pathological?'[35]

And yet, partly because of these distinctive factors, France was developing a counterculture of its own, as the next few months were to show. Although influenced by Anglo-American trends, this counterculture was a more directly political phenomenon, fuelled by specifically French experiences: the Algerian War, growing dissatisfaction with the overcrowding and conservatism of French education, and, more generally, a swelling resentment of Gaullist paternalism, satirised in the slogan 'be young and shut up'. So it was that of all the Western democracies experiencing the challenge of youth, France alone, apparently capable only of worshipping false idols, produced a youth movement which in 1968, rather than almost levitating the Pentagon, as American hippies claimed to have done, almost toppled the state.

Pop itself did not play a very great role in the uprising of May 1968, though some events took place which involved the music world, such as the États généraux des variétés (estates-general of popular music) held on 21 May, which attracted 600 artists, and a benefit concert for strikers which included on the bill Pia Colombo, Jean Ferrat and Georges Moustaki.[36] Musicians from classical to popular mounted a 'silence strike', displaying a degree of solidarity with each other unusual in the partitioned and individualistic world of music. Culture generally, however, in both artistic and anthropological senses, was very much at the heart of May. Its consciously ideological insurgents had been persuaded by Althusser and Bourdieu that high culture was an apparatus of bourgeois ideology and social reproduction, though they were equally opposed to mass culture since it too was deemed bourgeois, diversionary and alienating. But for those young participants for whom May was less to do with Marxism or Maoism than with personal liberation (from family, education or state), the revolt was more confusedly entangled with the looser Anglo-American counterculture behind rock: personal creativity and difference, sexual liberation, hippiedom. For them, the newer Anglo-American sounds from *Sergeant Pepper* through Dylan to the Grateful Dead, Hendrix and the Mothers of Invention – became not simply the soundtrack but the medium of 'contestation'. To this sector of French youth, *yéyé* was largely irrelevant. Despite Hallyday's *blouson noir* past, his switch to hippie styling, and a religious row in 1970 over a song which proclaimed Jesus Christ a 'hippie', he was no revolutionary. Like him, *yéyé* stars mostly found May bewildering – and irritating when money-spinning concerts or recording sessions had to be cancelled – and so opted for prudent conservatism. To the magazine *Noir et blanc* shortly after May, Hallyday confessed: 'At the moment, I must admit I can't make much sense of it,' while France Gall exclaimed 'Goodness me, I was so scared! [. . .] But today, I'm completely reassured. Everything has gone back to normal. I'm so happy!' Frank Alamo, on the other hand, felt able to offer readers the benefit of a political insight: 'a few thousand irresponsible people have almost plunged France into a dreadful crisis. Fortunately, General de Gaulle has shown himself to be up to the job!'[37]

Although *yéyé* was clearly sidelined by the May 'events', mainstream pop nevertheless continued to flourish. In a *France-Soir* poll of France's favourite singers dated September 1968, Mireille Mathieu, a Piaf soundalike who had risen meteorically under Johnny Stark's management, came top, followed by Sheila.[38] Hallyday, Sheila, Claude François, Françoise Hardy and France Gall were still big stars, and some – Sheila, Hardy, Vartan, François – went on to major success in the 1970s, or, in Hallyday's case, far beyond. None the less, what the 'events' revealed (and exacerbated) was the fact that French youth culture was no longer homogeneous – if it ever had been. By 1968, French popular music in fact had at least three discernible forms. In addition to *yéyé*, there was the text-song, which was steadily being canonised. Although Brel had given up live performance in 1967, he remained a star and, with Ferré and Brassens, rode out the *yéyé* storm. Bécaud and Aznavour, with a lusher, more commercial style closer to the US crooners, also continued to sell, and occasional newcomers joined the ranks of the singer-songwriter, such as Colette Magny or Georges Moustaki. Alongside the well-established interpreters of *chanson* like Gréco, new ones became associated with the genre, notably the actor Serge Reggiani, who in his forties began recording and performing the songs of Vian, Moustaki and others. Then there was *variétés*, which proved remarkably resilient in the face of *yéyé*. In 1968, Georgette Plana, for example, a music-hall star of the 1940s in the pseudo-Latin mould, had

a big hit with 'Riquita', and the pre-war crooner Tino Rossi still commanded an audience large enough to justify a double album of tango music. Maurice Chevalier and Josephine Baker also had shows on in Paris.[39]

Of course, no such crude typology is ever watertight, even in less tumultuous times. Mutual influences were frequent, particularly once television began to turn virtually everybody into sequined variety stars. The positioning of Bécaud or even Aznavour on an axis between text-song and *variétés* is not easy. Similarly, the line between *variétés* and the work of some *yéyé* stars – Claude François, for example, or Petula Clark – was also becoming harder to draw. Even Hallyday was steadily metamorphosing into the *chanson* star he is considered today. Some of these crossovers were startling. Perhaps the most fascinating instance was Serge Gainsbourg, the Left-Bank singer-songwriter of the 1950s who had even met Fréhel in his childhood, but who switched to pop to survive, famously claiming to have 'turned his coat' when he realised it was 'lined with mink'. He began writing literate, disingenuous *yéyé* for the demure France Gall, including a 1965 Eurovision winner, 'Poupée de cire, poupée de son' (Wax Doll, Rag Doll), which unobtrusively plays on words to deconstruct the *yéyé* industry, and the discreetly lubricious 'Les Sucettes' (Lollipops). He then launched his own career as a pop *provocateur*, coming out with, among others, the international *succès de scandale* of 1969, 'Je t'aime, moi non plus' (I Love you, Neither Do I) with Jane Birkin, and ten years later an equally controversial reggae version of the French national anthem. Today, more than a decade after his death in 1991, he is probably more highly regarded and influential than ever, his former home turned into a virtual shrine.

As Gainsbourg's crossover already betrays, pop was becoming the lingua franca of the young throughout the world by the end of the 1960s. French popular music's evolution since 1968 is therefore the story of how the 'barbarians' were finally 'civilised' and settled in, the story in fact of pop's authentication.

Notes

1. Peterson, 'Why 1955?' p. 97.
2. Christian Victor and Julien Regoli, *Vingt Ans de rock français* (Albin Michel, 1978), p. 16.
3. Farchy, *La Fin de l'exception culturelle?*, p. 57, and MPO's website: *http://www.mpo.fr/*.
4. Victor and Regoli, *Vingt Ans de rock français*, pp. 11–28 (quotation p. 11); Raoul Hoffmann and Jean-Marie Leduc, *Rock babies: 25 ans de pop music* (Seuil, 1978), Chapter 4.

5. Arthur Marwick, *The Sixties: Cultural Revolution in Britain, France, Italy and the United States, c.1958–c.1974* (Oxford University Press, 1998), p. 99.
6. Ibid., p. 95.
7. Doubt is occasionally cast on the truth of the 'myth' of broken seats at the Olympia, though not specifically about Bécaud. Of pop concerts generally, one of my correspondents writes: 'This is a myth, as solid as a myth: there have hardly ever been any seats broken at the Olympia.' There is also some uncertainty about whether Bécaud's famous appearance there took place in 1954 or 1955.
8. Jean-Charles Lagrée, *Les Jeunes chantent leurs cultures* (L'Harmattan, 1982), pp. 13–16.
9. My sources here are various: Maurice Achard, *Souvenirs, souvenirs . . .* (Flammarion, 1998), pp. 36–43; individual reminiscences included in the radio programme 'Le Rock débarque en France' ('Histoire en direct'), France Culture, 2 June 1997; and to a lesser extent Claude Fléouter, *Johnny: la dernière des légendes* (Robert Laffont, 1992). Long Chris had some justification for Americanising his name since his mother was Texan. Hallyday too had an entitlement of sorts. As a child, he had accompanied his aunt and two female cousins on tour as a dance act. In London, the act was joined by an American dancer (who married one of the cousins), calling himself Lee Halliday. As his career began, Johnny took the surname, though the spelling was accidentally altered.
10. Bertrand Bonnieux, 'Une Certaine Tendance du rock français', in 'Dossier rocks nationaux', *Écouter Voir* (January 1990), pp. 26–8.
11. English quotation from Iain Chambers, *Urban Rhythms: Pop Music and Popular Culture* (Macmillan, 1985), p. 38; Paul Yonnet, *Jeux, modes et masses: la société française et le moderne 1945–1985* (Gallimard, 1985), p. 158.
12. Teillet, 'Une Politique culturelle du rock?', p. 220.
13. Tony Dunn, 'The Evolution of Cultural Studies', in David Punter (ed.), *Introduction to Contemporary Cultural Studies* (Longman, 1986), p. 82.
14. Lucien Rioux, *Cinquante Ans de chanson française* (L'Archipel, 1994), pp. 138–9.
15. 'Le Rock'n'roll aujourd'hui', *L'Express*, 22 June 1961, pp. 44–5 (p. 44).
16. Later, once Taylor's career had flagged, he is reported to have discovered a sci-fi mysticism, becoming, so David Bowie recounts, the model for Bowie's character Ziggy Stardust.
17. Victor and Regoli, *Vingt Ans de rock français*, p. 37.
18. 'Le Rock débarque en France'.
19. *L'Express* quotation from 'Le Rock'n'roll aujourd'hui', p. 44; *Le Courrier du Parlement* quoted in Victor and Regoli, *Vingt Ans de rock français*, p. 24; de Gaulle quoted in Hoffmann and Leduc, *Rock babies*, p. 39.

20. Boris Vian, *En avant la zizique, et par ici les gros sous* (Pauvert, 1997; first published 1958), p. 58.
21. Jacques Pessis and Jean-Pierre Blamangin (eds), *Génération Mireille* (Édition° 1, 1995), pp. 37–8.
22. 'Le Rock'n'roll aujourd'hui', p. 45.
23. Contrary to what most accounts claim, the term *yéyé* could not have derived from the Beatles' single 'She Loves You', since it was already in use before the song was released in August 1963. It is more likely to have originated in the common refrain 'woah, woah, yeah, yeah' used by a variety of pre-Beatles singers from the Everly Brothers to Helen Shapiro.
24. Claude Fléouter, *Un Siècle de chansons* (Presses Universitaires de France, 1988), p. 72; 'Les Années Barclay' (TV programme), France 3, 14 September 1999.
25. Rioux, *Cinquante Ans de chanson française*, pp. 135–6.
26. Victor and Regoli, *Vingt Ans de rock français*, p. 22.
27. Marwick, *The Sixties*, pp. 104–9. See also Michael Kelly, 'Catholic Cultural Policy from 1944 to 1950: "Bande dessinée" and Cinema', in Brian Rigby and Nicholas Hewitt (eds), *France and the Mass Media* (Macmillan, 1991), pp. 20–36.
28. Papon, Bouvard and Charpy are quoted in *Salut les copains*, no. 13 (August 1963), pp. 3 (Papon) and 30. This issue also contains a more sympathetic account of the night: Claude Brulé, 'Un Croulant à la Nation', pp. 31 and 90.
29. Ibid., pp. 3–5 and 89.
30. Victor and Regoli, *Vingt Ans de rock français*, p. 16.
31. Edgar Morin, 'Salut les copains', *Le Monde*, 6 July 1963, pp. 1 and 11; and 7–8 July 1963, p. 12.
32. Françoise Hardy's 'J'ai jeté mon cœur' (I've Thrown My Heart Away), which she co-wrote, is just one example among many of a song in the *yéyé* style which crisply captures in suitably coded language the sexual anxiety of adolescence.
33. Michel Lancelot, *Je veux regarder Dieu en face: le phénomène hippie* (Albin Michel, 1968), p. 16.
34. Ibid., p. 23.
35. Ibid., p. 23.
36. Sylvie Coulomb and Didier Varrod, *1968–1988: Histoire de chansons: de Maxime Leforestier à Étienne Daho* (Balland, 1987), p. 18.
37. Ibid., pp. 22–4.
38. Ibid., p. 17. Mireille Mathieu must not be confused with Mireille Hartuch, whose stage name was simply 'Mireille'.
39. Ibid., p. 15.

– 3 –

From 1968 to the Present: Authenticity and *Métissage*

From the 1970s to the end of the century, the boundaries between *chanson*, *variétés* and *yéyé* become ever harder to mark out. For, if there is one word which summarises the stylistic evolution of French popular music since 1968, it is *métissage*: cross-fertilisation. This term is often reserved for the 'world music' of the 1980s and 1990s, ethnic styles fused with Western rock rhythms and instrumentation. But less dramatic forms of *métissage* evolved much earlier than this, as *chanson* and *variétés* began assimilating the international pop idiom, though this has not always been a one-way traffic. Paris has been a musical melting pot for a long time, and a sprinkling of expatriate Anglophones, playing with French musicians or singing in French, adopting and adapting French styles, had been lighting the way for cross-fertilisation for some years, in sometimes original ways which the myth of Anglo-Saxon invasion fails to account for: from Josephine Baker and Sidney Bechet, to Petula Clark (whose very name used sometimes to be gallicised as Petu La Clark), Jane Birkin and a handful of folk artists I shall come to shortly.

The sociologist Paul Yonnet provides a useful conceptual framework for the evolution of *métissage*. He reasons that the problem of cultural Americanisation was caused not by any inadequacy in the indigenous *chanson* but rather by its strength. In his view, the development in Western societies of an organic youth culture which transcended social, ethnic and national barriers to become the universal class-consciousness of modern youth was bound up with what he calls the 'transcultural' nature of rock'n'roll: the exchange of elements of black and white youth cultures, their musical forms and their behaviours.[1] Transculturalism created a new creative space which young Americans could occupy to forge an identity of their own. In France, however, where the existence of similarly diverse ethnic and regional communities offered similar opportunities, no such space became available. This, Yonnet argues, was because, in its heyday between 1953 and 1961, *chanson* was entirely monocultural, turned in on itself against new influences either from outside or within France: 'it was produced by and for the French [*une production franco-française*]; it synthesised absolutely nothing, [. . .] a one-dimensional music, with no entrance or exit, a music I shall call Jacobin'.[2] Young people were unable to gain any purchase on this compact monolith, to find any loose ends with which to weave a new generational music. *Chanson* therefore withered on the vine in the 1960s rather than being renewed, the young mostly turning to Anglophone pop instead, or French imitations of it.

How can this closure of French *chanson* during the 1950s be explained seeing that, before the Occupation, Trenet and Django Reinhardt had shown France to be perfectly capable of producing transcultural music? For Yonnet, it has to do with a defensive post-war reinforcement of cultural Jacobinism, in the context of decolonisation and 'the degaullisation of the structures of French society around a strong state'. During the 1950s and 1960s, he correctly notes, the time-honoured French 'ideology' of high culture was reinforced and disseminated by a movement dedicated to its democratisation: 'Improving oneself culturally did not yet mean watching television [. . .]; it meant reading the classics, going to classical theatre, a highly written theatre; and it meant listening to classical music, both highly written and highly rigidified, codified, reified [. . .].'[3] Artistic legitimacy in France, Yonnet goes on, was thus identified with a national literary tradition; so it was natural for singer-songwriters to build their reputation and self-image by identifying themselves with a high-cultural form, namely poetry: setting established poets to music as Ferré, Brassens and Ferrat did, having their own lyrics published by Seghers in its 'Poètes d'aujourd'hui' (Poets of Today) series, or recited by famous stage actors. From this elevated, lyric-centred vantage-point, rock and pop could only look crass and be dismissed, or be mocked for their illiteracy, as Vian did, rather than being absorbed and reworked. Yonnet therefore concludes that 1960s pop was a threat to *chanson* not because of American economic imperialism (as the UK's success in the USA demonstrates), but because of *chanson*'s imprisonment in an obsolete national hierarchy of aesthetic value, at a time when youth culture was open to the international.

Yonnet's reading of 1950s *chanson* is unsound up to a point, paying insufficient attention to the diversity and musical innovations of the immediate post-war generation. The influence of jazz, swing or other styles is audible in the work of Aznavour, Bécaud, Brassens and Brel, while Ferré was increasingly experimental musically. Then there are the influences of Brecht and Weill, Latin American music, and so on. None the less, Yonnet's basic thesis carries weight, illuminating the cultural-historical significance of *métissage*. By the early 1960s, *chanson* did seem to be hardening into a defensive national genre, the songs of Brel, Brassens and Ferré all appearing in the Seghers poetry series at the very moment when Anglo-Saxon pop began to be viewed as a 'threat' to French cultural exceptionalism. Yet pop's ascendancy, in tandem with the Sixties 'cultural revolution', can be understood more positively than this, Yonnet intimates: as interrupting this sclerosis, clearing the arteries and getting new influences pumping through *chanson* once again. Certainly, from the early 1970s one may detect – in *chanson* and in popular music generally – a drive to experiment by appropriating rather than imitating Anglo-American styles and rooting them in French experience, to restore authenticity by expressing oneself in a language (metaphorically and literally) of one's own but *reinventing* that language in the process. In this chapter, I want to examine the various forms this authentication took and the contextual factors which made it possible. I shall begin by looking at the immediate impact of May 1968 on pop and *chanson*, before moving on to a range of newer forms from the 1980s and 1990s.

Pop from 1968

As we saw, *yéyé* was breaking up by the late 1960s and the term soon ceased to describe an identifiable reality. The beginning of the 1970s therefore saw a revealing terminological shift, as the interchangeable anglicisms *la pop-music*, *la musique pop* or just *la pop* became established. These covered a more diffuse set of styles and acknowledged the influence of Anglo-American rock bands like the Rolling Stones, Pink Floyd and Jimi Hendrix. It was in fact in French versions of such groups that the rebellious spirit of the late 1960s mostly became lodged in French music. *Yéyé* had not been a band phenomenon, though a handful of rock groups had started up before 1968, such as Alan Jack Civilization or the Variations, in venues like the Golf Drouot.[4] Around 1970, there were some abortive attempts to bring *gauchisme* and pop together in some form. The Youth Liberation Front (FLJ) disrupted pop concerts in an effort to produce revolutionary happenings in the Woodstock mould, provoking violent confrontations with riot police and for a time making it hard to obtain municipal authorisation for such events. The FLJ was replaced in October 1970 by the FLIP, whose manifesto defended pop as a 'subversive weapon to change life and transform the world here and now'.[5] Simultaneously, a number of new bands emerged, mostly instrumental or singing in English and loosely identified with this subversive spirit to varying degrees. A few were directly political, such as Red Noise, formed by Boris Vian's son Patrick, or Komintern, which grew out of it and was behind the formation of the FLIP. Others, like Gong, Magma and Ange, saw themselves as revolutionary in a formal, 'progressive' sense, combining rock with free jazz, synthesisers, happenings and even, in one or two cases, the work of Brel or Brassens.

Magma and Ange were prepared to use conventional means of promotion like playing at the Golf Drouot or touring with Hallyday, even doing some

TV when they could. Accordingly they enjoyed a degree of success. Others preferred to reject the entire apparatus of the music business, which in any case rejected them since record companies were now sceptical of the viability of French-language rock and TV certainly would have nothing to do with them. Instead, living in communes or squats, supported by an underground press (*Le Pop* and the more successful *Actuel*) and by two underground labels, Byg and Futura, they sought to establish an alternative live-music circuit. This included the national network of youth centres, the MJCs (*maisons des jeunes et de la culture*), universities and Woodstock-style festivals. The first of these took place in autumn 1969, shortly after Woodstock, organised by Byg and the magazine *Actuel*, though after difficulties with the French authorities it had to switch location to Amougies in Belgium.[6] Further festivals ensued in 1970 and 1971, in Aix-en-Provence, Biot, Saint-Gratien and elsewhere, but in chaotic circumstances and sometimes despite local-government bans and clashes with police. The era of the improvised one-off festival in fact proved ephemeral, though from it grew more lasting initiatives like the annual 'Printemps de Bourges' event, which began in 1977 as a way of promoting *chanson* unknowns or marginals and which survives today with a wide mix of styles and talents; or the Transmusicales de Rennes (1979), which today makes room for electronic dance music. Furthermore, as we shall see, the political ambition behind the festival movement, which was to set up a parallel economy to that of showbiz capitalism, was one of several distinctive sequels of May 1968 in the French pop world which together provided new structures for new creativities.

Chanson from 1968

Chanson too was radicalised by May and its aftermath. In January 1968, the state-owned radio station France-Inter had been the most popular. In May, it was discredited when state censorship restricted its coverage of the events. Europe 1 then became the station to listen to, followed by RTL (formerly Luxembourg). By 1968, although the *Salut les copains* magazine was still flourishing, the radio show was not. In April, the station launched a new youth programme, Michel Lancelot's significantly named 'Campus', which came closer to the public mood, introducing listeners to more experimental, vaguely underground *chanson* artists like Catherine Ribeiro, Jacques Higelin and Brigitte Fontaine.[7] At the same time, the influence of Dylan, protest and folk-rock, mixed in with the events of May, stimulated a wave of topical songs. These were of variable quality. Shortly after the Woodstock and Isle of Wight Festivals, Michel Delpech, a *yéyé* artist with Barclay since 1965, released 'Wight is Wight', which, as the pun in the title grimly forewarned, was little more than a ragbag of Anglo-Saxon allusions. More seriously, Dominique Grange, who had started a music career in the early 1960s as a student at the Sorbonne, recorded a set of four songs about May shortly after the events, sold for three francs during demonstrations with earnest titles like 'Down with the Police State' ('A bas l'état policier') and 'Indefinite Strike' ('Grève illimitée'). Georges Moustaki wrote the sentimental 'Le Temps de vivre' (The Time to Live) inspired by the events, while Léo Ferré, already in his fifties but perennially transgressive and radicalised even further by May, released an album containing a number of songs which conveyed more complex responses to it: 'Les Anarchistes', 'Comme une fille' (Like a Girl) and 'L'Été 68' (The Summer of 68). He also began working with a progressive jazz-rock group called Zoo for two years, recording an album entitled *La Solitude* (1972), which included strange, amorphous declamations to an electronic accompaniment.

Ferré's innovations proved seminal, as did Gainsbourg's. Their examples, together with the popularity of American folk-rock in the late 1960s, helped drive *chanson* into the arms of pop. Lyrically at least, the French tradition of the singer-songwriter mapped quite easily onto the poetry and protest of folk-rock, though there was an abyss between them musically. This was precisely where change came with the next generation. While occasional French performers like Aufray diluted the American folk idiom somewhat, expatriate English speakers like the New Zealander Graeme Allwright and the American Steve Waring began transposing the songs of Dylan, Cohen or Tom Paxton more faithfully into French. As in the USA and UK, folk clubs also sprang up, starting with the Traditional Mountain Sound in Saint-Germain, while Paris's American Center furnished a base where performers like Waring and his music partner Roger Mason could both perform and teach. Another club, Le Bourdon, became the first devoted to a revival of French folk music, as some artists, following the examples of Pete Seeger and the Folkways label, sought a new authenticity by working with their own regional-minority heritage: the Alsatian Roger Siffer, the Occitan Claude Marti, the Breton Gilles Servat.[8] Especially significant in the context of *métissage* was Alain Stivell, who championed a Breton music revival. Stivell himself played the Celtic harp but his band brought together rock instruments and traditional ones, which he saw as an organic way of reinterpreting and reinventing a regional past.

At much the same time, new singer-songwriters emerged who reworked the 'national' *chanson* tradition in a similarly acoustic-folk or soft-rock style. Maxime Le Forestier (born 1949) found success from 1972 with songs which fused the lilting rhythm of folk with the spare arrangements of Brassens and the more romantic melodies associated with *chanson*. His combination of appearance (long hair, beard, jeans), themes (anti-militarism in 'Parachutiste', the hippie dream in 'San Francisco') and polished, sometimes precious verse made him probably the first newcomer of the *chanson* canon (he was hailed as Brassens's successor) made in the image of a late Sixties folk poet. Between 1973 and 1977, he was among the three best-selling album artists in France.[9] Others invoked Ferré as their inspiration: Alain Souchon (born 1945), Francis Cabrel (1953), Bernard Lavilliers (1946), Yves Simon (1945), Renaud (1952) and Jean-Jacques Goldman (1951). All of these used the pop or folk-rock idiom (hard rock in the case of Lavilliers) which they had grown up with, but remained within the French tradition by writing well-crafted songs in their own tongue drawing on their own experience. Renaud adopted perhaps the most original approach to national authenticity by blending the *chanson réaliste* of *belle-époque* Paris with contemporary pop but with a ludic, reflexive distance which allowed him to comment subtextually on contemporary music while observing contemporary France. With Renaud, *chanson* turned post-modern, which was to have some impact on the music of the 1980s and 1990s.[10]

As with early French rock, these post-1968 singer-songwriters were indebted to alternative structures for production and live performance: provincial cultural centres like the MJCs or the more bohemian venues in Paris such as Lucien Gibara's Pizza du Marais, where Renaud began performing. This was largely because the media became ever more obsessed with Anglo-American product and largely ignored *chanson*. One or two dedicated magazines kept the lamp alight, though they struggled to survive. Fred Hidalgo's *Paroles et musique* died once and was reborn as today's *Chorus;* a similar magazine, *Chanson,* launched in 1973, lasted only five years.[11] As for radio, the vinyl revolution put an end to live music broadcasts, as stations went over to playing records, but some still managed to stay true to *chanson* in different ways and assisted new talent. One was RTL, where Monique Le Marcis was in charge of music programming and helped launch Le Forestier, Michel Berger and others. On state radio, some quality programming from the 1960s went under, like the poet Luc Bérimont's 'La Fine Fleur de la chanson française' (The Flower of French Song), a talent contest for new poetic songwriting which had helped launch several new *chanson* careers.[12] But new programmes also sprang up, such as Jean-Louis Foulquier's successive shows on state radio (France-Inter): 'Studio de nuit' (Night Studio), 'Saltimbanques' (Entertainers) and 'Il y a de la chanson dans l'air' (Song is in the Air). It was on the last of these, in summer 1979, that Foulquier launched the term *la nouvelle chanson française* to describe the new wave of 1970s singer-songwriters, many of whom went on to become the established *chanson* stars of the 1980s and 1990s.[13]

One other media-related factor which helped this generation, and transformed the French music market into the bargain, was the creation of an official Top 50 in 1984. Charts of some description had existed since the 1960s, organised by radio stations like Europe 1 (via 'Salut les copains') or RTL. But these were unreliable as they were based solely on the preference of those listeners who took the trouble to write or phone in. From 1984, two polling agencies, IPSOS and Nielson, were employed to garner data more scientifically on sales of singles in record shops, chains and supermarkets, which Europe 1, the TV station Canal Plus and the TV magazine *Télé 7 Jours* then announced weekly. A Top 30 was also established for album sales. The impact of *'le Top'* was mixed. On the positive side, it created an opportunity for the latest *chanson* artists to demonstrate their popularity because it revealed that the dinosaurs of *variétés* were not the best-sellers their media exposure suggested, but that the new generation – Renaud, Cabrel, Lavilliers, Goldman – were. The down-side was that it encouraged the biggest retailers such as hypermarkets, which account for the majority of record sales in France, to stock only chart hits. This considerably reduced opportunities for new talent to reach a wide market and for small specialist retailers to make up for slow-moving stock by selling hits. Moreover, the chart began affecting rather than reflecting sales, influencing production too in that artists learnt to produce a biddable single as a way of promoting an album.[14]

By the second half of the 1970s, the cultural legitimation of *chanson* in France in its most ambitious forms was virtually complete. For evidence, one has only to look at the way record companies were looking to the repackaging strategies of book and classical-music publishers: re-editing neglected singers like the late Bobby Lapointe, and producing anthologies of complete works in box sets.[15] Furthermore, singer-songwriters were appearing who also wrote books: Yves Simon and Julos Beaucarne, or the lyricist Philippe Labro, who wrote for Hallyday among others. The academic study of Brassens and Brel had also begun. Yet as *chanson* waxed culturally, it waned commercially. The optimism about the 'new French *chanson*' was in truth a rearguard action in response to an equally publicised phenomenon: 'the crisis' in French *chanson*. Of the previous generations of legendary artists, Piaf was dead and Chevalier died in 1972, followed by Brel in 1978 and Brassens in 1981. *Chanson's* more recent manifestation as folk protest or hippie radicalism was soon over, as economic recession and youth depoliticisation took their toll. As for the newcomers like Renaud and Cabrel, their need initially to rely on an alternative live circuit had been partly due to the fact that the mainstream music-hall tradition of giving over the first half of a show to little-known support acts was dying out, especially as the biggest stars were by then beginning to perform in massive venues holding thousands of people, like the Palais des sports or Palais des congrès. Influenced by television, such events became prone to spectacle inflation, some stars in the 1980s even hiring top theatre directors like Jérôme Savary (Eddy Mitchell) and Patrice Chéreau (Jacques Higelin) to stage their shows. Obviously, such methods were beyond the means and often the talent of young unknowns.

This was all part of a growing sense in the 1970s and 1980s that the *chanson* as craft, interpreted by a solo artist accompanied by only one or two instruments, was of meagre entertainment value compared to the production values of the TV spectacular. In 1981, it was estimated that of some 3,000 singers in France, only 1 per cent appeared regularly on mainstream television.[16] Those who did had to mime to their records because it was cheaper. Dominated by the light-entertainment values of presenters like Guy Lux or Michel Drucker, public television (no private channels existed at the time) seemed incapable of handling *chanson* in anything other than the language of showbiz and promotion: a small circle of bespangled regulars chatting, giggling and miming to their latest releases before a complicit studio audience. The closest anyone came to an alternative was a show called 'Carnaval' hosted by Patrick Sébastien, though here the most promising representatives of *chanson*, Renaud or Francis Cabrel, were required to dress up in playful deconstructions of their public selves.[17] *Chanson* was indeed looking, in the words of a corrosive Gainsbourg on 'Apostrophes', like a distinctly 'minor' genre; or as Henri Salvador put it, as if it were dying of 'anglosaxonitis'.[18]

From Pop to Alternative Rock

Meanwhile, Anglo-American pop, sustained by developing technologies (smaller and better-quality hi-fi systems, cassette players, video), had become a multimillion-dollar global industry, now founded not just on the youth market but on 'adult-oriented rock' for Sixties veterans, creating a buoyant consumer base for reissues. Youth and its pleasures in fact started to become a universal value in the 1970s. From mid-decade, the kind of teen pop once represented by *yéyé* was reborn as disco, which swept from the US into Britain and continental Europe, boosted by the John Travolta film *Saturday Night Fever* (1977) and the Bee Gees' soundtrack, which sold over thirty million copies. As with early rock'n'roll, derivative French acts began springing up, including a number of repackaged *yéyé* stars. Sheila, managed from the first by impresario Claude Carrère and signed to his label, was still popular in the 1970s but growing stale. Carrère therefore relaunched her as a disco act (and himself as an international distributor) with the help of a group of black singers, under the alias Sheila B. Devotion, whose dance rendition of 'Singing in the Rain' became an international hit, even in the UK.[19]

A further threat to *chanson* came in the form of what became known as 'French rock'. This development, and the skein of meanings attributed to the term '*le rock*' by this time, have to be understood in the context of the evolution of the music industry worldwide and the arrival of punk. In market terms, as disco partly illustrates, the main feature of the global pop landscape in the mid-1970s was segmentation: the development of a mosaic of genres and sub-genres which in turn influenced or combined with each other to create further micro-divisions. Each genre or sub-genre had its own following in an ever-expanding market. Increasingly, these segments had little explicit content other than style, amounting to what one observer calls 'a series of fashions concerned about their brand image and offering consumers a variety of suggestions for identities': progressive, glam rock, punk, new-romantic, grunge, and so on.[20] Nevertheless, for want of a better word, all were initially classed as *la pop-music*, as we saw, but then, in another terminological shift, which took place from the end of the 1970s, as *le rock*. In practice, this clarified nothing whatsoever since, like *la pop-music*, *le rock* was a misleadingly singular label for an increasingly plural phenomenon. But the term's adoption as a *meta-genre* probably came about once it had been adopted as a *sub-generic* category covering a new phenomenon of loud, thrashing Francophone music produced in France by bands which in English would probably be called hard rock or even heavy metal. This musical evolution owes much to UK punk.

As seen earlier, rock groups did exist in France before punk, but they were beset with problems. Part of France's delay in developing a rock of its own can be attributed to the shortage of the kinds of infrastructure which have helped it flourish in other countries: rehearsal space where noise would not cause nuisance; bars or pubs where beginners could gain experience of performing; and recording studios.[21] In addition, the music press was infatuated with Anglo-American rock – particularly the left-wing daily *Libération*, at the forefront of fashionable metropolitanism – and French-language albums did not sell all that well. Few commentators have had any good to say about these early bands since, like *yéyé*, their music was considered inauthentic. In January 1981, the journalist Patrice Bollon wrote in *Libération* of 'the big sleep' of French 'rock' since the first Palais des sports festivals twenty years before, in terms which recall Lancelot's diagnosis of French responses to the hippie movement:

> French rock is rock made by the colonised, which has no roots other than imported and (or) mythical ones. A 'country-bumpkin' rock whose capital is a fantastical 'New York' or an imaginary 'London' and which retains of its models only a 'form' completely devoid of real 'meaning'. [. . .] A rock torn between complacency and nothing but vague impulse, with no profound authenticity.

Imitation is endemic, he adds, a symptom of French rock's 'hopeless provincialism'.[22] Like Lancelot's, Bollon's criterion for authenticity here is straightforward and explicit: genuine creativity. The rhetoric of colonialism serves as a metaphor not of American invasion but of French submission, a self-inflicted, masochistic abdication of creative input. Bollon accepts that all musicians start by copying as a way of learning their trade; but the apprenticeship has to come to an end eventually, the copy must be 'assimilated and reinvested with a meaning which was not there before in the original. What can you say when the copying goes on forever, when it sets itself up as an absolute value?'[23] Part of this 'neo-colonial' reading is a subtextual sense that pop remains a foreign language for French bands: they have mastered its basic grammar but can still only mouth platitudes. The latest evidence of this, in Bollon's estimate, is punk, which French groups like Stinky Toys (admittedly not a name to trigger moral panic) have transformed from a 'social movement', with 'a meaning and a necessity', into 'a pointless formal gimmick, no more than a speeded-up rhythm'.[24] Bollon's reading is perceptive and uncompromising (though his own form of submissiveness to the Anglo-Saxon might repay investigation), but it misses an important point where punk is concerned. In one sense, punk was the last of the collective youth movements begun in the 1950s, one which had its own styles, language and meanings. But like Dada, it was also a movement against movements. In this sense, it may be viewed as the ultimate disintegration of Morin's notion of a homogeneous youth culture and as furthering pop's segmentation. However, like Dada, it also appears to have freed up creativity. Certainly, punk did not have as profound an impact as it did in Britain (not immediately, at least) and was on one level just another high-profile foreign form ripe for imitation, as Bollon claims. Yet punk style – musical primitivism, lyrical aggressiveness, trashy iconography – was designed to delegitimate and deprofessionalise pop ('We want to be amateurs,' Johnny Rotten demanded), to place it back where it belonged, in the hands of snarling youth.[25] This DIY aesthetic seems eventually to have released French pop from its self-imposed 'colonial' treadmill, showing it how to appropriate styles and evolve its own permutations and meanings. The first of these was a more authentic French rock.

Most commentators agree that this began in the mid-1970s with Jacques Higelin, who proved that it was possible to combine Anglo-American instrumentation with articulate use of the French language, hitherto deemed incompatible with rock's simple duple chug. A number of reasonably successful bands then began to emerge at the end of the 1970s branded either rockers, like Trust, Bijou and Téléphone; punks, like Starshooter, Stinky Toys and Métal urbain; or new-wave, like Indochine. Some, chiefly those associated with hard rock, were still accused of being enslaved to Anglo-American models like the Stones. Many did not last, though Téléphone kept going for nine years. But the real flowering of punk came in the mid-1980s, with what became known as 'alternative rock'. It is at this moment that one can begin to talk of a true implanting of pop, of a musical graft which has taken and finally flowered in foreign soil. Several factors may be adduced to explain it.

Benetello and Le Goff point out that musically one of British punk's innovations was the rejection of US blues and rock harmonies based on the tonic/subdominant/dominant pattern, in favour of a more specifically 'British' sound using more varied chord sequences and underscored by an English rather than feigned American accent.[26] But there is also a case for suggesting, as the authors briefly do, that from this naturalisation arose a more European consciousness in pop. Certainly, it is since the punk era that a growing band of French acts have achieved recognition in Britain: Vanessa Paradis, Stinky Toys (signed by Malcolm McLaren), Les Négresses vertes and MC Solaar, before the techno wave took French music to unprecedented heights internationally in the late 1990s. Punk also helped restore one of the founding principles of rock'n'roll, which was that, at the furthest remove from progressive or stadium rock, music can be made with only a minimum of skill, training and equipment. This helps explain a remarkable proliferation of amateur and semi-pro bands, chiefly in the provinces, from the mid-1970s.

As the sociologist Patrick Mignon argues, this proliferation outside Paris was also the result of sociocultural factors which helped bring about a steady acclimatisation of pop. Unexpectedly, one of these was the French Communist Party. Despite its hostility to mass culture, the PCF, as we saw, was drawn to youth music quite early on because of its apparent dissidence. Hence the Party's launch of its youth magazine, *Nous les garçons et les filles*, in 1963. Later, in the early 1970s, the Party's annual bash, the Fête de *L'Humanité*, started booking top French and international pop acts, while local PCF events created performance opportunities for neighbourhood groups.[27] A second factor was the greater suitability of local environments to this kind of music. Given the shortage of suitable rehearsal space in densely populated areas, small towns and suburbs offered better opportunities because, alongside the traditional *bal* (an improvised dance or 'hop'), there were barns, garages and individual housing available, as opposed to blocks of flats where noise was often an obstacle. Hence rock's wider sociological recruitment in such areas.[28]

This decentralisation is related to another factor explaining the blossoming of alternative rock, which was the growth of an independent sector. France had already had a strong tradition of independent labels, including Carrère, Vogue and Barclay, though by the early 1980s these had mostly disappeared or been bought out. Here too, the DIY mentality of punk was an important driver, as a number of small, informally run companies sprang up enabling non-mainstream bands to avoid the interference and dispossession involved in working for the majors. In addition, the French indie movement had origins of its own in post-1968 Leftism, characterised by a self-management ideology and a culture of communes, squats and alternative circuits. For some, Mignon maintains, indie music was a way out the political impasse of the new Left, based on a belief that what is first needed to change society is personal liberation, 'driving out the cop inside your head': '[the ability to] constitute, within the interstices of urban life, places likely to become pockets of resistance or accumulated energy which society will be unable to control. Forming a rock band can signify this desire to achieve autonomy, and squats (empty flats or workshops which are occupied) can become the ideal location for these bands to express themselves.'[29]

Bondage Records (now known as Bond Age) was one instance of this spirit, starting life in 1982 as a non-profitmaking collective formed by 'Marsu', Philippe Baia and Jean-Yves Prieur. Its early days were typically chaotic. Relations with bands were based on trust rather than contracts, recording equipment was poor, and proceedings were occasionally disrupted by squat warfare or police raids.[30] Even so, the label survived and prospered, largely on the strength of its connection with a punk group, Les Béruriers (later Bérurier noir), managed by Marsu, who became one of the hottest indie properties of the 1980s. The label later acquired Ludwig von 88 and the Négresses vertes. Inevitably, however, Bondage became a limited company in 1986 and its founders left in 1989, feeling that it had become too much like a conventional business. A similar synergy came about between the rock group Les Garçons bouchers (the Butcher Boys), formed in 1985 by François Hadji-Lazaro, and Boucherie Productions, the label that he set up and ran. As this kind of DIY spirit spread in the 1980s and 1990s, technological innovations even allowed artists to self-produce in home studios, with all the added creative independence this gave them. Some insisted on supervising their own image too, maintaining control over everything from clothes and look to the design of their record sleeves.

The music associated with the indie movement was and remains diverse. One of its features was indebted to Renaud's post-modern recycling. Like him, several successful bands experimented with *métissage* by returning to the urban 'realist song', signified in some line-ups (Négresses vertes, Têtes raides) by the re-introduction of the accordion, producing 'a music that is so hybrid that it becomes brand new'.[31] The group Pigalle was formed in 1982 from folk-rock beginnings, again by the multi-talented Hadji-Lazaro, who fronted his two groups concurrently. Pigalle eccentrically hybridised punk and rock rhythms with folk, waltz and tango, using a wide variety of instruments including accordion, hurdy-gurdy and bagpipes. And like Renaud's, their early songs drew on and updated themes and locations from the 'realist songs' of Bruant, Fréhel and Piaf, underscored by knowing titles like 'Dans la salle du bar-tabac de la rue des Martyrs' (In the Bar on the Rue des Martyrs) and 'Marie la rouquine' (Marie the Redhead), both from their second album (1990).

But perhaps the most applauded product of this alternative scene is the duo Rita Mitsouko, also from a background of bohemianism and squats. Launching their career in 1980 at the Paris discothèque Le Gibus with an aggressively punk act intended to shock, Catherine Ringer and Fred Chichin had their first hit single 'Marcia Baïla' in 1985, reportedly the most played record ever on French radio. This was followed in 1986 by an acclaimed second album, *The No Comprendo*. They have also written for film, including the theme from Léos Carax's *Les Amants du Pont-Neuf* (1991). The duo has evolved an individual, eclectic manner which includes dance, theatre and video. *Le Nouvel Observateur*, announcing the release of their album *Cool Frénésie* in March 2000, described their style as a 'combination of lyrics full of imagery, often desolate or tragic, which dance to music that is always innovative, explosive mixtures of rock and Latin-American rhythms, jazz and popular waltz [java], funk and techno'.[32] Such representations are fairly characteristic of how alternative-rock artists generally are portrayed: there is a distinct sense that their avant-garde eclecticism places their music on a higher level of artistic ambition. Others working in a comparable popular-cum-experimental vein are the Têtes raides, Les Elles and, most successful commercially, Louise Attaque, who have achieved phenomenal success since the release of their eponymous 1997 album on the pioneering indie label Atmosphériques.

Despite such accomplishments, the alternative movement did not last long in its initial, anarchistic form, petering out by the end of the 1980s, as the founders of Bondage discovered. Their story is a fairly familiar one. Bérurier noir became famous and fell out with Bondage because they wanted a better deal, though they turned down offers from majors. Others had no such scruples and the independent labels often lost their most successful acts to majors, starting with La Mano negra, who moved from Boucherie Productions to Virgin in 1989. While Bond Age went on to open an international division and an experimental wing with its label Zelig and has now survived for two decades, Boucherie Productions folded as the century turned. In truth, the independents of the 1980s could rarely be fully independent anyway, since most were forced to sign distribution deals with majors as they lacked the sales force of the multinationals, though some were able to distribute their material via the French independent company New Rose. At the same time, although the post-punk era saw a multitude of groups find record deals, only a handful succeeded commercially and companies became chary of signing up more. The majors, though, should not be uniformly cast as villains. After Eddie Barclay sold his label to Polygram in 1979, it became the company's experimental wing under Philippe Constantin, a graduate of the prestigious business school HEC.

It was Constantin who signed Rita Mitsouko when he was at Virgin, as well as a number of other acclaimed artists working in similarly unclassifiable melting pots, for example Alain Bashung and the rock group Noir Désir.

The indie movement's main achievement, however, was to put an end to French pop's sense of inadequacy with regard to Anglo-America, as evidenced in this new readiness to rework popular French traditions. According to Enzo Enzo, a singer who herself looks back to the pre-pop *chanson*, the significance of this return to roots has to be set against years of trying to imitate Anglo-American music and of doing so badly: 'We have calmed down a bit and are coming back to a world that's more musical, more acoustic, towards something which touched us when we were kids, even if it belonged to our grand mothers.' The artist, argues Yves Simon on the same subject, is an 'archaeologist of knowledges, memories and imaginaries', reinventing the past and linking it to the present and future. Here too, one glimpses a subtextual rhetoric of past alienation and self-imposed colonisation, for example when Alain Stivell speaks of 'aesthetic tastes which were under-expressed, concealed, and repressed too. As people discover this, they rediscover a part of themselves, it's fantastic.'[33] The aesthetic motivation, then, would again appear to be a quest for authenticity, though of a special kind. For what also links such 'archaeological' acts as Renaud, Rita Mitsouko, Pigalle and Enzo Enzo is a post-modern irony, a self-conscious distance in which each of the contrasting styles – rock and the 'realist song', for example – functions as a ludic commentary on the other. In lesser groups, this reflexivity has become facile parody or derision, a sometimes embarrassing feature of French pop and a relic perhaps of imitation rather than appropriation. For the most talented, however, it has generated another of those 'transcultural' creative spaces identified by Yonnet.

World Music

Such experiments with authenticity took a different turn in the 1980s with world music ('*la world music*' in French, or sometimes *musiques métissées* or *la sono mondiale*), for which Paris has become a major centre. The term 'world music' was dreamt up in the late 1980s by a group of record producers led by Peter Gabriel who were looking for a tag with which to market the music from outside Europe and the English-speaking world that they had started to promote. It is also used to designate not simply non-Anglophone ethnic musics but a further form of *métissage* in which such musics are cross-fertilised with the sounds of Western pop and even occasionally *chanson*.[34]

In France, this form of cross-fertilisation took off in the late 1980s. From 1981 when private radio stations were legalised, community-based stations such as Radio Beur in Paris and Radio Galère in Marseilles began playing North African music particularly aimed at Beurs, second-generation immigrants of Maghrebi origin. This included Algerian raï, which became more widely known in metropolitan France with the first raï festival in France at Bobigny in January 1986. Raï began in and around Oran at the turn of the century as part of a popular oral tradition and by the 1960s was a celebratory acoustic music. Then, a new generation began fusing it with Western pop, which was flowing into the country after independence in 1962. This fusion was popularised in France by Khaled (formerly Cheb Khaled, born 1960), who first performed there at Bobigny. In 1991, he signed to Barclay and appeared at the WOMAD festival in Reading (UK). His single, 'Didi', sung in Arabic and hypnotically fusing North African, rock and jazz rhythms, became raï's first major hit in France in 1992, helping the eponymous album from which it was taken become an international best-seller. The end of the century found him still a star, with a big hit in 1999, shared with two other North African singers (Faudel and Rachid Taha), '1,2,3, soleil'. During the 1980s, such hybrids were seen as one of the voices of France's marginalised suburban communities, but also as offering the chance of a multicultural solidarity of young people, supposedly transcending post-colonial resentments. The anti-racist organisation SOS Racisme, set up in 1984 to encourage solidarity between young French people of diverse origins under the slogan 'Touche pas à mon pote' (Hands Off My Mate), particularly took this view and featured Khaled and other North African performers regularly at the series of outdoor concerts it organised from the mid-1980s. Musical styles from Sub-Saharan Africa also found success, for example Les Touré Kunda, Youssou N'Dour and Xalam, all from Senegal. So too did other styles, from Latin America like salsa, or from the Caribbean, in particular Guadeloupe and Martinique, where zouk is the favoured genre. Popularised by Kassav', a sixteen-piece band from Guadeloupe, zouk is, according to Rioux, 'born of local tradition and fed on North-American jazz, rock and funk, as well as Latin-American samba and salsa'.[35]

In most cases, the language of origin is retained, as with zouk (Creole) and raï. In others, a *chanson* standard may be reworked with some form of arrangement or sound which recontextualises it, as with the Egyptian Natasha Atlas's Arabised version of Françoise Hardy's 'Mon Amie la rose' (My Friend the Rose), or Carte de Séjour's 'Douce France' (Sweet France), an ironic take on the 1940s Trenet hit released in 1986 in response to Interior Minister Charles Pasqua's proposed Nationality Code. What distinguishes the group's interpretation is the Arabic inflexion in the singing and musical arrangement from the very first bars, and the aggressive punk delivery of the chorus: 'Sweet France, dear country of my childhood.' The topicality of its meaning was complex. In reworking a French classic of the Occupation which had expressed nostalgia for the old pre-war, rural French idyll, it both established an ironic distance from nationalist sentiment and simultaneously reclaimed the nation for a new, Beur generation. In a third configuration, some singer-songwriters (Lavilliers, Higelin, Renaud), following the controversial example of Paul Simon's 1986 album *Graceland*, set their own compositions to African accompaniments. The biggest success of this kind marked a come-back for Maxime Le Forestier with his 1988–9 hit, 'Né quelque part' (Born Somewhere), which, with its timely quotations from the Declaration of the Rights of Man of 1789, became an anthem of official multiculturalism at the time of the bicentenary of the French Revolution. A fourth slant on world music were the bands which combined several different languages and musical traditions in a post-modern melting pot: La Mano negra, sometimes classified as 'flamenco rock', the Négresses vertes, whose twelve original members were European and North African, or the Gipsy Kings, a group from Arles who sing in French and Spanish.

Why did world music catch on so extensively in metropolitan France? At one level, its dissemination was made possible by conjunctural or infrastructural factors. One of these was media enthusiasm, notably from *Libération*, *Actuel* and, once again, a favourable FM station, Radio Nova. Another was the existence of festivals: either broad-based ones like Le Printemps de Bourges which welcomed it, or those entirely given over to it, like Musiques métisses in Angoulême or Nuits blanches pour la musique noire.[36] Also vital once again were independent production and distribution structures which took up the musics: Sonodisc, Déclic and, especially, Celluloid, another label with roots in the extreme Left, formed by two former members of the post-1968 Proletarian Left group, Jean Caracos and Gilbert Castro. Starting off with post-punk new-wave acts, it soon moved into world music, signing Les Touré Kunda, Youssou N'Dour and others. However, majors again muscled in once the genre was established, notably Universal (which included Barclay under Philippe Constantin), Sony and Virgin, who distribute Peter Gabriel's Real World label.[37]

For young people specifically, the appeal of world music was essentially that of pop and rock. It seemed both to furnish young second- or third-generation immigrants with a sense of cultural identity and to free youths of Western origin from a rationalised, urbanised, technocratic world by restoring a sense of festive, communal wholeness. Writing about world music, the ethno-musicologist Isabelle Leymarie argues that in today's great conurbations popular musics 'crystallise the emotions of these young people, often torn between contradictory values, giving them the reassuring feeling of belonging to a community which extends beyond their direct environment, of redis-covering a planetary identity, where opposites are reconciled and tensions finally subside'.[38] World music seemed in fact to reflect the multicultural reality of post-colonial France, where immigration and urbanisation had brought about a rich ethnic mix in the big cities. France is often said to have a history of assimilating the musics of other cultures. In this, however, it is scarcely different from other Western countries and the argument misses an essential aspect of the French passion for world music, which was welcomed as much by the authorities as the public. Behind this passion was an awareness of resisting the global standardisation of music by favouring an alternative 'transculturalism' to that of pop. If the patrimonial *chanson* is to be opened up to outside influence, let the provenance of that influence be not simply America, where African-American forms have been diluted by white performers, then imposed by multinational corporations. Implicit in Francophone world music is the conviction that other cultures have as much to offer as the US and that France's historic connections with those cultures enable it to absorb their influences directly, without American mediation, whether in the French language, in French-lexifier Creoles, or indeed in any language other than English; and by choice rather than the fabled economic 'imperialism' of the United States. World music, then, is a way of rewriting national authenticity.

Not everyone, however, sees it as so uplifting an incarnation of inter-ethnic harmony. First, the idea that the existence of a Francophone 'community' makes the unmediated absorption of such musical styles somehow easier and more 'natural' for France is scarcely borne out when one considers that artists like Khaled generally only succeeded there once they had done so elsewhere, 'as if', writes Marie Virolle, 'a detour were needed, a mediation between reception in France and transmission in Algeria for the message to be understood. [. . .] there seems to be a difficulty regarding direct dialogue between the two cultures, a difficulty for the French scene (here, the music scene) simply to open up, to recognise the forms of enrichment it is being offered'.[39] Second, naming once again proves to be a culturally explosive operation since the term 'world music' is often denounced for disguising a post-colonial construction of 'otherness': 'for us', says Kassav', 'the only niche they have been able to find is world music. So as not to have to say the music of Third-World people!' As the black singer-songwriter Pierre Akendengue argues, Africa has suffered an 'identitarian eclipse' which has given African musics the image of an indistinct folk culture, 'with, as its postulate: Africa means dance, or that kind of stuff'.[40] The use of 'world music' to designate intercultural cross-fertilisations is no less problematic, since it is sometimes argued that the subtleties and complexities of indigenous musics have to be neutered to fit the regular pulse of pop and appeal to the jaded Western appetites which the majors and FM radio have produced, so that authenticity is reduced to packaged exoticism for musical tourists. In an issue devoted to reviewing new French music, the popular-culture weekly *Les Inrockuptibles* goes further still, provocatively asking whether Khaled's 'big cheerful moustache' (he is often pictured with a beaming smile) is all that different from the string of bananas worn by the semi-naked African-American dancer Josephine Baker in the 1920s, or her 'delightful "pidgin French"' which reminds the French of the might of their colonial empire and the availability of their natives'.[41]

These arguments carry considerable moral weight, though they also neglect the more empirical realities of career-making for non-Western artists. As Coulomb and Varrod point out, in the 1980s the music industry on the African continent was such that musicians from one country had difficulty breaking into the market of another without first making a name for themselves in Europe. A reputation in France meant airplay on Radio France Internationale and thereby exposure in other parts of Francophone Africa. Similarly, problems of piracy in Africa meant that selling records in Europe and becoming a registered member of the French SACEM were sometimes the only ways of making a living through royalties.[42] Added to which, Yonnet's 'transculturalist' argument can again be usefully applied here, in that the fusing of ethnic musics with global pop can become creative and empowering for the artists concerned. Youssou N'Dour feels that world music has in fact bifurcated in a promising way: 'Now, Africans aren't just the bearers of that traditional music which kind of represents the image people have of them from the outside; but they also have a new music fed by urban trends like rap or funk. This is what we're discovering and it has a lot of potential.'[43]

Either way, world music has today become one of the major sounds of France for the outside world, a change in which official or para-official discourses are complicit. Describing the melting pot of world cultures he had designed for a procession down the Champs Élysées to celebrate the 1789 bicentenary, Jean-Paul Goude claimed that 'the real revolution' is world music.[44] In 1991, Amina, a Tunisian singer living in France, represented her country of adoption at the Eurovision Song Contest with 'Le Dernier qui a parlé' (The Last to Speak), combining a French *chanson* with an Arabised delivery. In July of the same year, an open-air concert of world music was organised by the French Music Bureau in New York's Central Park featuring Khaled, Mory Kanté and the Gipsy Kings, none of them singing in French. In one sense, such representations show France flatteringly as modern, dynamic and multicultural, though precisely where French-language *chanson* stands in such representations is problematic, as we shall see in the next chapter. Yet in another way, a voice is occasionally heard suggesting that, in the eyes of the ever more hegemonic Anglophone world, France's entire range of popular musics is becoming one of those 'exotic', 'folk' cultures whose musics it has so readily assimilated. In record shops outside France, CDs of Parisian accordion music and compilations of Hallyday, Hardy or Brel are often found in the bins marked 'World Music' alongside African, Maghrebi and Latin American music. This goes some way to confirming the 'neo-colonialist' constructions of otherness but also indicates that France today may be as much a victim of such constructions as a source.

Rap

As world music reached an apogee of official recognition with Goude's bicentenary event, a new hybrid emerged that had been pupating since the mid-1980s and would eventually extend and compete with it. In 1990, a compilation was released by Delabel entitled *Rapattitude*, which showcased a number of little-known French rap and reggae artists: Assassin, Supreme NTM, Tonton David and twelve others. Two acts which did not appear on this first volume (a second came out two years later) were also beginning to take off at the same time: MC Solaar and IAM. These five – especially Solaar, NTM and IAM – would dominate the 1990s market, and the release of *Rapattitude* marked the beginning of French rap's meteoric rise. Rap was a hybrid before it reached France. Essentially African by inspiration, it grew from Jamaican reggae, which crossed into the USA to become the sound of the black ghettoes, of New York particularly. Although some contend that Jamaican reggae was itself influenced by black American popular musics, the basic techniques and technology which rap exploits were evolved by West Indian artists: dubbing and scratching (and later sampling), the sound-system, and what reggae artists call 'toasting' but which subsequently became rapping: half-talking, half-singing to the accompaniment of the rhythms issuing from the sound-system. In both reggae and rap, the DJ who operates the sound system is no longer simply a presenter of other people's material but is as creative as the rapper (or 'MC'), who, originally at least, would improvise a text over this sound. At the heart of both forms is a more or less spontaneous, creative recycling of existing sounds which, initially at least, could be achieved at minimal expense in terms of equipment and training.[45] Little wonder that rap, arriving on a French music scene which had already been experimenting with *métissages* in the form of alternative rock and world music, swiftly became established. As with these other genres, French rappers mostly broke with straightforward imitation and evolved their own styles in French. By the end of the 1990s, France had become the second largest market for rap after the USA, ahead, significantly, of the UK. Other industrial factors also help explain its assimilation. As we have seen, an independent production sector rejecting compromise with the majors had already developed in the 1980s, which rap was able to adapt to its own purposes: small independent labels (Arsenal Records, Plug It Records), self-production, fanzines (*Get Busy, Down With This*), associations dedicated to promoting rap.[46] As with the other genres I have looked at, this alternative economy was a way of preserving rap's authenticity and image. The rise of FM radio again played a role, in particular Radio Nova. The imposition of a 40 per cent quota of French music, imposed on all radio stations from 1996, was also crucial, since a number of stations were able to use French-language rap to make up the percentage.

At a different level, the social setting with which American rap had become identified – ethnic communities, social deprivation – translated easily to France's troubled suburbs, and rap quickly took root there. But it slotted just as neatly into French cultural traditions, much more in fact than did pop or rock. Its semi-spoken nature allows the stresses and cadences of French to be accommodated somewhat more comfortably since they are not constrained by a melodic line. Furthermore, its foregrounding of words sits more happily with the *chanson* tradition than do genres like rock or world music oriented towards dance. Typical of this kind of reading of rap is that of Serge Hureau, director of Paris's Hall of Song (Hall de la chanson), who makes an analogy between the rapper in his baseball cap and the cheeky street urchin Gavroche from Hugo's *Les Misérables*.[47] As rap has become assimilated, more complex cross-fertilisations have taken place, as with the Occitan rap of Claude Sicre and Ange B from Toulouse, who form Les Fabulous Trobadors; or the Massilia Sound System, another Occitan group based in Marseilles, whose regional label, Rocker Productions, also launched Les Fabulous Trobadors. Sicre finds parallels between rap and medieval Occitan music which Les Fabulous explore.[48] Equally important perhaps, the rap which migrated from America was part of a wider culture, hip-hop, which includes modes of dress, gesture, dance (most notably break dance) and graffiti art. Here too, it has proved relatively easy to establish organic links with other contemporary arts in France, for example dance, fashion and mural art. Of all the imported popular-musical forms, rap was probably the easiest upon which to stamp a label of French authenticity.

This is not to say that it was assimilated without problems. Its reputation in America for dissent, violence, antisemitism and sexism preceded it and made some in France wary. Their suspicions were fuelled by provocative performance styles, aggressive lyrics and band names like NTM, which roughly means 'motherfucker' (*nique ta mère*). Early work by some artists – Ministère AMER, NTM, Assassin – was banned from the air, while Ministère AMER were taken to court accused of insulting the police and even encouraging terrorism, following comments they made when promoting their 1995 piece 'Sacrifice de poulets' (Sacrificing Cops), written in conjunction with Mathieu Kassovitz's film *La Haine*. But it was NTM who experienced most trouble with the law. The controversy was bound up with the electoral successes of the extreme Right, which was and remains overtly hostile to rap, as it was to rock in the 1980s. Seven years before the astonishing presidential elections of 2002, the National Front (FN) of Jean-Marie Le Pen had already made disturbing gains, polling some 15 per cent in the 1995 presidentials and winning three city councils (Orange, Marignane and Toulon) in the ensuing local elections. In November 1996, the two members of NTM, Joey Starr and Kool Shen, were given a three-month custodial sentence and forbidden to perform for six months by a Toulon court for 'verbal outrage' (*outrage par paroles*) against the police. They were indicted for comments and gestures they had made when performing their song 'Police' at an anti-racist concert held in July 1995 near Toulon, to protest against the FN's recent successes.[49] The verdict caused uproar in cultural and Left-leaning circles, all the more so as NTM, and rap in general, were already at the heart of another conflict, also triggered by the FN's electoral showing, this time between Gérard Paquet's Théâtre national de la danse et de l'image in Châteauvallon and the FN Mayor of Toulon, during which Paquet was told by the regional Prefect to withdraw NTM from a rap festival his theatre was organising. Clearly, in 1990s France, popular music, despite the obvious commercial interests at stake, could still provoke fierce controversy, much as it had at various moments since 1789.

Even so, by the end of the century, rap had become an accepted, profitable form, as record companies had quickly hauled it into the mainstream. Production values for rap records are now as high as for pop generally. MC Solaar is acknowledged as a contemporary troubadour, and his and others' songs are studied by French and overseas academics. Another well-known Beur group, Alliance Ethnik, places stress on the festive aspect of rap rather than on contestation. Surveying French popular music at the turn of the twenty-first century, *Les Inrockuptibles* argues that bands like NTM are already the older generation for a new wave of rap artists – Time Bomb Commando being probably the best known – who are less directly political and less committed to hip-hop as a culture with its own values. According to Laurence Touitou, head of the Delabel label, which released *Rapattitude*, 'reducing the spectrum of the expression "hip-hop" to rap alone makes it a musical thing like any other, and therefore less interesting', though she admits that there are still people 'around the outside', designers, photographers, producers, who remain imbued with hip-hop culture 'and may take it into new and unexplored territory'.[50]

At much the same time as rap, a new American migrant, techno, was reaching France via Britain and causing a stir. I want to look at the techno movement separately in the concluding chapter, since it raises crucial issues about both the past and the future of French popular music. But what is already clear from pop's evolution since 1968 is that, as the idiom has gradually taken root, the music scene in France has become increasingly segmented, complex and cross-pollinated. Kent, former vocalist with the punk-rockers Starshooter, is today considered a *chanson* artist writing his own material, having realised that bands like his own had lost touch with the production values of the *chanson* world.[51] Bernard Lavilliers, whose lyrics have echoes of Brel and Brassens and who began as a Left-Bank cabaret singer, can adopt the sounds of hard rock, reggae and world music. Teen idols Étienne Daho from the 1980s or Patrick Bruel from the 1990s are today often included, like Hallyday, in compendia of *chanson*, and so on. Furthermore, the contiguity within metropolitan France of a growing number of genres has meant that they increasingly draw on each other as well as on non-French musics. The group Zebda fuses rap, raï and reggae; rap artists have produced an album of Renaud songs; Alain Stivell has been born again by assimilating techno into Breton music, while techno itself is merging with rap, *chanson* and even traditional folk (*ethno-techno*). As a consequence, the nature of national authenticity has been reconfigured in a post-national, post-modern perspective. In what might seem a paradox, authenticity is redefined as creative and even ironic *métissage*. What accounts for this is that *métissage* is almost unavoidably creative since, as Yonnet implies, transcultural mixing produces new spaces for expressive innovation. Authenticity thus comes to mean not so much cleaving to or pastiching *national* musics of one kind or another, but an aesthetics of permanently creative eclecticism, a playful, experimental, nomadic refusal of boundaries. And as one might expect in a country experiencing the resurgence of the extreme Right, this aesthetics is also an ethics and a politics.

Musically, then, the pop 'invasion' has ended up having a positive effect, albeit rather belatedly, by acting as a leaven. The result is that French popular music from 1958 to the start of the twenty-first century, and despite the inevitable presence of dross, has, I suggest, undergone a coming of age, achieving creative maturity, self-confidence and a density it had lacked. In the next two chapters, I shall explore conceptual rather than musical responses to pop, as they too have generally evolved from negative to positive.

Notes

1. Yonnet, *Jeux, modes et masses*: see article added as an annex to his chapter 'Rock, pop, punk': 'A propos de "l'impérialisme américain"': rock et chanson française', pp. 191–200. For the reference to pop as a class consciousness, see p. 181.

2. Ibid., p. 193.
3. Ibid., p. 196. I deal with the question of democratisation at greater length in Part II.
4. Victor and Regoli, *Vingt Ans de rock français*, pp. 90–2.
5. Quoted in Pierre-Albert Castanet, 'Les Années 1968: les mouvances d'une révolution socio-culturelle populaire', in Antoine Hennion (ed.), *1789–1989, Musique, histoire, démocratie*, 3 vols, vol. II (Fondation de la Maison des Sciences de l'Homme, 1992), p. 151.
6. Victor and Regoli, *Vingt Ans de rock français*, p. 93.
7. Coulomb and Varrod, *1968–1988*, pp. 17 and 193.
8. Maison des cultures du monde, *Les Musiques du monde en question* (Babel, 1999), p. 24.
9. 'Le Dossier: Maxime Le Forestier', *Chorus*, no. 15 (Spring 1996), p. 81.
10. See Kim Harrison, 'A Critical Introduction to the Work of the Singer-Songwriter Renaud', MA by research, University of Leeds, UK, 2000.
11. Pascal Ory, *L'Entre-deux-mai: histoire culturelle de la France mai 1968–mai 1981* (Seuil, 1983), p. 82.
12. Ibid., p. 82; Rioux, *Cinquante Ans de chanson française*, pp. 69–70.
13. This paragraph draws particularly on Coulomb and Varrod, *1968–1988*, Chapters 2 and 8.
14. Ibid., pp. 307–10; Gilbert Salachas and Béatrice Bottet, *Le Guide de la chanson française contemporaine* (Syros, 1989), pp. 150–2.
15. Ory, *L'Entre-deux-mai*, p. 84.
16. Patrick Delbourg, 'Sept Ans de culture: la chanson', *Les Nouvelles Littéraires*, 23 April 1981, p. 35.
17. Coulomb and Varrod, *1968–1988*, pp. 144–50.
18. Rioux, *Cinquante Ans de chanson française*, p. 384. 'Apostrophes' was a televised book programme hosted by Bernard Pivot.
19. Coulomb and Varrod, *1968–1988*, p. 66–70.
20. Henry Torgue, *La Pop-Music et les musiques rock* (Que Sais-Je?/Presses Universitaires de France, 1997), p. 37.
21. Anne Benetello and Yann Le Goff, 'Historique (aspects politique, économique et social)', in Gourdon (ed.), *Le Rock*, p. 35.
22. Bollon's article, 'Le Grand Sommeil du rock français', is reproduced in Coulomb and Varrod, *1968–1988*, pp. 239–45 (quotation from pp. 242 and 245).
23. Ibid., p. 242.
24. Ibid., p. 243.
25. Dick Hebdige, *Subculture: The Meaning of Style* (Methuen, 1979), Chapter 7 (quotation from Johnny Rotten, p. 109).
26. Benetello and Le Goff, 'Historique', p. 38.

27. Patrick Mignon, 'Évolution de la prise en compte des musiques amplifiées par les politiques publiques', in Adem-Florida (ed.), *Politiques publiques et musiques amplifiées* (Adem-Florida, Conseil Régional d'Aquitaine, 1997), p. 24.

28. Mignon, 'Paris/Givors: le rock local', in Mignon and Hennion (eds), *Rock: de l'histoire au mythe*, p. 205.

29. Mignon, 'Évolution de la prise en compte', pp. 24–5.

30. 'Les Joies du Bondage' (interview with the label's founders), *Les Inrockuptibles*, special issue 'Made in France', 7–27 July 1999, pp. 34–5.

31. Rioux, *Cinquante Ans de chanson française*, p. 413.

32. Sophie Delassein, 'Saga Mitsouko', *Le Nouvel-Observateur*, 24 February–1 March 2000, p. 54.

33. All three quotations are from 'Le Grand Forum de l'an 2000: la chanson de *Chorus*', *Chorus*, no. 30 (January–March 2000), pp. 90–1.

34. On world music, see Christopher Warne, 'The Impact of World Music in France', in Alec Hargreaves and Mark McKinney (eds), *Post-Colonial Cultures in France* (Routledge, 1997), pp. 133–49, on which this section draws.

35. Rioux, *Cinquante Ans de chanson française*, p. 408.

36. Maison des cultures du monde, *Les Musiques du monde en question*, p. 26.

37. Ibid., p. 43.

38. Isabelle Leymarie, 'Musiques du monde: le grand métissage', *Le Courrier de l'UNESCO*, March 1991, p. 11.

39. Marie Virolle, *La Chanson raï: de l'Algérie profonde à la scène internationale* (Karthala, 1995), p. 158.

40. Kassav' quoted in 'Le Grand Forum de l'an 2000', *Chorus*, p. 89; and Akendengue in ibid., p. 90.

41. Tewfik Hakem, 'Métèques et mat', *Les Inrockuptibles*, special issue, p. 41; quotation p. 40. For a similar view, see Denis-Constant Martin, *Politis*, 3–10 January 1991, pp. 42–3.

42. Coulomb and Varrod, *1968–1988*, pp. 276–7.

43. 'Le Grand Forum de l'an 2000', *Chorus*, p. 90.

44. Goude quoted in David Looseley, *The Politics of Fun: Cultural Policy and Debate in Contemporary France* (Berg, 1995), p. 182.

45. On this topic, see Georges Lapassade and Philippe Rousselot, *Le Rap ou la fureur de dire* (Éditions Talmart, 1996), Chapter 1; and Manuel Boucher, *Rap, expression des lascars: significations et enjeux du rap dans la société française* (L'Harmattan, 1998), Part I.

46. Boucher, *Rap, expression des lascars*, pp. 72–3.

47. Pascale Bigot, *Questions pour la chanson* (IRMA Éditions), 1996, p. 21.

48. See Joan Gross and Vera Mark, 'Regionalist Accents of Global Music: The Occitan Rap of *Les Fabulous Trobadors*', *French Cultural Studies*, vol. 12, no. 34 (February 2001), pp. 77–94.
49. The song had actually appeared three years before on NTM's 1993 album *J'appuie sur la gâchette* (I Pull the Trigger). See Boucher, *Rap, expression des lascars*, pp. 209–12 for an account of the NTM 'affair' and pp. 240–1, note 123 on Ministère AMER. Press coverage of the affair was extensive: see, as just one example, 'Les Mouvements de jeunesse veulent riposter à la condamnation de NTM', and other articles, *Le Monde*, 17–18 November 1996, pp. 6–7. In June 1997, an appeal court reduced the penalty on NTM to two months suspended sentence and a 25,000 franc fine.
50. Thibaud de Longeville, 'Le Combat continue', *Les Inrockuptibles*, special issue, pp. 38–9; quotation p. 39.
51. Kent quoted in 'Le Grand Forum de l'an 2000', *Chorus*, p. 91.

– 4 –

Chanson as National Myth: The Authenticity Debate

As the early responses to *yéyé* suggest, French public representations of pop were for some years largely negative. Even before the Place de la Nation event of 1963, the new youth culture was dismissed by the cultural establishment as fatuous, commercialised and socially dangerous. In a study of the *blousons noirs*, for example, published a year before Morin's articles, the Left-leaning intellectual Émile Copfermann displays a distinctly Adornian pessimism about pop:

> The feelings of the songs with their sentimental and rhythmic tunes can be shared by the listeners without their having to make any effort themselves. One only needs to have a bit of feeling in order to love; one only needs a bit of rhythm to dance. It is the fact that the majority of people find these things so easy to do that explains the whole process of how mediocrity is producing a levelling-down effect in society. [. . .] The entertainment industry [. . .] begins by gratifying people's vague aspirations. On the basis of these it provokes artificial needs and then caters for them in abundance, thereby creating its own profits and, at the same time, producing a standardised effect.[1]

Plainly, the criteria Copfermann applies to pop are aesthetic ones drawn from high culture. He condemns it as mediocre because it is a commercial product requiring no intellectual effort and aspiring to no moral improvement, seeking only to elicit the most basic response. But following the Nation event such artistic disapproval was overlaid with paranoia about public order. André Frossard, of the right-wing *Candide* and *Le Figaro*, wrote: 'three twist idols only have to appear for 200,000 Parisians under twenty to be thrown into furious agonies by an unlikely cult of worthlessness', while a writer in *Aux Écoutes* opined: 'Examined from a moral standpoint, the [Nation] affair can be seen as one of the most degrading so far recorded in the civilised world.' As the term 'civilised' suggests, there was a genuine sense in such writing that pop represented a threat to the Republic by an alien horde.[2]

Some of the negative responses to the Place de la Nation concert were of Catholic inspiration. In his column for *Le Figaro littéraire*, the Catholic writer François Mauriac spoke paternally of the need for today's teenagers to be given guidance, to be addressed with sympathy and gravity by their elders, for the cultural industries (records and cinema) are feeding parasitically on their naïve and natural passions. To rescue them, those with experience of life need to furnish them with a message of hope in their infinite possibilities, possibilities which will become clearer to them once the ephemeral moment of adolescence has passed and they face the real duties of national life and the human condition: 'O young people, it matters little if you "let your hair down" for a night or two, as long as you keep intact the faith in that part of yourself that is your soul, whose youth is eternal.'[3] Sincere as it is, the most remarkable thing about Mauriac's rhetoric here – the concerned patriarch counselling the callow youth – is its spectacular inappropriateness to the times. Typical of a brand of French Catholic humanism which might still have resonated in the early 1950s, a decade on it has aged by a century. Studying the Catholic youth magazines of the period, Marwick detects a similar untimeliness in their attempts to have it both ways, superficially acknowledging the new music but secretly undermining it, for example in record reviews which point out the poor quality of *yéyé* performers, or express a preference for acoustic over electric guitar: 'Wouldn't you like to learn pretty songs, songs which you would be happy later to teach to your little sister or to your little brother?'[4]

Even non-religious pop journalism did not always avoid such pieties. In an editorial in *Disco-Revue* from October 1964, Jean-Claude Berthon criticises *yéyé* and classic *chanson* equally: *chanson* because the songs of Brel or Ferré are too explicitly adult to be suitable for fourteen-year-olds; and *yéyé* because it is manufactured and over-commercialised. What he calls for instead is 'pure rock', French or 'foreign'. To illustrate what he means by pure rock, he cites Eddie Cochran, Gene Vincent, Chuck Berry and newcomers like the Beatles, the Stones and the Animals. However, it eventually dawns on the bemused reader that these names are being cited as instances of 'purity' not in the sense of musical authenticity as opposed to manufacture and commerce, but in a different sense entirely. Alluding to songs like 'She Loves You' and 'Can't Buy Me Love', Berthon sees the Beatles particularly (but also by implication the other stars mentioned) as talented artists singing about the real problems of young people, rather than about sordid subjects like sex. After all, he notes with evident admiration, the Beatles sing 'I want to hold your hand', not 'I want to touch your breasts'. 'No, the real singers of pure rock sing about something other than this, they sing about love in its purest, healthiest and most natural forms. That's what pure rock is!'[5] The very least one can say here is that at the time Berthon's grasp of the coded eroticism of English-language rock still needed a little work.

Nevertheless, animosity towards foreign pop was the product not only of bigotry, religious belief or cultural misunderstanding but of its being judged, consciously or not, against the existing standards of quality and authenticity applicable to French popular music. Despite its American origins and some heated Parisian exchanges in the 1930s and 1940s, jazz, for example, was widely accepted in France by the late 1950s.[6] Initially, some jazz fans took to rock'n'roll because of its roots in be-bop and blues. But its coarseness and unruliness began to offend the more sensitive enthusiasts. The jazz specialist André Francis wrote in 1958 that rock'n'roll was merely 'a vulgar copy of the rhythm and blues style, made by a gang of white louts', while Vian denounced it as a 'a sort of ridiculous tribal chant for an audience of idiots'.[7]

However, pop, I believe, was primarily found wanting from the implied vantage-point of *chanson*. In the rest of this chapter, I want to illustrate this by examining the meanings and values attached to *chanson* by *chanson* people: singers, songwriters, the specialist press, and so on. My sources will include a volume by Marcel Amont, *Une Chanson, qu'y a-t-il à l'intérieur d'une chanson?* (A Song, What's Inside a Song?), which combines his own reflections with those of 110 writers and composers of all ages with whom he has conversed; and also 'Le Grand Forum de l'an 2000', a special millennium issue of the *chanson* periodical *Chorus*, which collates extracts from past interviews in the form of an imaginary round-table on Francophone song. I shall also examine the discourses of specialist commentators such as the academic linguist and semiologist Louis-Jean Calvet, the only French writer to my knowledge to have produced something approximating a theory of *chanson* in his book *Chanson et société* (Song and Society); and a variety of books by music journalists. Taken together, what such sources reveal is that there is an identifiable rhetoric of *chanson*.

Chanson versus Pop

On the surface, *chanson* is a straightforward generic category; but it also connotes a web of assumptions and expectations relating to the core notion of authenticity. Arguably, *chanson* only becomes fully aware of itself as a genre in negative, defensive opposition to its 'other': initially easy-listening (*variétés*), then to a much greater extent pop. The most respected *chanson* stars are only what they are by virtue of what they are not; negative representations of pop, therefore, were and to an extent still are mediated through *chanson* rhetoric.[8]

One exceptionally vigorous instance of this binary can be found in the very first editorial by Fred Hidalgo of *Paroles et musique* (Words and Music), forerunner of *Chorus*, in 1980. *Chanson*, he insists, is above all 'expression', not just entertainment: expression of life, society and the human condition. It thus has 'no connection whatever with syrupy *variétés*, oozing soppiness and mediocrity and consumed passively'; nor do its 'singer-poets' have remotely the same conception of success as 'those cardboard "idols" whose futility is only equalled by the thirst for stardom or wealth in a dehumanised society'.[9] As the term 'expression' suggests here, Hidalgo's premise is that *chanson* is an authentic creative art. A subtler instance of an 'art discourse' is Jacques Bertin's *Chante toujours, tu m'intéresses* (Carry on Singing, I Like You), published in 1981. As a singer-songwriter himself in the Left-Bank tradition, Bertin has developed a following since his first record release of 1967 but has remained marginal and pursued a parallel career as a journalist, one of that cohort of talented newcomers in the 1960s whose music careers were held back by the rise of pop. His work, consisting of his own compositions and occasional settings of poets like Aragon and Giraudoux, is an instance of *chanson* at its sparest and most poetic, an aesthetic position from which he makes a plea for *chanson* as art and craft.

   Like Vian's *En avant la zizique* (On With the Music) in the late 1950s, *Chante toujours* is a polemical snapshot of the state of the music industry in the late 1970s. It also exemplifies the discursive dichotomy between the industry and the mind-set of *chanson*. Like Vian's, Bertin's perspective is based on a polarity between '*le Métier*' (literally, the trade), which refers to the frivolous, unreal world of the music business, and the humbler but greater '*le métier*' (lower-case), that is, the industrious, authentic craft of *chanson*, a skill which has to be learnt. *Le métier* is at the furthest remove from *le Métier*, which involves the essentialist notion that singing and songwriting are a matter of instinctive 'genius', not of the high seriousness and labour which literature entails. Showbiz genius is recognised by its irresponsibility and the kind of savvy which enables a performer to rattle off a hit on the back of a cigarette packet. You can even become a showbiz genius without writing anything at all, as long as your sound-system is loud enough and you have a rock'n'roll lifestyle of crazy antics and preferably drugs. Clearly, the butt of Bertin's irony here is contemporary pop as it is commonly represented. Such representations are damaging, he feels, because they stop singing and songwriting being recognised for what they really are: a serious profession exercised by 'art-workers' (*des ouvriers de l'art*).[10] As he reminds us, song and literature have a common origin in *la chanson de geste*, though by the end of the eleventh century lyric poetry had bifurcated into popular and aristocratic forms. Originally indistinguishable from music, poetry steadily became the preserve of those who could read and song the preserve of those who could not, downgraded by a Bourdieusian ruling class anxious to distinguish itself by its more refined tastes. What is needed now, Bertin concludes, is for *chanson* to sever all connection with *le Métier* and be restored to its rightful dignity as 'the other poetry, that which one gives with the voice'.[11]

This commonly identified aesthetic and moral superiority of *chanson* helps turn it, like the Tour de France for Barthes, into a national myth, reinforced by the internalising of the English use of the word *chanson* to designate a genre explicitly French, which allows *chanson* people to see themselves through the eyes of the world. This heightened self-awareness means that *chanson* in its general sense, including singers well known in the Anglophone world like Mistinguett, Chevalier and Piaf, is easily constructed as a distinctive national heritage. As music journalist Claude Fléouter writes, for example, 'nobody in French *chanson* expresses the popular soul better than Piaf, the feelings, the passions and the amorous philosophy of a people'.[12] Such representations of *chanson* are commonplace and express a perception of its quintessential Frenchness. Exploring that 'Frenchness of *chanson*', Hawkins rightly singles out one core characteristic: 'the foregrounding of the lyrics, which are often interpreted in the manner of a dramatic monologue accompanied by music. This is much less the case with Anglo-American popular music, where the tune is all-important, and more recently the "sound".' Hawkins goes on to suggest that one reason why *chanson* has generally failed to make much impact in the non-Francophone world is the fact that the literary refinements of the lyrics written by its greatest practitioners such as Brassens and Ferré can only be fully appreciated by 'a sophisticated practitioner of French' and imply 'an informed listener'. Thus, he concludes, 'they create a complicity among their target audience, who are self-selecting and can share the subversive pleasures to be gained from an appreciation of their work'.[13] I want first, then, to explore this national specificity further.

Although in France the term *chanson* is often used unselectively, the status of myth is mainly reserved for the elite of singer-songwriters who, as we saw, continue the Trenet tradition by stretching the resources, mood and range of the lyric. Culturally, this mythic form within a form is very potent and all singers who write their own material are gilded by it. At its centre is the trinity of Brel, Brassens and Ferré, with Trenet as the forerunner. The national significance of such performers is evidenced, and at the same time intensified, by the media coverage when they die. The treatment of Trenet's death in February 2001 by the public TV channel France 2 was a form of embalming, painstakingly bringing out his role in unifying the nation ideologically and culturally. 'Today', intoned the voice-over, '[Trenet] attains the status of a monument before which everyone bows.' Chirac described him as a 'symbol of a France that is smiling, imaginative'. The term 'poet' was persistently applied and particular prominence was given to his famous song 'L'Ame des poètes' (The Souls of Poets, 1951), which celebrates how the 'songs' of dead poets live on in the popular memory, neatly intimating that Trenet's own work had now acceded to that same immortality. This literary transfiguration, ironically denied him in life when he was turned down twice for membership of the Académie Française, was completed by a persistent stress on the complexity of his work, the subtext of melancholy beneath its sanguine surface.

Trenet's death and Bécaud's at the end of the year were the latest in a melancholy litany and, given their ages (eighty-seven and seventy-four, respectively), did not have quite the impact of some earlier departures. The premature deaths of Brel and Brassens in fairly close proximity (1978 and 1981, Brel was not yet fifty, Brassens was sixty) were the most critical in evolving the *chanson* myth. Emerging from the Left Bank of the 1940s and 1950s, and looking further back to the 1930s via their debt to Trenet (without whom, Brel once remarked, 'we would all be accountants'), they had faced down pop and remained true to themselves and French song. They were known abroad – in Brel's case even in the enemy's lair. They could thus be constructed as universal and timeless and their demise came to signify the end of the grand narrative of a distinct French tradition in popular song, just as France's record industry went into crisis. On the brink of the 1980s, their existing standing as quasi-literary figures (alongside Ferré), begun in the 1960s with the menace of *yéyé*, finally solidified into a comforting patrimonial legend. Certainly, earlier greats like Chevalier and Piaf had helped shape that legend, but they do not possess in the public imaginary the same gravitas as the Brel–Brassens–Ferré trinity, which today functions as a national signifier, a benchmark not only of aesthetic excellence but also of authenticity and truth, against which other French artists must be measured and measure themselves. What they were sets the parameters for what *chanson* is always capable of being.

So what were they? White, male, solo performers initially leading somewhat bohemian Parisian lives, accompanying themselves on guitar or piano as befitted the intimate Left-Bank cabarets where they began, and writing songs whose lyrics were remarkable for their polish, complexity and wit, their dissidence and political incorrectness, their combination of personal emotion and social criticism. This is still *chanson*'s Platonic ideal. Non-white singer-songwriters classed as *chanson* artists are still rare, particularly since the 'world music' tag has effectively segregated ethnic Francophone song in a category of its own. Comparatively rare, too, are women who have built successful careers on singing their own work, like Barbara or Anne Sylvestre, though this is changing, as the success of Véronique Sanson, Enzo Enzo and the all-female group Les Elles testifies. Even so, it is often noted that the standard career path of the female *chanson* star continues to be as a performer of work written by men. In terms of legitimacy, this gender distinction is to the detriment of female artists. Precisely because the cultural exchange-value of the singer-songwriter paradigm is set so high thanks to the esteem in which Brel, Brassens and Ferré are held, singers who do not write are less valued, somehow inauthentic, as we shall see later. The paradigm is also gendered in a different way, by the fabled misogyny of the big three. Masculinities of one kind or another (Michel Sardou and the muscular Lavilliers at one extreme, Souchon and Goldman at the other) are today written into the persona of the singer-songwriter, whose rugged sensitivity – or so a hundred lyrics would have us believe – is the result of a heart brutalised by disappointment in love. During their famous meeting in 1969, the big three were asked whether women were 'capable of bringing something important to men'. Amid some laddish chuckling, Ferré replied with a straight no, and Brassens and Brel waffled about the difficulties of love.[14]

Within this paradigm, songwriting is conventionally represented as both art and craft, combining spontaneous inspiration with a punishing regime of polishing and perfecting. As Bertin's term 'art-workers' suggests, his view of the *chanson* profession is an earthy, modest one. Often from humble back-grounds (he furnishes no evidence of this), singer-songwriters take very seriously the privileged access to self-expression which songwriting affords, approaching it as a trade to be learnt. Authenticity in Bertin's conception is plainly associated with labour and persistence. At the same time, it is this craft aesthetic which, in his typology, makes songwriting as much an art as literature. This is a familiar rhetoric. 'The authors of songs,' writes Fléouter in similar vein, 'like "real" writers, wrestle with language and know the anguish of the blank page.'[15] Here too, Brel, Brassens and Ferré are the paradigm. Brel, we are told by his pianist and occasional composer Gérard Jouannest, was a perfectionist, always scribbling in an exercise book wherever he found himself, in search of a word, a colouration, a rhythm. Brassens too, according to his friend Éric Battista, 'would write little, slowly, laboriously. [. . .] He would redraft his lines, pruning a good deal, progressing by successively altering and recasting, making a clean copy of his work each time.'[16] It is such craft representations that allow Bertin to dismiss the facility with which the pop writer rattles off a new number. Yet even the next generation of singer-songwriters who quite plainly do write in the pop idiom – Cabrel, Goldman, Renaud, Souchon – have followed their masters' example. As their careers develop, their production rate slows and some need as much as five years between albums. Goldman, for example, echoes Bertin: 'I think that the fact of writing and composing songs, that moment when you work with a pencil and a guitar, remains fundamentally a form of craftsmanship, a moment that's very authentic.' It is true that Renaud claims to have written his first hit, 'Laisse béton' (Leave It Out), on the back of the legendary cigarette packet; but his biographer reveals that such moments are generally the result of a long maturation.[17]

Clearly, a slow gestation and painstaking, auteurist perfectionism are the core *chanson* values. There is little suggestion of the singer-songwriter deploying similar care in composing. Indeed, *chanson* is again identified here by a binary opposition, this time between the solitary writing of the lyric and the social creation of a sound by orchestra, pop group or studio. As the ex-rocker Kent observes: 'There need to be several of you to make rock music, identity has to do with the group, the pleasure of spending time together; people listen first to the music and the sound. But when you take your own name, you become a singer, and then people listen to the words first.'[18] However, as Goldman's evocation of writing *and* composing hints, the claimed primacy of the lyric over melody in *chanson* is actually less clear cut. Ferré wrote symphonic orchestrations for his later work, conducted, and constantly experimented with sound. Brassens's homely tunes and guitar work involve much more complex chord changes and rhythmic patterns than they appear to. He himself once revealed: 'Music makes me shiver with pleasure. I have never experienced this joy with a text, not even by Baudelaire or Rimbaud.' Brel's later songs were often lavishly orchestrated and Jouannest recalls that 'it was always the music which triggered the ideas'.[19] For the next generation too, there is little suggestion of an immutable hierarchy. Some, like Bashung, write the words first, others – Le Forestier, Cabrel – the music. Renaud believes his best songs are those where lyrics and tune arrive at the same time.[20] This wide variety of opinion and practice is rationalised by the sociologist and singer Chantal Grimm (also known as Chantal Brunschwig) and the psychoanalyst Philippe Grimbert. Both see melody and lyrics working at different levels: the music appealing to the group, the text to the individual. Grimm in fact suggests that the individual listens more cerebrally than the group, looking for a personal return from the lyrics.[21] Calvet, too, refutes the primacy of the lyric by positing the existence alongside it of an alternative text, present in the music and in other non-verbal signifiers such as gesture, voice and the spatial organisation of the stage.[22]

Another commonly evoked dimension of the words–music debate is whether the French language can 'swing'. This goes back to jazz's arrival in France, when it was sometimes said that 'the French simply could not play jazz', because of the rift between French 'civilisation' and the supposedly 'primitive' nature of early jazz.[23] More recently, the question has been whether American-isation has ushered in rhythms shaped by the phonetics and stress patterns of English, to which French is said to be ill-suited. Simon Frith, popular-music academic and critic, writes:

> musical forms have, in practice, adapted themselves to languages, to ways of speaking. This is particularly obvious in the global movement of rock music. There

are clearly ways in which rock musical conventions, in terms of melodic form, use of verse/chorus, mode of vocal attack, and so on, reflect – or at least gesture at – patterns of Anglo-American and Afro-American speech [. . .]. These musical conventions may not be appropriate for other languages.[24]

Even Trenet, who claimed always to set his songs to a syncopated rhythm, takes much the same view, believing that 'when you put American songs together with French lyrics, it doesn't fit. You have to respect the tonic accent of our language, which is very attractive.'[25] Yet those surveyed by Amont often insist that French is perfectly capable of swinging, and the work of Trenet, Brassens and singer-songwriter Michel Jonasz, 'Mister Swing' himself, is cited in evidence. Goldman also seems to be making the same point in his 2001 album entitled *Chansons pour les pieds* (Songs for the Feet), where each song is arranged in the style of a particular dance rhythm: jig, tarantella, disco, 'swing fanfare', and so on. Goldman writes in the sleeve-notes: 'This is the sole ambition of these songs: to make people get up, look at each other, talk to each other, brush against each other, sing and dance. Just songs for the feet.' Here again, one senses a desire on the part of a *chanson* artist to break free of a restrictive dichotomy deriving from a uniquely 'literary' representation of the genre.

In his brief treatment of *chanson* in *Performing Rites*, Frith partially accepts the centrality of the lyric, using an article by Ned Rorem to argue that French *chanson* is 'the most obvious narrative song' and that 'it was always as much a verbal as a musical form'. *Chanson* singers, Frith goes on, 'effectively " 'talk' their tunes, beguiling through anecdote rather than through a formal development of sound"'.[26] And yet, he still sees *chanson* as subject – just as much as 'the most meaningless house or rave track' – to the principle that lyrics in popular music generally are not just words but 'words in performance' or 'speech acts'. Therefore, 'song words are not about ideas ("content") but about their expression'; and 'the craft of the lyricist is [to] find the word which both sounds and means right'.[27] Song lyrics are not poetry, Frith insists, because poetry 'scores' itself for performance or reading, through its rhythm and meter, whereas in song the lyric is 'scored' by the music.[28] Frith is reinstating the importance of sound (amongst other elements of performance) in much the same way as Calvet does, and as some French *chanson* artists do. Véronique Sanson, to cite just one instance, argues that 'the idea comes directly from the sound itself. The words of a song are written to be sung, they have to have their own musicality, as well as a profound meaning.'[29] Clearly, though, there are limits to this principle for most of them, particularly for the older generation. Amont, for example, adopts a comparable position to Frith but only so far. He draws the line at the kind of aesthetic expressed by Mick Jagger, who maintains that he does not worry too much about making lyrics comprehensible when he sings, because listeners can always add their own meanings if need be. Amont considers this conception, which for him reduces 'words *solely* to their value as *SOUNDS* or as a rhythmic element', to be 'very Anglo-Saxon', and from a French *chanson* perspective it is natural that he should do so. As he points out, it is even enshrined in the fact that in the States a melody attracts more royalties than a lyric, whereas the SACEM treats them equally. But he is dismayed to see it developing in the younger generation in France too. If the sonorities of a lyric are a bonus, he has no objection. But if the preoccupation with sound 'starts to be applied to the detriment of ideas, of the spirit of the language: danger!'[30]

Although Amont himself is not a major figure in French popular music, the distinction he makes here between *chanson*, which attempts to *harmonise* sense and sound, and Anglo-American pop (or its French derivatives), which *sacrifices* sense to sound, is a feature of *chanson* discourse generally. This distinction points to a difference between the 'theories' of reception which underpin French *chanson* and Anglo-Saxon pop, respectively. Seeking to define the principle behind Jagger's comment, Amont writes:

> As with those believers who prefer mass in Latin, a vague understanding helps foster a certain mystery, which intelligible words shatter. Intelligible, intelligence. The communion is all the better if one lets an element of the unconscious over-ride the intelligence. Hence the mass *ceremonies* whose officiants are pop and rock stars. As André Malraux said: 'A myth does not appeal in us to reason but to complicity.'[31]

Amont's underlying premise, that pop communicates by provoking only affective communion while *chanson* does so by working on both the emotions and the intelligence, has characterised French discourse on pop from the first, among a generation of French commentators like Amont who saw pop arrive. From it flows a web of further oppositions upon which the belief in *chanson*'s distinctiveness is built. No single commentator will necessarily articulate them all, but taken together they refine our sense of how *chanson* is discursively constructed.

One is an opposition between *chanson* and dance music. As Jeffrey Jackson observes, the establishment of jazz in France in the 1920s was seen as a threat in some circles. This was often for very material reasons, as with those musicians who resented jazz because it cut across their own musical styles and threatened their livelihoods. But others saw it as a threat to a way of life based on a defining belief in French 'civilisation'. Jackson writes: 'The wild dancing it encouraged threatened to undermine older values of sobriety and self-control. At the same time, it was some of the most "modern" music of the day, imported from an

Chanson *as National Myth*

America which embodied the mass-produced, machine culture that lacked any sensitivity to the nuances of civilization such as a sense of good taste.' Paul Claudel was one who made this analogy, relating the bump and grind of early jazz to the rhythms of American mass-production, 'this pulsation, rhythmic and nervous like the pistons of a steam engine punctuating the cyclic drone of the dynamo, which makes itself felt throughout the whole of American life and of which jazz is the supreme expression'.[32] Years later, at the end of the 1950s, the absurdist playwright Ionesco, scarcely a fervent rationalist, was nevertheless appalled at Gilbert Bécaud's frantic stage act and its effect on his audience, though here the analogy was with the animal rather than the mechanical. No doubt with his latest play *Rhinocéros* (1958) in mind, where the characters turn into rhinoceroses, he fumed: 'Bécaud's power to make crowds go hysterical is exercised with no other aim than a pitiful fame, a pitiful exhibitionism . . . When he saunters about with the gait of a deranged monkey, two thousand people are transformed into deranged monkeys.'[33]

This kind of animus against American dance music and the physical modes of performance associated with it has not gone away, though it has assumed different forms. One of its more dyspeptic exponents is Pierre Delanoë. His quarrel, though, is not with either jazz, which he enjoyed in his youth, or rock, since he was among the first to adapt Presley songs into French. Rather, his enemy is the awfulness of American civilisation as a whole, a civilisation which has contributed nothing, only destroyed, whose values are the antithesis of French humanism: 'this civilisation of consumption, of money, which completely fails to understand the other values in life, i.e. friendship, love, the basic units which make up society: family, job, where you come from'.[34] Rather than being part of the natural ebb and flow of civilisations, Delanoë feels, American influence has been artificially imposed, since the US majors have cynically occupied France via the back door of youth music. The ideological opposition between culture and commerce translates into one between words and music, or, more accurately, words and rhythm. France's strength, he argues, has never been music but lyrics. In America, the opposite is true. Apparently forgetful of the Ira Gershwins, Oscar Hammersteins or Johnny Mercers, he insists that 'the Americans have never said anything interesting in their songs, apart from Bob Dylan, Leonard Cohen [a Canadian in fact] and two or three others. The lyrics of American songs are so banal! *The moon is blue, up above* . . . There's nothing original . . . Just love songs!' But what Americans have brought to France in abundance – and for Delanoë this is no compliment – is rhythm, that of the African slaves and even, he asserts without a trace of embarrassment, the 'scalp dances' of native Americans. Today, the young are exclusively interested in dance, not words, which for him is 'a considerable intellectual regression!'[35]

Such flagrant ethnocentric resentment is admittedly an extreme instance but has also become embedded in less overtly retrogressive discourses. Serge Dillaz, author of *La Chanson française de contestation* (The French Protest Song), regrets that the rise of the first jazz bands playing dance music (the One Step, the Shimmy, the Charleston), together with the success of the 'Revue nègre', which made Josephine Baker a star, had by the 1930s killed off the home-made song ('*la chanson artisanale*') and the traditional street singer, both associated in his view with a 'noble' tradition of popular protest:

> Dance therefore represented the final stage of *chanson*'s subjugation before its complete industrialisation, signalled by the arrival of the microgroove record. By taking further a process begun with the *caf' conc'*, in which music had gradually replaced words, [record] publishers are killing off not only the literary song but also the political song by linking the [song] form to the dance phenomenon.[36]

Dillaz here overlays the distinction between sound and sense with a subtextual representation of dancing as intellectually inferior to listening.

For some critics, this trajectory has worsened of late, from the 1970s craze for disco to house, techno and today's club culture (which I shall return to in Chapter 10). Lucien Rioux, for example, believes that clubbing, where nobody listens properly to either words or music, is at the furthest remove from the *chanson* experience. Paradoxically, though, his ideal model of listening is not necessarily that of the solitary record fan listening intensely to Brel or Brassens on the home hi-fi: 'Entering a jazz club [. . .] means going in search of others, communicating, joining the party. Going into a dance club is the very opposite.'[37] Listening, then, can clearly be a convivial experience, whereas clubbing imprisons and isolates the individual through noise and lights, the lack of physical contact in the dancing, overcrowding, alcohol and drug abuse. (Rioux apparently forgets that these last two are not exactly absent from jazz clubs either.) What ultimately condemns the contemporary dance scene is its lack of 'authenticity', a word Rioux uses frequently. It meets no genuine need, he insists, but is imposed on the young by fashion and FM radio. Against such contrivance and decadence, he holds up zouk, 'an *authentically popular* West Indian music' (my emphasis), which he evokes lovingly in a lexis suggesting naturalness, sensuality – and indeed dance. But what authenticates zouk dancing specifically, one can only assume, is the presence of acoustic instruments (no synthesisers here), a local tongue (Creole) and spontaneous fun, 'an atmosphere of jubilation and pleasure'. This does not, apparently, have to mean good clean fun, but it is fun which is evidently healthier to Rioux's way of thinking than clubbing: vivacious, sensual, happy, provocative, 'zouk presents itself as the amiable face of love and desire'.[38]

Manifestly, Rioux sees such exotic and gregarious musics as falling within the *chanson* tradition, or at least compatible with it. This rather unexpected connection can be explained by another opposition, familiar throughout Western twentieth-century popular music, between live and reproduced music. For a significant number of French performers and commentators, the authenticity of *chanson* is historically and ontologically tied to stage performance, in front of a flesh-and-blood audience. Even Jean Sablon's introduction of the microphone into his stage set in the 1930s caused him to be booed, because it transformed this direct relationship, shifting public judgement from the quality of the voice to the personality and intimacy of the singer.[39] Although the demand for authenticity is no longer taken this far, the unmediated experience of live communication remains a core value. For Michel Jonasz, 'there is something irreplaceable in a music hall [*salle de spectacle*], which television can't re-create. Because *chanson* is a physical exchange of vibrations; it's on stage that songs are really born, that they come alive. In this sharing, this emotion in the air.' For Georges Moustaki, a freewheeling concert tour 'offers a kind of truth, because I know, when I give a performance somewhere, that I shall never give the same one again'.[40] Even Calvet the academic, whose analysis in *Chanson et société* is carried out in the style of scholarly neutrality, makes it plain where his own preference lies: 'For me, the stage more than the record is the privileged space for receiving *chanson*, because all discourses are combined there, the discourse of shadow and light, of the voice, of clothes, of gesture, and of the audience too.'[41]

As these statements demonstrate, a dominant rhetoric of uniqueness, naturalness, exchange and craft is used to describe live performance, in opposition to the contrivance of electronic reproduction. Be it broadcasting or recording, such reproduction is represented as manufacture, the intimacy between performer and audience being falsified by mediation. Alain Bashung admits that it is only on stage that he has any sense of being a singer: 'In the studio, I feel as though I'm writing a book.' For Jean-Roger Caussimon, 'what counts is writing, and singing in public. Because radio and television are like making films, they're frozen food; a record is frozen food too . . . Nothing replaces the stage, the emotion of the moment, it's a really extraordinary feeling of exchange.'[42]

This deep-freezing of what *chanson* quintessentially is begins of course in the recording studio, with the dark arts of production. Bernard Estardy, sound engineer of the French studio CBE, complains about the latest studio technology: 'We're sold machines which all do the same thing and, these days, the danger is of everyone using the same constituents to produce the same song, and afterwards you fall back on mixing and remixing.' He himself has worked for months on processes that have produced 'a perfection of sound which left no chance of error and dehumanised everything'.[43] Next, there is broadcasting, which fares no better: television is slated by virtually all serious *chanson* artists: 'I can't see the point of doing TV programmes which serve no purpose other than to support some twat and his rubbish programme every time!', fulminates Lavilliers in a characteristic turn-of-phrase.[44] The intensity of such sentiment derives from French TV's indifference to new talent and its obsession with vapid spectacle and a coterie of established stars, but also its consistent resort to miming. Finally, there is the army of music-business intermediaries, from publishers to radio programmers, press agents and critics, who also mediate between song and public.

What is ultimately at issue in such condemnation is commodification, where technology and economics come together. Recording and broadcasting can capture a concert as an event but not as a unique, shared experience: they reify it as an item for purchase. Worse, this reification has contaminated live performance itself. Moustaki argues that in the modern concert, the pop idol – physically remote on stage and psychologically distanced by the coded rites of formal performance – is fetishised through the objects associated with him or her (and, today, through merchandising): 'Affectively undernourished, condemned to love at a distance, [the fans] communicate by consuming. That is all that they are expected to do. They have no choice anyway: consumption is the only means left open to them of getting close to the object of their adul-ation. The singer–audience relationship has been twisted into a manufacturer-customer one.'[45] In the same year as Moustaki (1973), Dillaz argues that industrialisation eliminates the public as agent in a different way. What he sees as the true, historical significance of the *café-concert* is that, with the noise and bustle brought by much bigger numbers in a café setting, singing along to songs whose lyrics were of some organic, collective significance died out and songs became more facile. The public, now listening and watching rather than singing along, became more apathetic. This is what made the transition seamless from *café-concert* to the formalised spectatorship of the music hall described by Moustaki and the passivity of listening to radio or records. Little wonder that in the West we rarely sing but merely listen; and even that we do badly: 'industrialised song means industrialised listening', Moustaki laconically remarks.[46]

These are clearly serious matters for Dillaz and Moustaki. Not only does song cease to be an authentic emanation of a community, produced and owned by it, but the ability of the public to make aesthetic judgements is also gradually diminished. In the economy of the pre-industrial song, the concert audience was a social arbiter of the quality of a flesh-and-blood performer. But as commercialisation developed, Dillaz laments, the audience's ability to discriminate began to atrophy, as the singer Yvette Guilbert had already recognised as early as 1913, in terms which anticipate Adorno:

Songs are manufactured today on the Boulevard de Strasbourg just as furniture is in the Faubourg Saint-Antoine. This is certainly a productive industry, too productive in fact because the public does not have the time to choose with care. Scarcely has it begun to retain a melody [. . .] than a new refrain rings out relentlessly in its ears; and so it ceases to react and puts up with being simply a phonograph recording everything it hears, without trying to sort the good from the bad.[47]

Today, however, matters are perceived to be even worse by music's Jeremiahs. With recorded music dominant and artists miming on TV rather than bothering to appear live, with so much mediation in the form of marketing hype and repeated airplay, who can say where the public's preference really lies, what public 'demand' really is?[48] Moustaki sees the 'people' as doubly alienated by mediation, as music is brought to it pre-selected and encoded, by marketing managers, radio programmers and critics: 'Removed not only from the elaboration of the product but also from its reception, listening by proxy and moved vicariously, [the public] has no direct leverage on the events it surveys. Popular song has ceased to be the expression of the people.'[49]

Despite the somewhat antiquated Adornian-Marxist rhetoric in much of the above, such questions regarding the people cannot be dismissed as the laments of an older generation unable to adjust to audiovisual post-modernity. They are in fact central to contemporary debates about aesthetic value and discrimination in popular-music and popular-culture studies, which I shall return to in the Conclusion. But a problem that Dillaz's and Moustaki's arguments do raise is that they appear to depend on an essentialist conception of popular taste which, we are led to believe, exists in a 'natural', unmediated form that today is being distorted and damaged by the interposition of the music industry. Yet public taste has always been in some way mediated and configured by whatever music 'institutions' have existed at a given time, be they the *goguette* and the *caveau* or the record and the rock stadium. Indeed, in *Politics and Popular Culture*, John Street problematises the very concept of 'the people', who in his view 'are as much a rhetorical as a political fact'. Today's blind faith in market populism – in giving 'the people' what they want, in either politics or culture – is an illusion since the market is not, as is commonly claimed, 'a neutral instrument, it is a political arrangement', just as the music industry is: 'The people do not have a "voice" [. . .]. The people are made; they do not just exist.'[50] This being so, there is a flaw in the whole live/mediated dichotomy. For if not only the record and the TV appearance but even the public and 'the people' from which it springs are fabrications, surely the 'popular' authenticity, the 'naturalness' of the live performance itself needs to be questioned?

In a sense, however, the myth of the big three comes to the rescue here, for it can again be deployed as proof that authenticity does exist. They represent *chanson*'s pre-industrial, cottage-industry ideal, against which the falseness and alienation of today's music business can be measured. This ideal rests on two conditions. One is that the singer must perform 'his' own compositions, thereby creating a ring of integrity. The male singer-songwriter is seldom constructed as an entertainer; he is above all an *auteur*. Félix Leclerc thinks of himself not as a singer but as a man who sings what he writes. For Jonasz, self-composition, not singing ability, is the condition of directly communicating true emotion: 'you can get your emotions, your feelings across in your voice, your way of singing, but there will always be something missing if you're not singing your own words'. This is not so much an aesthetic imperative as an ethical one; or rather the ethical and the aesthetic cannot be separated since it is a question of being honest with oneself and one's audience: 'I'm somebody who above all is in profound agreement with himself and what he sings,' Lavilliers asserts, with an edge of smugness matched by Jean Moiziard: 'When I write, it's as if I were looking at myself in the mirror. I find out who I am. And sincerity can be easily spotted. It's authenticity that creates quality and elicits emotion.'[51] Those unfortunates who fall short of this state of grace, for the most part female singers as we saw earlier, respond in different ways. Some, like France Gall, persuasively defend their qualities as sensitive interpreters of other people's work, pointing out the doubtful quality of many self-penned outpourings. As Catherine Sauvage observes, 'you feel dishonoured if you don't write the words and music yourself. But often, even if the lyrics aren't bad, the music is nothing to write home about!' But others live in the shadow of the big three, whose songs they dare not touch: 'I don't know whether it's humility or fear,' admits Catherine Lara; 'I say to myself, how could anyone do better than Léo [Ferré], Brel, Brassens?'[52]

The other condition is that the singer-songwriter, incarnation of the lone artist in the Romantic mould outlined by Farchy, must be able to accompany himself, if only in a rudimentary, DIY way, irrespective of musical competence. One important consequence of this, as Calvet notes, is that it limits the use of the hands and immobilises the singer (to an extent), who is usually caught in a single spotlight.[53] Stage space itself is thus a metaphor of both artistic sincerity and solitude. Self-accompaniment also signifies a DIY, anti-star discourse. More pragmatically, it means that the musician is mobile and travels light, that he is easy to hire and available to perform at a moment's notice. Symbolically, then, it speaks of both reduced circumstances and an irresistible desire to communicate despite those circumstances, even if this means that the musical or spectacular quality of the performance is limited. The classic instance here is Brassens, famously taciturn on stage, visibly uncomfortable and sweating copiously, one foot stolidly placed on a stool to support his guitar (a pose suggestive of amateurism), and a luxuriant peasant moustache veiling what an exposed mouth might unconsciously reveal; an icon of the non-iconic. Ferré too, even when he abandoned accompanying himself on the piano, still sang motionless, hands by his sides, staring intently or accusingly ahead, facial muscles involuntarily twitching and his long white mane stark against the bohemian black of his stage attire. Once the US folk boom reached France in the mid-1960s, this Left-Bank trope was overlaid with a more fashionably youthful, American look, that of the early Dylan, as with Maxime Le Forestier. But what still linked Le Forestier to Brassens or Ferré was that with all three the look was consistent with the content of the songs. Of course, authenticity here is still 'fabricated', as Richard Peterson says of American country music.[54] Fabrication does not necessarily imply insincerity, but the line between insincerity and fabrication can be wafer thin. Even a Brassens, when famous, will acquire a constructed persona and thereby share the fate of the Abbé Pierre, the charity worker discussed in Barthes's *Mythologies* whose famously plain appearance in the early 1950s testified to his unstinting dedication to the poor but who was soon condemned to dress up as himself once appearance became a media-generated sign of that very dedication. Nevertheless, it is a fabrication based on an auteurist principle which is taken very seriously and still has currency.

Plainly, the model of the self-sufficient, self-contained, male singer-songwriter enshrined in three celestial talents weighs heavily on *chanson* artists, a benchmark which cannot be ignored. Amont's remarks even hint at a certain complex in the profession. He clearly feels obliged to defend the comic *fantaisiste* singers (amongst whom he figures) against unidentified antagonists, insisting that 'laughter, gaiety, entertainment do not deserve the disdain in which they are so often held'. For him, to entertain is a fine and noble thing and he resents those high-minded souls, like the singer-songwriter from Quebec Gilles Vigneault, who say: 'If I'm doing nothing more than entertaining people, I want to drop dead today, this instant [. . .]. I much prefer "alerting" people.'[55]

Amont is sceptical about *chanson*'s ability to alert, or educate, or bring about change, particularly now that it has become a consumer product. Even so, its educational or developmental potential is quite commonly placed above its function as entertainment. For Vian, writing when the Brel–Brassens–Ferré phenomenon was just beginning, this educational dimension is of an aesthetic rather than political order. His guiding value is educating public taste, which he believes the French music industry refuses to do because it has adopted the American market ideology of the customer as king. Yet the public, he confidently asserts, is 'what you turn it into'.[56] Unlike in the car industry, where it is more costly to produce a Rolls than a VW Beetle, quality in popular music costs no more than mediocrity, so why trade only on the latter? Once more, the singer-songwriter is Vian's model, in this case Brassens and Trenet, both of whom have successfully created a massive market for quality, extending their public rather than diminishing it. This for Vian is the way forward: 'Give people back a taste for lyrics that are a little better turned than those of the rhyming-dictionary hack. And where the music is concerned, let us try developing a little the "vocabulary" of the ordinary mortal.'[57] Popular taste could be improved if the education system were willing to teach the public to be more discriminating and, crucially, if the radio were not busy doing the very opposite by letting programming be determined by customer demand, his point (blunt and politically incorrect by today's standards) being that only the stupid write in to radio programmes. Behind his anarchic humour, this is the crux of Vian's position and it is meant seriously. If public taste is to be improved – and it can be – the state radio service must assume its educational mission: 'Education means selection, choice; a choice made by those who educate, not by those who are being educated.'[58]

A similar though more tactful discourse of improvement is found in Calvet's *Chanson et société* (1981). Despite its scholarly tenor, this is a book with a mission, which is to see *chanson* included not among the high arts but alongside other legitimated forms of popular culture like cinema and comic strips. For song, Calvet contends, has never achieved a sufficiently high status among the French intelligentsia to merit serious study, except as a popular form of poetry, with no attention paid to anything other than lyrics. Yet outside education, song is part of our daily lives; and even politicians are realising the value of being seen to appreciate it, as in the case of Mitterrand (then the leader of the Socialist Party), who in 1976 confessed to a liking for Sheila, because she had 'rhythm' and a voice he appreciated.[59] Hence Calvet's book, which introduces ways in which song can be analysed, based on the assumption that the song recital follows much the same semantic strategies as language.

Calvet denies having any polemical intent, but a discursive position does emerge, paradoxically from his stated desire to avoid the covertly ideological discourses of others. An instance he cites is Mitterrand's affection for Sheila's 'rhythm', in which Calvet, close to Bourdieu here, recognises a latent disdain for *chanson*. So fatuous a comment implicitly devalues popular music by assuming that one can express an opinion on it without knowing anything about it. This, Calvet insists, is the disdain of an entire cultured class. The critical methodology Calvet has devised is therefore an attempt to define a different discourse. This is founded upon a distinction between active listening and mere hearing, just as film criticism, he argues, distinguishes between looking and seeing. What is needed is an alternative gaze 'which, by analysing works, can slowly teach the public to listen to them'.[60] For Calvet, inventing what he calls a 'responsible critical discourse' would therefore appear to be an ethical imperative, his ambition being to lift reception above mere consumption, beyond records alone, and certainly beyond the kind of alienated passivity which makes today's audiences accept the spectacle of a live artist miming to a record.

Like Vian's, Calvet's pedagogical voluntarism is a distinctively French voice. It stands out from the branch of cultural studies which considers the consumption of mass-cultural forms to be creative in its own right, to be active and even subversive. And it stands out equally from the disingenuous indulgence of Mitterrand's remark. To some, it may sound like the voice of pre-1960s cultural paternalism, from Arnold to Leavis. More accurately, it is the voice of a long tradition of republican, missionary educators and *animateurs* who have made up the French popular-culture movement, which I shall return to in Part II. As such, it is also the voice of French cultural exceptionalism.

So, what conclusions can be drawn from *chanson* discourse about what *chanson* is? As I have said, the term *chanson* is promiscuously used, its meanings forming a kind of palimpsest. Beneath its common-sense surface meaning can be glimpsed a much less comprehensive sense of a national genre, a chain of prescriptions and expectations of what *French* song *ought* to be. This is an identikit picture rather than the view of any single commentator, coming close to what Bourdieu calls a 'field' and Howard Becker an 'art world'; and it is by reference to it that taste distinctions in popular song are usually made. Assumptions about *chanson* in its purest, Platonic form prioritise lyrics, critical listening, live performance, creativity and sincerity, and consciousness-raising or even education. Conversely, they demote sound, dance, technological mediation, and entertainment for its own sake. In the process, *chanson* achieves national authenticity: it is something which 'the French' do 'naturally' well, and which, in some ineffable way, makes them who they are. The theoretical position these assumptions most readily recall is that of the Frankfurt School, with the caveat that, unlike Adorno, French commentators attribute high-cultural virtues to a popular form. These assumptions are adopted not only by singers and songwriters but also – and especially – by critics and other mediators. Indeed, there is a case for suggesting that they are voiced much *more* by the likes of Calvet, Dillaz and Rioux, or by performer-commentators of a certain age like Vian, Amont and Bertin, than by younger artists who grew up with pop and are often more relaxed about the place of sound, technology and even commerce in music today. To demonstrate this, the position adopted by *Chorus* is worth a closer look before we leave the subject.

By adopting *Les Cahiers de la chanson* as a subtitle, the magazine deliberately recalls *Les Cahiers du cinéma*'s role in the emergence of a new *auteur* cinema in the 1950s, self-consciously awarding itself a badge of cultural credibility. Its house style, however, treads an awkward line between an art discourse, marked by an underlying exasperation that *chanson* is not treated with the same respect as film, and the pieties of the minority fanzine, with its complicitous inverted commas and indignant exclamation marks. The introduction to 'the grand forum of the year 2000' is a case in point. Here, the magazine's claims for the importance of *chanson*, and for its own role as defender of the faith, are on occasion too shrill, calling to mind the righteous hyperbole of the doomed partisan:

> This difficulty (euphemism!) involved in creating a Francophone song magazine and above all keeping it going in minimal conditions of professionalism and competence is all the more paradoxical as the subject under consideration – the most popular form of expression there is – constantly produces statistics – as many people go to live shows as buy records – which are absolutely mind-boggling. A paradox explained of course by the pejorative reputation attached to the very term *chanson*: a form of leisure, pleasure, a pastime, certainly, anything you like . . . except an art [. . .]. [Yet] those words sculpted in flesh and blood, those words which depict the human condition, those melodies which make them dance by con-structing every kind of architecture, classical, modern, avant-garde, 'they're nothing much, just a song' (Ferré), 'but its story is the same as our own' (Trenet). And when the 'souls of the poets' [Trenet] join those of the people, there is no form of artistic expression more eloquent and authentic, more durable and sensitive, more worthy and honourable, in a word more noble than this.[61]

Flushed with self-belief, *Chorus* thus enters the fray over the good, the bad and the ugly in *chanson*. Throughout the fictional forum, such certainty as there is lies not with the interviewees but with the imaginary interviewer, who constantly, though perhaps unconsciously, tries to steer the discussion towards the journal's own slant but repeatedly fails. Some of the questions asked are perfectly open-ended, but others are more like statements. Today, we are informed, song 'is above all a vehicle for ideas'. As this assertion meets with only lukewarm agreement and one overtly hostile response ('I myself don't trust ideas one inch', cries Henri Tachan), *Chorus* tries again, this time with a proper question: 'Is it also ideas which guide the writing of a *chanson*?' Receiving a much more resounding 'no' here, *Chorus* then gets provocative: 'So apparently sound is just as important as sense?' Again, the answers are frustratingly inconclusive: yes, no, and a cryptic parable from Guy Béart about a marriage of the blind and the paralysed. Possibly as mystified by this as the reader is, *Chorus* nevertheless tries to run with it, again with an unequivocal statement: 'Husband and wife are equal, no doubt . . . but each spouse has a specific role to play. And the role of the text remains fundamental in French *chanson.'* Thus corralled, the respondents agree; but when *Chorus* asks what the role of music therefore is, a different set of results is obtained, leaving the 'interviewer' to remark, now with an edge of exasperation: 'It's difficult developing a set of convictions with you! For some, the text plays the dominant role, for the others it's the music, or the voice.'[62] Of course, as the 'forum' is entirely staged and structured by *Chorus* itself, the magazine is clearly pointing up these contradictions and is good-natured about them. None the less, its own position on the definition of *chanson* is quite transparent, unlike that of the performers it is interrogating.

One might justifiably conclude, then, that while Brel, Ferré and Brassens are unquestionably the Olympians of post-war *chanson*, it is principally a committed critical discourse which guards the flame, servicing their memory as evidence that Gods once walked the earth and that *chanson* can be art. Measured against such deities, pop can only be found wanting. This is an ambivalent situation. Certainly, having such models to look up to has generally kept the standard of French songwriting high. But it may also have locked *chanson* in a patrimonial, idealist discourse which makes it difficult to move on. *Chanson* has never existed in some pure, atemporal state but has always been constructed by its spatial, social, industrial and technological contexts, as Calvet demonstrates. Yet *chanson* rhetoric is founded on a pre-industrial, Romantic notion of the 'sacralised' artist, as Farchy puts it, an inspired creator working alone with his or her imagination. It is this idealism which Becker deconstructs in his notion of 'art worlds'. In reality, no artist works alone since all art forms, including those usually seen as the most reclusive, like painting or poetry, are in some sense social, requiring the intervention of others, either directly as technicians (in cinema for example) or indirectly as the guardians of a patrimonial tradition (critics, academics) or as society or the state.[63] Although, occasionally, a specialist like Calvet will also acknowledge this, there has yet to be a major epistemological shift in the French notion of *chanson* towards Becker's kind of reasoning. Irrespective of commercial or industrial realities, *chanson* artists are ultimately perceived to work alone, if only in so far as they are deemed to be trying to please nobody but themselves. Constructions of Brassens particularly, I suggest, are vital to this process. His archaic versification and vocabulary, his deceptively artless melodies and aesthete's remoteness from fashion and the material world, in a sense authorise the essentialist, authenticist readings of *chanson* exemplified in Vian, Bertin, Amont and *Chorus*. The industrial, commercial dimensions of popular music are seen not as determining but as contingent and ultimately external to the creative process.

Arguably, then, what one finds in French *chanson* discourse generally, and in representations of Brassens particularly, is the conflation of two of the three 'taste groups' identified by Frith (who extrapolates from Becker and Bourdieu), that is, the three 'discursive practices' according to which music is valued: art discourse, folk discourse and commercial discourse. Deliberately kept apart from commercial values, *chanson* is represented as having features of art music, being produced by skilled, creative individuals and providing the audience with 'a transcendent experience'. But it is also constructed as having what Frith describes as 'the folk value of the natural, the spontaneous and the immediate'.[64] This distinctively French rhetorical hybrid allows discriminatory judgements to be made regarding what I am calling the national authenticity of music, and it helps us arrive at a better understanding of the difficulty France has experienced in assimilating pop. Particularly striking from an Anglo-Saxon perspective is how remote this discourse is from the perspectives of cultural studies, which has never properly established itself as a disciplinary category in the French academic world. Even so, the handful of academic sociologists who have addressed the subject of popular music have shown a readiness to tackle the social, cultural and industrial dimensions of popular music which cultural studies addresses. It is to them that I now want to turn for an alternative perception of popular music, which opens up quite different ways of constructing authenticity.

Notes

1. Quoted and translated by Brian Rigby, *Popular Culture in Modern France: A Study in Cultural Discourse* (Routledge, 1991), pp. 165–6.
2. Both quotations are from *Salut les copains*, no. 13 (August 1963), p. 30.
3. 'Le Bloc-notes de François Mauriac (samedi 6 juillet)', *Le Figaro Littéraire*, 13 July 1963, p. 18.
4. Marwick, *The Sixties*, pp. 106–7 (Marwick's translation).
5. Gilles Verlant (ed.), *Le Rock et la plume: une histoire du rock par les meilleurs journalistes français 1960–1975* (Éditions Hors Collection, 2000), p. 22.
6. On early jazz in France and the accompanying debates, see Jackson, 'Making Enemies'; Nettlebeck, 'Jazz at the Théâtre Graslin; and Philippe Gumplowicz, 'Au Hot Club de France, on ne faisait pas danser les filles', in Gumplowicz and Klein (eds), *Paris 1944–1954*, pp. 167–82.
7. Francis is quoted in Fléouter, *Un Siècle de chansons*, p. 64; Boris Vian, *Derrière la zizique* (Bourgois/Livre de Poche, 1997), p. 280.
8. A good deal more research needs to be done on this idea of a self-conscious *chanson* discourse, by examining not only writing about *chanson*, as I am attempting to do here, but also the songs themselves. At the University of Leeds, a doctoral student, Kim Harrison, has begun working in this area by studying 'reflexivity' in the French *chanson* form.

9. Fred Hidalgo, 'Un Cri dans le silence', *Paroles et musique*, no. 1 (June–July 1980), p. 3.
10. Bertin, *Chante toujours, tu m'intéresses* (Seuil, 1981), p. 154.
11. Ibid., pp. 138–41 (quotation p. 140).
12. Fléouter, *Un Siècle de chansons*, p. 40.
13. Hawkins, *Chanson*, quotations from pp. 54, 61 and 62, respectively.
14. Reproduced on the occasion of Ferré's death as '1969. Ferré, Brel, Brassens, trois géants se rencontrent', *Paris Match*, 29 July 1993, p. 55.
15. Fléouter, *Un Siècle de chansons*, p. 110.
16. Both quotations are from Marcel Amont, *Une Chanson, qu'y a-t-il à l'intérieur d'une chanson?* (Seuil, 1994), pp. 69 and 70, respectively.
17. 'Cabrel, Goldman, Simon et Souchon: Chorus met ses "parrains" sur la sellette' (interview), *Chorus*, no. 1 (Autumn 1992), pp. 10–32 (quotation from Goldman, p. 14). On Renaud, see Amont, *Une Chanson*, p. 61.
18. Bigot, *Questions pour la chanson*, pp. 14–15.
19. Amont, *Une Chanson*: Brassens, p. 77; Jouannest, p. 74.
20. Ibid., p. 80.
21. Brunschwig and Grimbert are cited in Bigot, *Questions pour la chanson*, p. 28.
22. Calvet, *Chanson et société*, see especially Chapters 3, 4 and 7.
23. Jackson, 'Making Enemies', pp. 182 and 186.
24. Simon Frith, *Performing Rites: Evaluating Popular Music* (Oxford University Press, 1998), p. 175.
25. Trenet's last radio interview, France Inter, 25 October 1999, repeated on the morning of his death, France Inter, 19 February 2001.
26. Frith, *Performing Rites*, p. 170 (the inner quotation is from Rorem).
27. Ibid, pp. 164 and 173, respectively.
28. Ibid., p. 181.
29. Amont, *Une Chanson*, p. 89.
30. Ibid., pp. 86–7 (quotations p. 87).
31. Ibid., p. 87.
32. Jackson, 'Making Enemies', pp. 182 and 190 (Claudel).
33. Quoted in Coulomb and Varrod, *1968–1988*, p. 100.
34. Delanoë, *La Chanson en colère*, pp. 124 and 27 (quotation).
35. Ibid., pp. 110 and 126, respectively.
36. Dillaz, *La Chanson française de contestation*, p. 75.
37. Rioux, *Cinquante Ans de chanson française*, p. 408.
38. Ibid., pp. 407–10 (quotations pp. 408 and 410, respectively).
39. Chocron, 'Les Enjeux économiques du rock', p. 121.
40. 'Le Grand Forum de l'an 2000', *Chorus*, pp. 85 (Jonasz) and 131 (Moustaki).
41. Calvet, *Chanson et société*, p. 47.

42. 'Le Grand Forum de l'an 2000', *Chorus*, pp. 131 (Bashung) and 129 (Caussimon).
43. Amont, *Une Chanson*, p. 140.
44. 'Le Grand Forum de l'an 2000', *Chorus*, p. 85.
45. Georges Moustaki (with Mariella Righini), *Questions à la chanson* (Stock, 1973), p. 121.
46. Ibid., p. 122; Dillaz, *La Chanson française de contestation*, p. 45.
47. Dillaz, *La Chanson française de contestation*, p. 75.
48. Ibid., pp. 117–8.
49. Moustaki, *Questions à la chanson*, pp. 125–6.
50. John Street, *Politics and Popular Culture* (Polity Press, 1997), pp. 16–18.
51. 'Le Grand Forum de l'an 2000', *Chorus*: Leclerc, p. 96; Jonasz, p. 96; Lavilliers, p. 82; Moiziard, p. 81.
52. Ibid., Sauvage, pp. 119–20; Lara, p. 121.
53. Calvet, *Chanson et société*, pp. 50–61.
54. Peterson, *Creating Country Music*, pp. 3–11.
55. Amont, *Une Chanson*, pp. 115 and 114, respectively.
56. Vian, *En avant la zizique*, p. 118.
57. Ibid., p. 128.
58. Ibid., p. 121.
59. Calvet, *Chanson et société*, pp. 10–11.
60. Ibid., p. 18.
61. 'Le Grand Forum de l'an 2000', *Chorus*, pp. 73–4.
62. Ibid. All quotations are from pp. 91–9 passim.
63. Howard Becker, *Art Worlds* (University of California Press, 1982).
64. Frith, *Performing Rites*, pp. 35–42.

– 5 –

Denationalising Authenticity: The Sociological Debate

French social-scientific writing on pop is still relatively scarce, but what there is has, like cultural studies, become increasingly interested in reception rather than production. This perspective opens up quite different ways of constructing authenticity. Its earliest exponent is Edgar Morin.

Morin's 1963 articles in *Le Monde* stand out amid all the cod sociology and moral earnestness of the early hostility to pop. This is because he strives to approach *yéyé* unburdened by ulterior motives or youth-club paternalism, but with the anthropological empathy of the participant observer. He readily accepts *yéyé*'s exploitative, economic face but chooses not to stop there. Instead, he explores it as the manifestation of a deeper sociological trans-formation, in which mass communications – first cinema, now pop – have played a big part by furnishing myths and models. As we saw, *Salut les copains*'s early pop journalism was, like most, hagiographic, written from the perspective of a 'we' comprising young people, their idols and the magazine concerned, all brought together as *copains*. This 'we' particularly fascinates Morin. He interprets it as the reflection and vehicle of a new form of class-consciousness based not on socio-economic status but age. *Yéyé*, he argues, is the sign of a relatively homogeneous 'age-class' which has been welded together as a youth *culture* by shared musical tastes, fashions, rituals, language and values, and quite simply by a shared awareness of not being old, which is its ultimate meaning, 'as if it possessed in youthfulness a quality that is immutable and inalienable'.[1]

However, as this last remark indicates, Morin is not blind to the movement's self-delusion or ambivalence. He recognises that it shares some of the nihilism of mass culture and that its primary purpose is to prepare French youth to become docile consumers in a capitalist economy. But what intrigues him is its other face: the Dionysian quality of the hysteria caused at the Place de la Nation event, the way it glorifies play, pleasure and a musically induced 'gratuitous frenzy' (*frénésie à vide*), 'a message of ecstasy without religion, without ideology, which has come to us via a prodigious injection of black energy, of uprooted negritude, into American civilisation and which has infused twentieth-century humanity'. Evidently, Morin sees this aspect of *yéyé* as one expression of a shift in alienated Western culture generally:

> through the rhythm, this chanted, syncopated music, these cries of yeah yeah, there is a form of participation in something elemental, biological. Is this not an expression – only slightly more intense among adolescents – of an entire civilisation returning to a more primitive, more basic connection with life, as a way of compensating for the continual growth of the field of abstraction and artificiality?

But although this nihilism may only be the bovine individualism of self-gratification, it also contains an embryonic revolt against dominant values the revolt of the beatnik or the *blouson noir* against 'an adult world from which seeps bureaucratic boredom, repetition, deceit, death'.[2] At present, Morin sees individualism as the dominant meaning, but he argues that this dominance does not suppress the other meanings and that in the future youth culture could go either way.

On one level, May 1968 proved Morin right about the revolt at the heart of *yéyé*'s blandness. However, his identification of a homogeneous generational culture beyond class was already looking threadbare by the end of the 1960s. As another social scientist, Erik Neveu, argues, drawing on Frith, the rebellious themes identified with late-1960s pop in fact express a disaffection with the post-sixteen education system which only a minority of adolescents were in a position to experience. But the polysemy of pop ideology allowed it to be *read* as universal, crossing class divides. Nevertheless, Morin's articles did prefigure the rise of more analytical forms of pop commentary than the fanzine writing of *Salut les copains*, beginning with the appearance of *Rock & Folk* and *Best* in the late 1960s. Born in the 1940s, the journalists writing for these magazines, like Alain Dister, François Jouffa or Philippe Constantin (future talent scout and head of Barclay), had grown up with jazz, rock and pop, lived in the USA in some cases, and displayed an encyclopaedic knowledge of Anglo-American music. Morin also seems to have set the agenda for such pop writing, much of which similarly constructs pop's content in terms of a hesitation between subversion and submission.

A good example is the slim volume of a well-known cumulative encyclopaedia series (Que Sais-Je?), entitled *La Pop-Music* and published in 1975 by a social scientist and musician, Henry Torgue.[3] Throughout these re-editions, Torgue proposes a basic anatomy of pop using four analytical perspectives summarised as 'history', 'message', 'music' and 'politics'. Like Morin, he focuses on pop's subversion but he gives it more prominence. Separating 'message' from 'music', he undertakes a standard content analysis based on the lyrics of the Beatles, Dylan, Hendrix and Pink Floyd, since he considers that pop's dissidence was established during the years 1964 to 1977. Inevitably, this corpus proves more and more misleading as the editions go by, and there is an overall naïvety about this kind of writing, which sometimes invests unremarkable lyrics with a literary subtlety more appropriate to *chanson* and may leave the Anglophone commentator slightly sceptical. One also senses in such writing, though only occasionally in Torgue's own case, the same wide-eyed admiration of Anglo-American pop as was shown by its first French imitators. Nevertheless, Torgue does go beyond straight content analysis to suggest that pop's radicalism has also to do with the sense of power, energy and violence its rhythm provokes. Like Morin, he sees the music as about rediscovering the body and the festive but, separated from him by the collapse of May 1968, Torgue is even more aware of pop's ideological ambivalence: 'The ambiguity of this music becomes clearer: on the one hand, it is revolutionary in the sense that it carries subversion within it and reveals revolution to be the great absentee; on the other, it limits revolutionary action by providing satisfaction of a post-revolutionary nature but contained, and of no lasting consequence for the system in place.' Pop's homogeneity is in fact only ephemeral, limited to the ludic moments of the concert or the festival, after which the class origins of participants inexorably restore social boundaries.[4]

Another analyst who takes Morin's reading further is Paul Yonnet in his seminal book *Jeux, modes et masses* (Games, Fashions and Masses). Like Torgue, Yonnet, as we have seen, makes use of content analysis to construct a historiography of pop, and, like Morin, he sees pop as broadly homogeneous from the late 1950s until punk. Against all expectations, Western youth during this period broke with the rules and structures imposed upon it by institutions like the Scouts and Guides, trades unions, and political parties, as if it realised that it could only constitute itself as separate and autonomous by depoliticising itself. In their place, pop became its real 'class' consciousness, as counter-exemplified by the continuing dependency of young people in countries where pop has been actively repressed.[5] This theme is pursued by Yonnet into the music itself. Once rock'n'roll was transplanted into European societies, it lost its racial potency and gave birth to the more anodyne styles of pop. Despite the variety of such styles, 1960s pop became a meta-genre characterised by a 'collective giddiness' (*un vertige collectif*). What this means is threefold: amplification, consciousness-expanding drugs and festive events like Woodstock. This echoes Morin's interest in the ludic nature of pop, but Yonnet points up more explicitly its political implications for public and private life: 'Pop, unlike rock 'n' roll, would not be recreational music but a music leading to all-embracing life solutions, proposing new modes and norms of living meant from the outset to go beyond the simple framework of new leisure time.'[6] Only with punk does pop approach Morin's 'gratuitous frenzy' since, synthesising and transcending the mask of rock and the eschatology of pop, punk is above all *about* music, in its revolt against technical virtuosity.

Yonnet's book both updates and challenges Morin's thinking, concluding that, over the thirty years it surveys, adolescents have indeed formed a separate, largely autonomous group organised around pop but have reversed the traditional adult–child power relationship by contaminating the tastes, fashions and ideas of adult society while remaining apart from it. This is because, like any integrated social group, it has its own system of communication, to which pop is crucial, challenging the abstract, verbal rationalism of the West. This unified culture does not, however, make youth a social class in the proper sense of the term, Yonnet argues, since it has no economic homogeneity. Nor will he call youth an 'age-class' as Morin does, chiefly because the frontiers of adolescence are impossible to generalise. What youth is, however, is 'an international ethnic group, a cosmopolitan nation', a 'people'.

Morin, Torgue and Yonnet, then, all share a belief in the broad homogeneity of youth culture and in the culture's potential for inducing change, though Torgue is more equivocal on both scores. Methodologically, all three base their analysis largely on 'content': lyrics, music, styles and values. To this extent, all three draw conclusions about pop's reception largely by examining its production (though not exclusively in Morin's case). This approach has it limitations. First, as seen earlier, Frith argues that treating lyrics as words rather than sounds restricts the sense that can be made of popular music. Second, textual analysis is limited by the polysemous nature of pop lyrics, as Neveu's commentary suggests. Lastly, and most importantly from the point of view of my argument here, content analysis pays scant attention to those who 'use' or 'consume' the music. The 1980s and 1990s, in France as in the English-speaking world, saw attempts to reverse this situation, following the lead given by two prestigious French social thinkers of the post-war period, Pierre Bourdieu and Michel de Certeau, both of whom are concerned with the consumption of popular- or mass-cultural forms. French sociological accounts of how pop is used can in fact be loosely divided into two clusters: the pessimistic, gathered to a lesser or greater extent round the work of Bourdieu, and the optimistic, gathered round Certeau. However, these two categories need to be qualified a good deal.

Bourdieu and Co.

One of the principal preoccupations of French social-scientific inquiry into popular culture has been the statistical measurement of cultural practices in relation to the variables of age, gender and class. An early pioneer of such work was the sociologist of leisure Joffre Dumazedier in the late 1950s, but he has been somewhat overshadowed internationally by Bourdieu, who began his own empirically based studies in the early 1960s. Building on his early findings published in *The Love of Art* (1966), where he maintains that high culture is so encoded as to be incomprehensible to those not conditioned to decipher it, *Distinction* (1979), his major work on taste, sets out to plot 'the social uses of art and culture' and reveal how cultural practices are at their deepest level related to class struggle.[7]

Using data from a survey carried out in 1963 and complemented by a further study in 1967–8, Bourdieu contends that cultural tastes are determined by social origin and education. Those whose family circumstances have enabled them to grow up with an easy familiarity with the 'legitimate' (or high) forms of learning and culture benefit from social advantage over those who have not. Schooling can theoretically compensate for this imbalance, but only partially and usually unsatisfactorily, since those who have inherited 'cultural capital' from family are predisposed to learn and deploy the formal codes needed to decipher the canonical narratives to which they are exposed in the French education system; and because the bourgeoisie, anxious to retain the lead its cultural capital gives it, devalues the kind of culture acquired through schooling alone, seeing it as artificial, pedantic and incomplete. Inherited cultural competence is in fact represented in charismatic terms, as a form of grace bestowed on some and not others. This is where the notion of distinction comes in. Bourdieu sees class struggle in post-industrial societies as a struggle for cultural power. Each class – and within it, each class fraction – uses taste in art and lifestyle as a means of displaying its difference, constructing its aesthetic 'disposition' as both 'natural' (rather than historically conditioned) and superior. This 'distinctive' strategy is deployed particularly with regard to each class's closest neighbours. This is not necessarily a conscious process but it is written into a complete system of taste: constructing one's own taste as natural automatically implies that the other's taste is not.

Clearly, in such a perspective, there is no place for the homogenisation identified by Morin. Although Bourdieu does not examine popular music at any great length in *Distinction*, he does consider that 'nothing more clearly affirms one's "class", nothing more infallibly classifies, than tastes in music', and that popular song in particular is ideal for the purpose. As we have already glimpsed at the discursive level (Chapter 4), song is in fact at the centre of a complex web of 'distinctive' practices and 'calls for particular vigilance from those who intend to mark their difference', because, like photography, its virtual universality makes it a lingua franca with which to draw the world's attention to one's social position.[8] In both classical and popular tastes, he demonstrates, differences in educational capital are associated with taste differences involving genres (for example opera and operetta), periods (classical and contemporary) and composers or works. Thirty-one per cent of working-class respondents with no or few qualifications list Petula Clark among their three favourites, while only 3 per cent of highly qualified upper-class respondents do, whereas for Brassens the results are 38 per cent and 90 per cent, respectively. Educational attainment also generates differences *within* classes. Among those in the working class with at least a basic level of qualification, the liking for Petula Clark is halved and appreciation of Brassens soars (from 38 per cent to 61 per cent). Ferré, meanwhile, appears to be an especially exclusive taste. Fewer than 25 per cent of the unqualified in either class appreciate him but almost half of the highly qualified upper-class do. Brel's output, on the other hand, although constituting 'one of the major works of the minor arts' according to Bourdieu, turns out to be a ' "middle-brow" taste', alongside Bécaud. As represented by Johnny Hallyday, rock, still incipient at the time of Bourdieu's main survey (1963), is more of a working-class taste, chosen by 17 per cent as opposed to only 7 per cent among the middle classes and 5 per cent among the upper classes (*classes supérieures*).[9]

From these data, Bourdieu draws a number of important conclusions. Intellectuals, artists and university lecturers are wary of opting for *chanson* as a social marker because it sends out mixed messages. For some, it is too middlebrow for their distinction-making needs, though others adopt an attitude of 'selective acceptance' (of Brassens, for example) which allows them to demonstrate the generosity of their taste horizons. They are, in fact, the only social group with enough cultural confidence to combine their 'natural' taste for legitimate culture with even a partial liking for those popular forms which are still only in the process of being legitimated, like *chanson*, cinema and jazz. Further along the scale, employers and professionals have little use for this kind of ' "intellectual" song', so have to demarcate themselves from those they consider beneath them 'by rejecting with disgust the most popular and most "vulgar" singers, such as Les Compagnons de la Chanson, Mireille Mathieu, Adamo or Sheila, though they make an exception for the oldest and most consecrated singers (like Édith Piaf and Charles Trenet) or those closest to operetta and bel canto'.[10]

But it is the middle classes who make most use of *chanson* to jockey for position and who, in Bourdieu's reckoning, have the most expert grasp of the fine distinctions at work in popular music's social meanings. They, too, carefully reject the favourite singers of the working class (Mathieu, Adamo, Aznavour, Rossi), opting instead for those who 'endeavour to dignify this "minor" genre'. It is, for example, through *chanson* that primary-school teachers are best able to flag up their educational superiority over other fractions of the petite bourgeoisie and workers, by adopting those like Brassens who 'offer populist poetry in the primary-school tradition'. Given the modesty of their educational capital, they are more comfortable with elevating a popular form than with throwing their lot in with legitimate art, dominated by the better educated, who are of course busy distinguishing themselves from the likes of primary teachers.[11]

Bourdieu's analysis invites two remarks. First, readers of *Distinction* may find themselves wondering whether it is only his respondents who are in the business of making distinctions of value. Since no other major source is cited, it would appear to be Bourdieu's own system of classification which separates the wheat from the chaff, the 'intellectual' Brassens from the 'vulgar' Mireille Mathieu, Adamo and Sheila; or which associates stars like Petula Clark, Guétary and Mariano with 'songs totally devoid of artistic ambition or pretension'.[12] In which case, Bourdieu's place might surprisingly be with other convinced distinction-makers like Vian, Bertin and *Chorus*. Be that as it may, Bourdieu's analysis certainly implies that the popular-music consumer makes aesthetic choices dynamically, in opposition to the choices of others, Brassens and Ferré being the strongest currency to flaunt when one wishes to publicise one's position at the top of the tree. This maps onto the tendency identified in *chanson*'s producers and apologists to define *chanson* against other, lesser forms. Second, what lends Bourdieu's commentary an authority which much French cultural theory lacks is its empirical starting point. But one of the limitations of this empiricism is that he was drawing conclusions in 1979 from data gathered in the 1960s. Hence the common criticism, summarised by Rigby, that *Distinction*'s gloomy deductions are better suited to 'a time when there was still a relatively unified and stable notion of an acknowledged high culture (classical music, great literature, grand masters, etc.), which people considered it necessary to know about, or at least to want to know about, if they were to think of themselves, and be thought of, as successful members of society'.[13] Similarly, just as the traditional class boundaries on which Bourdieu's arguments rely have shifted (even if they have not vanished), so too have the subdivisions within popular music, as we saw in Chapter 2.

However, by the time of *Distinction*'s publication, a new source of data had appeared: the Ministry of Culture's research department, the SER, headed by Augustin Girard, which had begun the statistical measurement of cultural practices in the early 1960s, partly with Bourdieu's collaboration since *The Love of Art* had developed from work that it had commissioned. The first full survey of cultural practices by the Ministry was carried out in 1973, followed by a second in 1981, a third in 1988–9 (including a separate volume of minute comparisons with the 1973 and 1981 findings) by Olivier Donnat and Denis Cogneau, and a fourth in 1997 by Donnat alone. As Donnat acknowledges, the surveys have inevitably been influenced by Bourdieu's interpretations and methodology.[14] As such, they expose the largely unsubstantiated generalisations made by Morin, Torgue and Yonnet about homogenisation.

The surveys' principal finding over the years is that there has been a shift in the 'centre of gravity' of cultural practices. In Bourdieu's perspective, France's high culture sets the agenda, with popular culture defined as its negative opposite and the newer popular forms like jazz and cinema having as it were to apply for admission to respectability. But the surveys show that this polarity is steadily being switched, as television-watching, music-listening and a growing demand for amateur activities elbow their way to the centre and nudge high culture to the periphery. The result is that the later surveys, while still using Bourdieu's lexicon and methods, adopt a post-Bourdieu perspective by updating and to an extent challenging his pessimism about culture and class. They confirm that social position and educational level are central in determining access to legitimate culture – though the 1988–9 and 1997 volumes do attempt to avoid ideological phraseology by dividing cultural practices into two 'neutral' categories: the 'culture' of going out (*culture de sorties*) and that of staying in, or 'apartment culture'. Outings involving traditional cultural activities (theatre, concerts, museums) 'remain, in 1988 as in 1973, the most "distinctive" practices', determined by class, education and geography.[15] And as Bourdieu also stresses, the fullest cultural lives are still led by the small minority which has enough economic and cultural capital to combine high-cultural outings with excursions to cinemas or discos, with visiting friends and eating in restaurants, while the opposite end of the social spectrum is still confined to an apartment culture consisting of television. But increasingly the surveys outgrow Bourdieu by showing that this is no longer the complete picture.

With the ever-growing sophistication of audiovisual and information technologies, the notion of cultural access is in fact being redefined. The increase in supply of TV programmes via satellite and cable and in the number of sets per household; new gadgets like personal stereos, video and DVD, remote control and interactive TV; the commercialisation of high-quality digital reproduction of sounds and images; and of course the Internet – all of these are profoundly altering the nature of apartment culture. But more importantly from our point of view, music is a key dimension of this revolution, though one which, in the authors' view, has not been as well publicised as the broadcasting revolution. The 1988–9 and 1997 surveys put this right by underscoring a 'boom' in music-related activities since the 1970s. Listening to recorded music has increased enormously, with frequent listening tripling between 1973 and 1997.[16] Admittedly, the degree of frequency does still vary with educational level, location, income and age,[17] and it must have come as no surprise to Bourdieu that, although between 1973 and 1988–9 the audience for recorded classical music went up by 7 per cent, its social composition changed little;[18] or that, by 1997, 81 per cent of the population had still never been to the opera.[19] But in all four surveys, it is *chanson* which is the undisputed queen of listening habits, despite the inroads made by Anglo-American pop. In the 1997 poll, the category 'French *chanson* and *variétés*' accounts for the biggest proportion of record collections (84 per cent) and is by far the most frequently listened to, its score (44 per cent) double that of 'international variety' and almost 4.5 times that of rock.[20]

These findings are not quite as conclusive as they seem, though, because they are undifferentiated. For example, the use of gender as a variable reveals that *chanson* is a predominantly female taste in both 1988–9 and 1997, while rock, hard rock, rap and punk are male.[21] Furthermore, as Donnat admits, the *chanson* category used in the surveys is misleading since it is very broad and its definition changes from survey to survey, making comparison impossible. More helpful is the section which asks which *kinds* of song are listened to most. Here, in both 1988–9 and 1997, one sub-category was defined as 'French "text-songs" (Brel, Brassens, Ferré . . .)'. This easily came first with approximately half the votes,[22] though this does not automatically mean that 'text-song' is the nation's indisputable favourite, since those who prefer it represent not half of the entire sample but half of those who listen most to 'songs'; and in any case this is again an undifferentiated proportion. When socio-professional status is taken into account, the likes of Brel, Brassens and Ferré are shown to be most highly prized by management and the 'higher intellectual professions'. When age is factored in, 57 per cent of text-song lovers in 1997 turn out to be over sixty-four, and fewer than a quarter between fifteen and nineteen.[23] What the surveys in fact reveal is that, if *chanson* remains a site for distinctive strategies, the most vigorous distinctive practices have now moved into pop, and that distinction-making is now generational as well as class-based. Both the 1988–9 and 1997 exercises demonstrate that somewhere between the ages of twenty-five and thirty-five, among those who choose songs as their favoured genre, text-songs begin to catch up with and eventually overtake either 'English or American songs' in 1988–9, or 'French hits of today' in 1997.[24]

Denis Cogneau explores this finding further in his section of the 1973–89 comparative study. Underlying his analysis is the idea that Bourdieu's postulate that tastes are socially classifying now applies as much to popular culture as to classical, because today the traditional polarity between the two, which *Distinction* assumed, has largely disappeared. Cogneau's point is that those with a taste for more complex or experimental forms in *either* category, popular or classical, are those with the most cultural and educational capital and who go out most. Pop, he deduces, is far from being the 'federalising' music Yonnet claims. The survey does, he admits, provide some evidence of a broad and distinct adolescent culture, due to the shared experience of schooling and unemployment. But he predicts this will prove temporary as the adolescents concerned reach adulthood, rather than fundamentally controverting the variables of class, gender and cultural capital which generally account for the social reproduction of taste.[25]

Cogneau also tackles Yonnet directly in three articles published in the popular-music magazine *Yaourt* in 1990, where he has more opportunity to develop his arguments. Here, Cogneau can be seen working towards an analytical model which does not limit itself to production as Yonnet's does but allows a more rounded sociology, akin to Simon Frith's for example. Yonnet's error, Cogneau believes, is that it infers the homogeneity of pop's adolescent consumers from the recurrence of themes and iconography across the field of pop-cultural production. But although 'le rock' is convenient as a marketing category and may be meaningful to musicians, historians and critics, it corresponds much less, in Cogneau's view, to young people's own classification practices. In the 1988–9 survey, only 53 per cent of those who listened most to 'sung music' called what they listened to 'rock' and only a small proportion of these could actually name a rock band they liked, which already suggests the term's irrelevance as a generic category. In the *Yaourt* articles, Cogneau uses the artists they did cite to refine his analysis of pop tastes, producing four basic types of pop fan. The first is the 'highbrow trendy' (*le branché cultivé*) who likes both 'classics' (mainly 1960s–1970s groups) and 'musts' (1980s rock stars who are still popular but are steadily being classicised) but eschews the latest one-hit wonders. This is the most Parisian type, with extensive cultural capital. The second is the 'classic', who likes only the well-established acts of the past. Both of these types include rock within an eclectic pattern of taste (including classical), their high-cultural capital having equipped them with wide-ranging deciphering skills. The third type is the specialist, a minority who likes mainly musts and is equidistant from the Top 50 and the classics. And lastly, of course, there is the hapless 'consumer', consisting of adolescents or older FM listeners who prefer the 'mass' stars like Madonna and Hallyday, as well as soft rock or heavy metal, in short everything which the first two categories despise. It is to one or more of these four configurations, Cogneau argues, that the various strategies and iconographies of pop performers correspond, not to some mythical notion of a unified youth culture.

Like cinema, Cogneau concludes, pop is destined for further stylistic and social differentiation, though with commercial success still depending on the mass public and art status and posterity still conferred by a cultural elite. It is therefore better sociology in his view (better, that is, than Yonnet's) to approach pop not as the class-consciousness of a unified social movement but as an art-form like any other, 'shot through, like the novel, with irreducible differences, between periods and generations, but also between legitimate forms and popular or mass forms'.[26] It is this steady process of classicisation and even 'heritagisation', as pop secretes its own history, which explains why Bourdieu's games of distinction are now being played out in the arena of popular culture. This implies the establishment of operational criteria of value, and Cogneau's contention would appear to be that this has now come about.

Overall, popular music, and indeed music as a whole, emerge from the surveys as a particularly dynamic and problematic sector in contemporary French cultural life, one that has probably seen the biggest shift in practices and values. As Donnat has revealed, in 1997 music was virtually the only category where comparison with 1988–9 had to be sacrificed because the categories used in the earlier survey were no longer applicable less than a decade later.[27] Here more than in other sectors, the rapid complexification of styles, the rise of audiovisual and more recently digital practices, and the development of amateur activity are transforming the landscape. Other sociologists, however, have begun to examine this complexity without adopting Bourdieu's perception of the popular as a dominated culture. Despite the visible influence of Bourdieu on the Ministry surveys, Donnat does not consider himself a pure Bourdieusian but situates himself alongside those who acknowledge their debt but have moved on. His own editions of the survey were in fact an attempt to find a middle way between the author of *Distinction* and those commentators who are willing to look more positively on popular practices. Amongst these he includes Joffre Dumazedier and Michel de Certeau.[28] Of these two, Certeau would seem to have had the greater influence on the sociology of pop.

Certeau and Co.

Certeau shares certain concerns with Bourdieu but his ideas have different ideological implications. Although he acknowledges the social forces which shape cultural practices, he does not see them as determining those practices in a monolithic way. Behind his work is a perception that social science has in fact identified the forces but ignored those often surprising 'trajectories' which individuals and groups describe within their circumscribed spaces. For between the plurality of social forces which for Bourdieu irresistibly *produce* cultures, Certeau locates gaps, cracks and flaws, a margin of play in the machine. Such gaps are present in any system, undermining its plenitude, letting in a shaft of daylight which enables culture to develop. For Certeau, a common element in all cultural activity, be it writing or reading, composing or listening, is creativity. The finished products of creative artists are only one of the forms

this creativity assumes and are specific to a privileged elite, though contemporary power relations allow this particular variant to dominate. Creation
actually pullulates all around us, springing up even in the tiniest interstices of
our public and private existences, and it is therefore characterised by its
impermanence, its perishability. Elitist art discourses try to freeze this
impermanence in the notion of an eternal art object, but for Certeau everyday
creation is about acts, not objects.

Such acts are ultimately subversive, a kind of 'poaching', as he describes it.
Contrary to what mass-culture theory would have us believe, the consumer
is not a helpless victim. We invisibly appropriate and customise the 'texts' which
those with power have mapped out, be they authors or authorities, town-
planners or the producers of mass culture, twisting and shaping them to our
own designs, producing a text of our own. Such 'poaching', however, is
ultimately a social act, for 'what is creative is the gesture which allows a group
to invent itself'.[29] Creation thus becomes essentially convivial, festive. Certeau
points out the greater interest being taken in the years following 1968 in
process rather than product, in happenings, street theatre, rock concerts. The
purpose underlying such events, in his reading, is not to perform a work, but
to 'allow a collectivity to constitute itself momentarily in the act of representing
itself'. Any artefacts such events may leave behind – the film of Woodstock,
say, or a live album – are no more than a 'residue' of these ephemeral cultural
moments.[30]

One important impact of Certeau's writing has been to prompt social-
scientific research on how popular-cultural artefacts are used.[31] In particular,
he has influenced three French sociologists who have worked on pop and
youth culture in recent years: Patrick Mignon, Pierre Mayol and Antoine
Hennion, the first two of whom also collaborated with him on his book *The
Practice of Everyday Life*.[32] All three take up his notion of creative consumption,
though they mostly jettison the post-1968 ideological baggage which
accompanies it. As Mignon points out, one obvious way in which Certeau's
influence is visible in French studies of popular music is simply the willingness
to take pop seriously, to show that it 'means' something.[33] Between Morin's
1963 articles and Certeau's writing in the 1970s, the few who already did so,
apart from fans, were either Marxists in some form (PCF or Leftist) or
sociocultural *animateurs*. But both paid attention to pop for utilitarian reasons.
The music itself was of little intrinsic interest to them, but there was a chance
that the sense of revolt it expressed, and young people's energetic investment
in it, might be harnessed to social change. Certeau was the only major theorist
in the 1970s to encourage the exploration of such popular-cultural practices
for their own sake. Under his influence, Mignon, for example, set to work
studying pop as a participant observer, going to see how rock was made and
used in towns and cities across France like Le Havre and Givors; the kind of

amateur or semi-pro rock which was never heard on radio or read about in magazines like *Actuel*.

Much of Mignon's work is concerned with socio-historiography and hinges on his understanding of pop as, in part, the result of an ongoing process of collective creation by a variety of agents (individuals, groups, institutions) who make up one of Becker's 'art worlds'; and, in part, a discursive category. Like Cogneau, Mignon challenges Yonnet's identification of a 'people of rock'.[34] Rather, rock is like an onion which, when all its layers are peeled away, has no musical or cultural centre. The meaning of rock is ultimately in the eye of its users; it is socially produced. There is no stable aesthetic definition of it, only a dynamic social construction which is the result of a working 'compromise', as he calls it, between the various definitions of all those involved in it, the artists, consumers, amateurs, critics, record companies and institutions. Each of these brings to it different expectations, practices or skills which make them construct rock in different ways; hence its heterogeneity. Yet in the cooperation and interaction which comes about between them (to make a record or start a band, for example), each is none the less aware of and accepts, in a kind of social contract, a continuously renegotiated sense of what *le rock* means. Rock history, then, is the history not of a form but of 'the way in which a multitude of social agents have invested the field of popular music and created something which has then been called "rock'n'roll"'. Pop culture can in fact be thought of as an 'imagined community' (Benedict Anderson).[35] It only truly came into being, Mignon suggests, once it was conceptualised and codified, which first happened in the mid-1960s when a 'theory of rock' began to develop in specialist American writing. From then on, its claim to authenticity was established and theorised until the mid-1980s, when competing authenticities appeared in the form of punk, rap, world music and techno. Having thus fragmented, it has ceased to be the bearer of universal values.[36]

One further preoccupation in Mignon's thinking is the importance of *national* rock forms, which for him preserve an authenticity of a kind by acting as the experimental wing of the global pop market, the local scene learning the international codes of rock but resisting the 'American steamroller' by reappropriating them.[37] In France, he argues, despite the dominance of the indigenous *chanson* tradition, French-language rock remains crucial. But this does not seem to me to be a concern on Mignon's part with *national* authenticity as it was understood in the previous chapter. For him, the preservation of the French language in rock, rap and reggae is important not as a means of national identification but as a 'local' form of cultural exchange for a specific social group, the young.[38]

However, Mignon describes himself as close to Certeau in that he also does not idealise pop, as he accuses other social observers of doing: Yonnet, clearly, and also Gilles Lipovetsky, whose book on post-modern culture, *L'Ere du vide*

(The Era of the Void), made a mark in the early 1980s.[39] Although Lipovetsky only mentions pop in passing, he argues that 1980s consumer culture offers a new form of democracy and liberation, empowering individuals to person-alise and customise their cultural lives rather than having culture imposed upon them. But in Mignon's view, both Yonnet and Lipovetsky owe such one-sided interpretations to a simplistically Tocquevillian conception of democracy, while he, like Certeau, takes up a position between this hyper-optimism and Bourdieu's pessimism, reading popular culture as essentially contradictory, as attempting but failing to lead an aesthetic existence entirely independent of consumption: 'The dynamic of rock is the tension between two principles: the principles of pop (to please, to sell), the principles of the society of mass production generally; and the Romantic ideal of a different way of producing music, as an artist, and of consuming it, as a community.'[40]

Pierre Mayol has a similarly mixed view of pop, which also owes much to Certeau. In his book *Les Enfants de la liberté* (The Children of Freedom), he criticises a tendency he detects in French post-war fiction and sociology to depict French youth negatively, when to his mind the picture is more complex. Young people are morally and culturally autonomous earlier than they were in previous generations, yet economically and educationally dependent for longer. This generates frustration but also what Certeau called 'inventivity'. This inventivity is most apparent, in Mayol's opinion, in the young's cultural practices, where, despite an indisputable conformity, they often surprise us with 'their lucidity, liberty, courage and creativity'.[41] Mayol devotes considerable space to how pop (specifically, rock and rap) is used and reappropriated, drawing his evidence from amateur, suburban, hard-rock concerts, which is where, for him, the 'essence' of the music is located. That essence is its quasi-religious nature. At the furthest remove from the solemnity of a classical recital, the rock concert seizes its audience with its first deafening notes and holds them in thrall until the end. This does not make it any less an aesthetic experience. It is simply that the rock aesthetic is of a singular kind, located not so much in the music itself as in its relationship with the collective fervour of the crowd. In live rock, there is no critical distance or knowing anticipation of delights to come, as there is in a symphony or an opera. Rock takes the audience unawares and ravishes it until it experiences 'the loss of self' and 'the subjective void, wherein lies the ordeal of initiation which rock demands'. '*The listener becomes sound and rhythm* and, in the process, turns into the actor of his [sic] own listening, listens as an act.'[42]

Nevertheless, as Certeau came close to saying in the early 1970s when he spoke of an '"exile" which unites', this subjective experience requires the presence of others. Mayol defines three major characteristics which account for this. The first is the intensity just described. The second is its festive apartness, like the *fête* of old or Bakhtin's 'carnival'. It is a special occasion, a collective ceremonial of belonging signified by ritualised attire and ornament-ation (badges, body-piercing, and so on). The third element is transgression, again as in the carnivalesque analysed by Bakhtin. Established musical and cultural codes are wilfully infringed through style, volume and dance, though all of these are similarly codified in their way. Ultimately, in Mayol's reading, the concert becomes a kind of liturgy of pleasure ('*jouissance*'), Certeau's 'collective ecstasy', and a form of 'communion' in the etymological sense of being united with others, 'in order to experience the same intensity in a collective fusion [*rassemblement fusionnel*]'.[43]

Mayol's evident fascination with the communal abandonment of self is common in French readings of pop music. In a seminar which he led in 1994, it was developed by another participant: 'In our societies, where individualism is growing and timidity with it, where there are no longer any social codes which allow us to get in touch with others or harmonise naturally with them, rock welds individuals together again and creates an undeniable well-being, a feeling of communion.'[44] The sociologist Olivier Cathus has analysed the 'federating' importance of noise in pop music, breaking down concert noise into that which the audience demands from the artist and that which the artist invites the audience to return, by screaming, chanting, and so on. These two noises fuse, 'and it is this confusion which founds a people's "art of living"': collective participation and communion'.[45] Such readings are not necessarily condemnatory. On the contrary, one may sense in them that writers like Mayol are irresistibly drawn to them, as if attracted by a hope that young people might be rediscovering a collective mysticism which could bring France back from secular rationalism into a life more spiritual.

Even so, Mayol's fascination is not unconditional, as is clear in his account of rap. In one sense, rap and hip-hop are a good example of Certeau's creative consumption. First, they are festive like rock, with a stress on participation and dance, and rap concerts have similarly ritualised, quasi-religious connotations. In the concept of hip-hop as a movement ('*le mouv*'), no clear line is drawn between performers and their followers, who together form a 'network' (the posse, crew or tribe). Second, hip-hop is an urban culture par excellence. In the city or suburb, the networks assemble and roam, dance, rap or tag. Like walking in the city for Certeau, these are subversive acts, ways of customising and reappropriating an urban space not meant for them. Yet this is not Mayol's last word. Both rock and rap, he argues, while undoubtedly contributing to 'the flowering of freedom' for the young, are also fashion-led and conformist, for example hip-hop's strict dress code. Worse still to Mayol's mind, rap is too often 'dominated by mediocre texts larded with clichés, its musicality and rhythmics are approximate, its belief in spontaneity attractive but lazy'; and graffiti and tagging have become equally formulaic.[46] What rap often lacks is 'the labour which makes the work and the accompanying sense of respons-ibilities'. What concerns him is the possibility that such conformity will trap some young people in a 'symbolic and aesthetic poverty such that it increases their difficulties without giving them the means of overcoming them', particularly the disadvantaged, since for them hip-hop may be the only choice available.[47] The implication is that rap, like other aspects of youth culture, can easily become a form of particularism and closure. Here, Certeau's 'culture in the plural', a phrase Mayol invokes in opposition to such closure, takes on the meaning of a need for such particularist cultures to reach out beyond their own boundaries and open up to other cultures. Mayol thus ends up with a discreet call for a return to conventional universalism.

Antoine Hennion arrives at a somewhat less guarded position than Mayol by investigating music reception in its entirety. Hennion has been involved in the sociology of music since the late 1970s. His central preoccupation is what he calls the sociology of mediation. In particular, he is interested in the ways in which sound technologies like the record and CD have transformed our relation to music, a process he refers to as 'discomorphosis'. While investigating this theme, he has gradually shifted his focus from production to consumption. In 1981, he was among the first in France to pay serious sociological attention to the French music industy, in his study entitled *Les Professionnels du disque* (Record Professionals, 1981), based on two years of field research in the record business. Even here, it is already clear that he is fascinated not only by the professionals he is observing but by what makes a pop record successful with the public, an enigma which, he claims, cannot be understood by those who do not share a passion for mass culture.[48] Later, in the equally pioneering volume which he edited with Patrick Mignon, *Le Rock: de l'histoire au mythe* (From History to Myth, 1991), he examines the differences between a rock concert and an opera performance. If Mayol interprets the concert as the essential rock experience because of the direct interactivity between audience and artists, Hennion chellenges this apparent directness, arguing that 'inter-mediaries' like the record and the radio in fact mediate and construct this relationship.[49] His most recent research is on the place of such mediation in reception and amateur practice. It is this work which I am concerned with here, as it points to a critical interrogation of the conclusions reached by Bourdieu, Hennion arguing against too crude an application of *Distinction*'s sociology of taste.

Rejecting the familiar polarisation between the alleged *passivity* induced by recording technologies and the *activity* involved in playing an instrument or singing, Hennion focuses instead on the 'intermediaries' at work in our relationship to music (the record, the score, the instrument, the fan club). His

originality lies in his placing *all* the various forms of practice these intermediaries imply, including listening to records or live music, on an equally *active*
footing. The French language takes the first step for him, since the word *amateur*
means both those who sing or play without payment and those who are music
'lovers', a term usually connoting listeners with a degree of informed competence. Hennion argues that representations of the amateur need to change to
take account of how she or he listens. Listening is an active practice just as
playing and singing are, and he is interested in how these three modes of
practice articulate. The amateur, he concludes, cannot be reduced to the cliché
of either the second-rate imitator (the embarrassing uncle who murders the
tuba at family parties) or the couch potato absorbing whatever the global
market imposes. In fact, there are no passive amateurs, he insists, only 'music
users', who creatively mix and match the various types of access to music they
individually have – listening to records, membership of a band or fan club,
concert-going – to make their own individuated space. Hennion endows the
amateur with a variable, post-modern degree of creative freedom, without
which the professional music world would have no purpose.[50]

In a paper delivered in Nashville in 1999, Hennion takes this argument
further by focusing more precisely on the kind of 'activity' involved in listening
to a concert, a CD or the radio. This requires a history of listening. As we saw,
for Donnat and Cogneau, listening technologies have transformed access to
all musics. Hennion's argument is that they have also transformed – and in a
sense *created* – the act of listening, which did not come about naturally but had
to be learnt. Originally, music's function was ritualistic or religious; and the
history of listening is primarily that of music's detachment from this function
to become a commodity of leisure and pleasure. As recently as the nineteenth
century, concert-goers listened quite differently from today. Since a piece of
music might only be performed two or three times in an average lifetime,
virtually all audiences were new to the piece. Today, however, with technologies
which capture such performances and an economy which makes them freely
available, Western audiences have access to music's entire history, and the
audience at any given concert is likely to be hearing a piece it already knows.
Listening today, then, is rarely innocent but is mediated by this familiarity; it
is an acquired skill. We listen by comparing and contrasting different renditions
(two different recordings of a piece, or live and recorded versions).

To test this hypothesis, Hennion has carried out empirical research into how
people listen. It is here that we can see more clearly what distinguishes his
analysis from Bourdieu's in *Distinction*. Whereas Bourdieu pays no attention
to the affective experience of cultural practices, only to their social value,
Hennion takes such experience seriously, and as realities not strategies, though
he still treats them as socialised rather than purely private. Like Mayol, he sees

the live concert (popular or classical) as having a special, almost mythical status because of the moments of intensified experience it affords, and which are its raison d'être. Also like Mayol, he sees the essence of the concert experience as the 'altered state': being transported by 'passion'.[51] But he analyses this experience more closely than Mayol does, in both social and psychological terms. The passionate state cannot be achieved without the familiar feeling, just before the concert begins, of resistance, of intellectual detachment from the performers and other audience members, of reluctance to let oneself enter into the collective spirit and be sublimely transported. Indeed, it is because of this preliminary detachment that the listener *needs* to be transported; and it therefore serves as the index of the success or failure of the occasion.

Hennion's lyrical evocation of these rare moments is a long way from Bourdieu's curmudgeonly dissection of social jockeying, and indeed, at times, from sociological discourse generally, to the extent that he can seem to be describing his own concert-going experience. At any event, snobbery, he insists, has no place in the thesis he is outlining, which applies as much to a 'good gig' as a classical music concert. But the essential feature of his argument is that this rapturous moment of listening – the kind of direct, immediate experience which Mayol describes – is not in fact a given but a social process. 'Immediacy is the paradoxical result of a lengthy sequence of mediations', of preparation, effort and action on the listener's part. A concert therefore is a performance by everyone involved, both artists and audience, and this is its paradox. It is an 'active process of putting ourselves in the right mood so that something can happen, [a] meticulous activity whose aim is to achieve complete passivity: a state in which we can be carried away, be taken up by something. [. . .] Music enables us to formulate a theory of passion.'[52]

There is one last instance of sociological inquiry that I want to touch on very briefly. Taken together, Mayol's and Hennion's interest in the intensity of the concert experience bears some resemblance to the thought of another sociologist, who has acquired notoriety in recent years: Michel Maffesoli. He too adopts a non-Bourdieusian perspective akin to Certeau's thinking and welcomes cultural change. Like Lipovetsky, he sees contemporary culture as characterised by a shift from the dour and oppressive rationalism of modernity to a post-modern 're-enchantment' of the world through passion, ambivalence and spontaneity, from the cognitive to the affective. Yet in contrast to Lipovetsky, he sees one of the characteristics of the post-modern age as not the rise but the decline of individualism, evidenced in 'l'être-ensemble' (the being-together), a dynamic relationship between the self and the other which is central to what he describes as a new tribalism: 'that proliferation of sects, cults, networks, sporting and musical communities [. . .] which has become such a prominent feature of the contemporary "mégapole"'.[53] For Maffesoli, contemporary techno music and the raves associated with it are a case in point. Techno 'reactivates – in the strong sense of the term – the festive aspect, that desire to lose oneself in the other, even to fuse with the other'. And in the intensity of this creative fusion, he detects 'all the characteristics of authenticity'.[54]

Indeed, all of the instances of affectivity, festivity and intensity examined in this chapter seem to add up to a definition of authenticity as the opposite of alienation, as a wholeness restored. For Morin, the thrill of listening to *yéyé* comes from a shared Dionysian celebration of youthfulness, and a rediscovery of the ludic and the elemental which is its deepest meaning. For Hennion, listening is not passive but active and creative. And for Maffesoli, the new tribalism at work in techno is a reactivation of the affective and the collective. As Max Silverman puts it: 'proximity and empathy, fusion and confusion are the order of the day, not distance, distinction and the patrolling of boundaries'.[55] New tribalism thus transcends the calculating games of social positioning identified by Bourdieu, becoming a new form of warmth and solidarity, of 'social connections' (Maffesoli).

What we have seen throughout Part I are four basic positions on the question of the authenticity of popular music, which I shall summarise as two conceptually linked pairs rather than in chapter order. On the one side, there is the assumption that authenticity is national (Chapters 1 and 4), in so far as a popular music must somehow draw on and express a conception of Frenchness, a cultural and linguistic heritage which gives French audiences a frisson of recognition and a sense of who they are as a people. Hence the perception of pop as alien and intrusive. Second, for the 'pessimists', from Adorno to Bourdieu (Chapter 5), popular tastes like pop are essentially inauthentic if they do not emerge 'naturally' or 'organically' from within a community but are manufactured from without or are the dominated products of class distinction. Hence the perception of pop as barbaric. These first two definitions are related to the extent that both hinge on the idea of pop as imposed, like a colonial ruler. On the other side, there is the more recent conception that music production can make itself authentic by taking the form of a 'transcultural' melting pot (Chapter 3) in which global pop is one ingredient and the diverse ethnicities and tastes of the national community are another. A new synthesis and new creative spaces are thereby formed, as Yonnet propounds. And last, there are the 'optimists' close to Certeau (Chapter 5), for whom authenticity is not about production but about music reception, about personal or collective response. And these last two definitions are also related to the extent that, in both production and reception, a new creativity and a new intensity are identified.

What also links all the social theories dealt with in this chapter, to a lesser or greater extent, is a tendency to 'denationalise' authenticity by fragmenting, pluralising or personalising it in some way. Curiously enough, this process was more or less contemporaneous with its renationalisation by the new Socialist government in 1981, which recognised pop as an authentically French rather than imported music. This was the work of a new Minister of Culture, Jack Lang, his advisers and his successors, all of whom worked in a Culture department whose creation in 1959 had coincided exactly with the coming of pop, and which had since become the most important agency of cultural legitimation in France. What I want to explore in Part II, therefore, is how the Ministry has constructed and acted on pop and what this has meant. Doubtless, the professional, intellectual and academic discourses sketched in Part I have influenced the Ministry to a degree. But both policies for popular music and the mixed reactions they have provoked have also produced discourses of their own: on music generally, on popular music specifically, and on the whole conception of authenticity.

Notes

1. Morin, 'Salut les copains', 7–8 July 1963, p. 12.
2. Ibid., p. 12.
3. The first edition appeared under the name Henry Skoff Torgue and the title *La Pop-Music*. Several updated editions have appeared since. The most recent, which I use here, is listed as Henry Torgue, *La Pop-Music et les musiques rock* (Que Sais-Je?/Presses Universitaires de France, 1997).
4. Ibid., pp. 102–6 (quotation p. 105).
5. Yonnet, *Jeux, modes et masses*, p. 181.
6. Ibid., pp. 161–9 (quotation pp. 165–6).
7. Pierre Bourdieu and Alain Darbel, *The Love of Art: European Museums and Their Public* (Stanford University Press, 1990); Bourdieu, *Distinction: A Social Critique of the Judgment of Taste* (Routledge and Kegan Paul, 1984), p. xi. I shall not discuss this work in any detail here, or look at the evolution of Bourdieu's thought, since it is from his writings on culture of the 1960s and 1970s that the 'classic' Bourdieu position comes. My chief purpose, with both Bourdieu and Certeau, is to use their work as a yardstick for examining other positions, adopted in sociological writings which address popular music directly and in more detail.
8. Bourdieu, *Distinction*, quotations pp. 18 and 60, respectively.
9. Ibid. All statistics and analysis are from pp. 14–18, 60–1 and 533 (short quotations p. 16).

10. Ibid., p. 60.'Operetta and bel canto' presumably refer to the likes of Luis Mariano or Tino Rossi.
11. Ibid., p. 60 (including quotation). Bourdieu does not appear to provide the complete statistics from his survey, so it is not always possible to see how he derives his analytical comments from them.
12. Ibid., p. 16. For a fuller treatment of this question, see Rigby's chapter on Bourdieu in *Popular Culture in Modern France*, Chapter 4, particularly pp. 112–13.
13. Rigby, *Popular Culture in Modern France*, p. 123.
14. Personal interview with Olivier Donnat, 20 July 2000. Denis Cogneau also writes of their findings in 1988–9 that 'many of the hypotheses expounded by Pierre Bourdieu in his book *Distinction* turn out to be confirmed', Donnat and Cogneau (Ministry of Culture), *Les Pratiques culturelles des Français 1973–1989* (La Découverte/Documentation Française, 1990), p. 285, note 44. To help the reader keep track of all the volumes with similar titles that I am using here, I shall in future refer to this volume as 'Donnat and Cogneau, *1973–1989*'.
15. Donnat and Cogneau, *Nouvelle Enquête sur les pratiques culturelles des Français* (statistical volume) (Documentation Française, 1990), p. 8. I shall refer to this volume as 'statistical volume, 1990'.
16. 1973 figure (9 per cent): Donnat and Cogneau, *1973–1989*, p. 59; 1997 figure (27 per cent): Donnat, *Les Pratiques culturelles des Français: enquête 1997* (Documentation Française, 1998), p. 110. I shall refer to this volume as 'Donnat, *enquête 1997*'.
17. Donnat and Cogneau, *1973–1989*, p. 63, and Donnat, *enquête 1997*, p. 110.
18. From 16 per cent to 23 per cent: see table, Donnat and Cogneau, *1973–1989*, pp. 63 and 67.
19. Donnat, *enquête 1997*, p. 248.
20. Ibid., pp. 104 and 157.
21. Compare Donnat and Cogneau, *1973–1989*, p. 66, with Donnat, *enquête 1997*, p. 160.
22. Statistical volume, 1990, p. 109; Donnat, *enquête 1997*, p. 165. For the exact wording used in the two questionnaires, see pp. 217 and 335, respectively.
23. Donnat, *enquête 1997*, p. 165.
24. Statistical volume, 1990, p. 109; Donnat, *enquête 1997*, p. 165. Again, accurate comparison is not possible because of the different categories used in the respective surveys.
25. Donnat and Cogneau, *1973–1989*, pp. 272–6.
26. Cogneau, 'Le Rock existe: les sociologues l'ont rencontré. A'queu c'en est [*sic*]!', three articles: *Yaourt*, no. 5 (July–August 1990); no. 6 (October–

November 1990), pp. 34–5; no. 7 (December 1990), pp. 32–4 (quotation, no. 6, p. 34).

27. Personal interview with Donnat, 20 July 2000.
28. Ibid.
29. Michel de Certeau, *La Culture au pluriel* (Seuil, 1993; first published 1974), p. 214.
30. Ibid., pp. 214–15 (quotation p. 214).
31. One would naturally call this an investigation of *reception*, were it not for Certeau's insistence that this term assumes that the consumer is passive, not creative.
32. Original French version. Certeau, *L'Invention du quotidien*, 2 vols. I. *Arts de faire* (Gallimard/Folio, 1990); II: co-authored by Certeau, Luce Giard and Pierre Mayol, *Habiter, cuisiner* (Gallimard/Folio, 1994).
33. Personal interview with Patrick Mignon, 20 July 2000.
34. Mignon, 'Rock et rockers: un peuple du rock?', in Alain Darré (ed.), *Musique et politique: les répertoires de l'identité* (Presses Universitaires de Rennes, 1996), pp. 73–91.
35. Ibid., pp. 77–9 (quotation p. 77).
36. Mignon, 'Existe-t-il une "culture rock"?', *Esprit*, July 1993, pp. 140–2.
37. Ibid., pp. 146–7.
38. Mignon, 'Y a-t-il une culture jeunes?', *Projet*, no. 251 (Autumn 1997), pp. 67–8.
39. Personal interview with Mignon, 20 July 2000.
40. Mignon, 'Existe-t-il une "culture rock"?', p. 150.
41. Mayol, *Les Enfants de la liberté: études sur l'autonomie sociale et culturelle des jeunes en France 1970–1996* (L'Harmattan, 1997), p. 21.
42. Mayol's italics, ibid., p. 201.
43. Ibid., pp. 203–4. On carnival, see Mikhail Bakhtin, *Rabelais and His World* (Indiana University Press, 1984).
44. Matthieu Calame, in Pierre Mayol, *La Planète Rock: histoire d'une musique métisse, entre contestation et consommation* (Fondation pour le Progrès de l'Homme, 1994), p. 18.
45. Olivier Cathus, 'Les Flonflons d'la balle', *Cultures en mouvement*, no. 21 (October 1999), p. 28.
46. Mayol, *Les Enfants*, pp. 212–13 (quotation p. 213).
47. Ibid., pp. 213–14 (quotations p. 214).
48. Hennion, *Les Professionnels du disque: une sociologie des variétés* (Métailié, 1981), p. 13. See also his *La Passion musicale: une sociologie de la médiation* (Métailié, 1993).
49. 'Scène rock, concert classique', in Mignon and Hennion (eds), *Rock: de l'histoire au mythe*, pp. 101–19.

50. Hennion, 'L'Amour de la musique aujourd'hui. Une recherche en cours sur les figures de l'amateur', in Darré (ed.), *Musique et politique*, pp. 41–50.

51. Hennion, 'Music Lovers:Taste as Performance', read as a paper at Social Theory, Politics and the Arts conference, Nashville, USA, October 1999, subsequently published under the same title in *Theory, Culture and Society*, vol. 18, no. 5 (2001), p. 14.

52. Ibid., pp. 14 and 13, respectively.

53. I draw here on Max Silverman, 'The New Democracy: Michel Maffesoli and The Analysis of Everyday Life', in John Marks and Enda McCaffrey (eds), *French Cultural Debates* (Monash Romance Studies/University of Delaware Press, 2001), pp. 121–33 (quotation p. 123).

54. 'Entretien avec Michel Maffesoli', in Michel Gaillot, *Sens multiple: la techno: un laboratoire artistique et politique du present* (Dis voir, 1998), pp. 101 and 103, respectively.

55. Silverman, 'The New Democracy', p. 123.

PART II

Politicising Authenticity

Every musical matter is a matter of state

(Maurice Fleuret)

– 6 –

Music and Politics before 1981

May and June 1981 saw a step-change in French political life, when François Mitterrand and the Socialist Party (PS) came to power in the first victory of the Left in the twenty-three years of the Fifth Republic. One impact of this was that the 1980s became the seminal decade of government intervention in popular music. The factors too easily advanced to explain this, as would later be the case when the first Blair government underwent a similar conversion in the UK, were electoralism and careerism. For the new President, so the story went, the young had become an important source of votes after the age of majority had been lowered to eighteen in 1974 and they had helped him win the presidency. For Jack Lang, the new Minister of Culture, who was to occupy the post for ten years (1981–6, 1988–93), popular music offered an important symbol of modernity and an arena in which to attract media attention.

No doubt there is a measure of truth in both explanations but neither is sufficient. Beyond the self-interested motives of individuals or parties, state recognition of pop was virtually inevitable by 1981. Even the rather conservative Jean-Philippe Lecat, Lang's predecessor under President Valéry Giscard d'Estaing, had lately turned his mind to it, albeit ineffectually. Equally incomplete is the standard historiography which depicts central government as the driver of the policy. As Philippe Teillet notes, the genealogy of pop policy was in reality polycentric, involving the Ministry and various local and regional agencies.[1] In this chapter, I shall explore that genealogy further. In the following two, I shall examine the new policy in some detail, because it is an exemplary story in terms of both cultural principles and political practice. In the final two chapters, I shall analyse some of the debates it gave rise to.[2]

Before 1959

During the Third and Fourth Republics, responsibility for the arts fell to an insignificant Beaux-Arts unit within the monolithic Education Ministry, but in reality there was no cultural 'policy' to speak of for most of that time. The unit had responsibility for ensuring that the arts, letters and heritage were a public service, but its remit was mostly limited to overseeing training in specialist establishments and preserving the heritage, while the Education Department itself had responsibility for a rudimentary art and music provision in state schools, which in some parts of the country was virtually non-existent. Though progress has been made since then, the shortcomings of this provision remain an issue in the French education system. Beyond this, the liberal ideology characteristic of the Third Republic meant abandoning contemporary artistic creation to private sponsorship and the market. Consequently, popular music, the record industry and the associated media were largely unregulated other than in the form of censorship, public order and copyright legislation. Nor was there any pro-active government concern before 1936 with what would later become known as cultural democracy. A movement was nevertheless stirring on the Left which would eventually alter this state of affairs, based upon a distinctive conception of popular culture.

In nineteenth-century France, the rising middle class set the nation's cultural agenda by writing the books, newspapers, history and curricula of the time. From these, the segregated proletariat was mostly absent.[3] Government attempts to combat this neglect began with the setting up of free, compulsory primary education in 1882 and the first flowerings of Socialism towards the end of the century. But for decades, primary schooling remained rudimentary and uninspiring, while secondary education was not yet either free or compulsory. Hence the emergence of a popular-culture movement, which reached its peak between 1945 and 1968. Up to a point, popular culture meant proletarian culture, particularly after the French Communist Party was formed in the 1920s. But the movement's chief concern was broadening workers' access to middle-class culture in various ways, particularly after the Liberation of 1944.

One of these ways was 'popular education': evening classes, amateur dramatics, sports and various other kinds of community action for leisure, which would later become known as 'sociocultural animation'. Another was democratising access to the arts specifically; and a third was recognising youth as a coherent area of institutional concern, involving a disparate collection of ex-Resistance, left-wing or Catholic thinkers, government inspectors and cultural organisations such as Joffre Dumazedier's Peuple et Culture.[4] These three interpretations of popular culture were connected by an ecstatic ideology of humanism, voluntarism and universalism, founded on the belief that a full cultural life was a human right. What they especially shared was an anxiety about the potentially reductive impact of the mass media, on the young particularly. In France as elsewhere, intellectual disapproval of mass culture intensified after the Liberation, as new means of communication – transistor radios, vinyl records, television – appeared to be implacably standardising leisure, and Europe became haunted by Americanisation. This disapproval was close to Adorno's insistence that the 'culture industry' led to uniformity and passivity, purveying the vulgar and alien forms of commercial entertainment associated with Hollywood and Tin Pan Alley, which were now being imposed on the defenceless French by the economic muscle of a superpower.

Although the popular-culture movement was particularly identified with theatre, song too was an important element, the two milieux having close ties. The 1930s singing duo Gilles and Julien had trained with the famed theatre director and theorist Jacques Copeau. Workers' agit-prop groups, like Jacques Prévert's Groupe Octobre, included song in their performances in the manner of Brecht. Then, during the Popular Front of 1936–7 and the Vichy regime under Nazi occupation (1940–4), those involved in popular education, together with Catholic or secular youth movements like the Scouts, the Youth Hostel Association and Jeune France (Young France), advocated both amateur dramatics and community singing, preferably outdoors round a campfire. Not unlike the incipient American folk movement at roughly the same time, this world of hearty singsongs and drama productions provided a seedbed for the post-war Left-Bank *chanson*. Les Frères Jacques are a case in point. These four male *chansonniers* used costumes and props to dramatise their mostly comic songs. The group's founder, André Bellec, had taught drama to young people and now worked with the Communist-dominated Travail et Culture (Work and Culture) organisation. Phenomenally successful, Les Frères Jacques also became the house act at La Rose rouge, a Left-Bank cabaret in the rue de la Harpe, then the rue de Rennes.[5] In Belgium, Jacques Brel came from a similarly invigorating background – scouting, Catholic youth club and amateur dramatics – prompting the mischievous Brassens to nickname him Father Brel.

Such youth activity during and after the Occupation also produced a surprisingly large audience for Left-Bank *chanson*, which set itself up as the antithesis of showbiz capitalism through its bohemian topography (Saint-Germain-des-Prés, cabarets, cellars), its spare, craft aesthetic (untrained singing voice, acoustic guitar or piano) and its often self-penned songs of a demanding, poetic or satirical nature.[6] This audience was a cosmopolitan mix of students, fans of American jazz and dance music, poets, painters, intellectuals and other singers. As we saw in Part I, it was from this milieu – La Rose rouge and other legendary clubs like L'Écluse, L'Échelle de Jacob, and one or two on the Right Bank with Left-Bank credentials like Milord L'Arsouille – that the post-war singer-songwriter paradigm emerged. Here too, a democratising ambition, though not an anti-American one in this instance, was often at work in attempts to raise standards in popular song, not usually musically but by using a simple melody as a vehicle for popular poetry, with lyrics which spoke of love, politics, society and morality in more complex ways and more carefully wrought French.[7] Some performers, particularly Ferré, Brassens and later Ferrat, went further by putting established French poets to music, while contemporary poets, notably Prévert and Queneau, worked with composers like Joseph Kosma to produce songs.

At government level, the popular-culture movement had little tangible impact until the 1960s, other than during two exceptional periods: the brief Popular Front interlude and the Liberation. The Front had big plans to democratise leisure, setting up France's first dedicated government department for the purpose under Léo Lagrange. In the same spirit, the Liberation in 1944 saw the beginning of the national network of culture and leisure facilities for young people called the MJCs; the creation of a directorate in the Education Department for youth and popular education, which eventually became the Ministry for Youth and Sport; and the first five decentralised national drama companies, the Avignon Festival in 1947 and the TNP (National People's Theatre) in 1951, both directed by Jean Vilar. Simultaneously, a battle over cinema was underway. Liberated France badly needed American economic aid, and one of its conditions was the lifting of trade barriers. Liberation therefore brought a flood of Hollywood movies. The Blum–Byrnes agreement of 1946 attempted to regulate this influx by introducing a 'screen quota', but this was widely seen as an abdication. In the same year, however, a public body was set up, the CNC, to protect and promote the domestic film industry more effectively, and a bill to provide subsidy to the French film industry was voted through two years later. These two state initiatives, for theatre and cinema, proved historic, helping establish the principle of state voluntarism in defence of an authentic national culture, which in 1959 would lead to the creation of a full Ministry of Cultural Affairs at the start of de Gaulle's new Fifth Republic, housed in the Palais Royal on the rue de Valois.

Government action for music, however, was slower coming. State intervention in music had existed since the time of Louis XIV but was mainly limited to a handful of flagship Parisian institutions such as the Opéra de Paris, founded in 1672 by royal patent and nationalised in 1939, and the National Conservatoire of Music created in 1795 (later the Higher National Conservatoire).[8] Composition was ungenerously assisted by state commissions, or by the state broadcasting body, the RTF (later the ORTF). Small government subsidies also went to Parisian symphony orchestras, though, before the 1930s, financing such organisations had mainly fallen to private sponsorship, or again the RTF, which set up its own National Orchestra of France in 1934. Outside the capital, music provision was mainly the job of the city councils, the larger conurbations like Bordeaux, Lyons, Marseilles or Toulouse having their own conservatoires, music schools, orchestras and opera houses. Musical life also flourished in the regions thanks to numerous associations for symphonic music, wind or brass bands, and choirs.

By the 1950s, however, while live music was thriving in comparable Western countries, in France it was in decline. Private sponsorship had dwindled after the crash of 1929; and as competition from records, radio and television grew, demand for live music had shrunk. The quality of Parisian opera and symphonic performance was widely considered inferior to that of other great capitals, and in both Paris and the provinces, such work was struggling to attract audiences. New compositions could not always reach the concert platform and rarely did so more than once. Not surprisingly given the high unemployment rate and the pay disparities between Paris and elsewhere, the number of professional musicians fell between 1946 and 1962 by 27 per cent and continued falling subsequently. Relatively few composers could make a living from composition. At amateur level, the enthusiasm for choirs, brass and wind bands was also on the wane. Clearly, it was time for a co-ordinated, wide-ranging and nation-wide music policy

The ideological seeds of such a change had already been sown in the first decades of the twentieth century. After their defeat in the Dreyfus Affair, the anti-republican nationalist leagues of the extreme Right looked to culture as a way of pursuing their defence of 'essential French values'.[9] At stake here is a directly *political* conception of authenticity, rather than the cultural and sociological conceptions examined in Part I. The national becomes a criterion of aesthetic judgement, in the sense of what Jane Fulcher describes as 'a return to tradition and an elevation of classicism as the French "national style"'.[10]

The far Right saw literature as the chief manifestation of this authenticity, 'expressive of "the ideal form and fundamental nature of the national community and the people"'.[11] However, their determination to conduct their political struggle on the symbolic front prompted them to politicise all the arts, especially music, since, as Fulcher writes, it 'was valuable as a symbol, for these nationalist leagues were well aware of all it could evoke when framed by a discourse that imbued it with ideological meaning: it could engage the realm of what Freud refers to as "primary process thought", or what is associated with "projection, fantasy, and the incorporation of disparate ideas"'.[12] Such symbolic benefits were hard to refuse, and both republicans and the Socialist Party of 1905 soon followed the nationalists' example, turning music in the early decades of the twentieth century into an ideological battleground. This is exemplified in the founding of the 'Fêtes du peuple' (People's Festivals) in 1914. Associated with syndicalism, the Fêtes were the brainchild of a young composer, Albert Doyen, who had written what he called a *fête* entitled *Le Triomphe de la liberté*, a monumental score based on part of Romain Rolland's play about the French Revolution, *Le Quatorze Juillet,* and influenced by Rolland's conception of popular theatre. It was conceived for open-air performance with the participation of professionals, amateurs and the crowd, drawing on Wagner, legend, the mystery play and the *fêtes* of the Revolutionary period. Its principal actor, Fulcher points out, was the 'people'.[13] Doyen's and Rolland's idea of the festive thus became integral to the cultural ideology of the Left and, more specifically, to the Popular Front's strategy for culture and leisure, which was to lay the foundations for France's cultural policy from 1959. The setting up of the Ministry of Cultural Affairs was to be a watershed in the relationship between music and the state, eventually.

From 1959 to 1981

Now that music had ceased to be one of France's foremost cultural assets, it looked set to play only a minor role in de Gaulle's project to rebuild the nation, and this was to a large extent the case. The President himself was known to be bored when his duties took him to the opera. On the other hand, his Culture Minister, André Malraux, had a metaphysical belief in high culture and had written of music specifically that it 'alone can speak of death', which in his intense cosmography was a distinct advantage.[14] His main ambition was to democratise high culture by establishing a network of regional arts centres called Houses of Culture (*maisons de la culture*); but most of these had theatre, not music, at their core. Thus, although the Malraux decade (1959–69) is forever associated with democratisation in this sense, during much of it music was the poor relation. Even so, in 1966 a modest but autonomous 'Music Service' (Service de la musique) was set up, which in 1969 became a full ministerial directorate for both music and dance. After some heated rivalry between Pierre Boulez and the more conventional composer Marcel Landowski, stewardship of the new Service was given to the latter. Shortly before he resigned in 1969, Malraux announced the implementation of a ten-year plan for music which Landowski had drawn up. A long-term strategy of this kind was essential if the shortage of regional orchestras, the training of professional musicians and the inadequacy of music tuition in state schools were to be properly addressed. The 'Landowski Plan', implemented by Jacques Duhamel, Minister of Cultural Affairs between 1971 and 1973 while Landowski was still in post, revolutionised music institutions in France and helped stimulate the 1970s boom.[15]

No ministerial support mechanisms were recommended for commercial popular music, though. As Mireille had complained in the 1950s, 'there are conservatoires for everything, except for *chanson* ! [. . .] Where can the young poets, lyricists, musicians and singers meet up? Nowhere.' Having taken her complaint to the then head of state radio, Paul Gilson, she had been able to launch a private training school of her own linked to a weekly radio broadcast, soon to become famous on 1960s television as 'Le Petit Conservatoire de la chanson'. Numerous future stars passed through her hands: Hugues Aufray, Pascal Sevran, Serge Lama, Françoise Hardy, Alain Souchon, Colette Magny, Sapho, and others. Mireille, according to one commentator, 'is the mother of modern *chanson*'.[16] But she was never invited to continue her work in a national conservatoire, carrying on unaided into extreme old age.

Government's main impact on popular music before the 1970s was through taxation and censorship. After the Great War, Ministers realised that the soaring demand for live entertainment offered the chance to recoup some of the public funds lost during the conflict. From 1920, heavy taxes were imposed on box-office receipts: 16 per cent in theatres, 20 per cent in music halls and, when music accompanied a meal, a staggering 50 per cent. One predictable result was the accentuation of the tendency to profitably frivolous entertainment. Similar levies were imposed on gramophones and records.[17] These burdens were to cripple live performance and the record industry for decades. As for censorship, this had particularly targeted the *goguettes* and cabarets. In 1850, a Prefect of Police warned the Ministry of the Interior that 'popular song is haughty and threatening, it makes people get excited, carried away, it is often more violent than the prose of periodicals. Instead of consoling people, it makes them bitter.'[18] Shortly afterwards, in a decree of 29 December 1851, Napoleon III regulated drinking houses and many were closed.[19] Yet political censorship did not end with the coming of a republic in 1870. Vian's song 'Le Déserteur' was outlawed in the 1950s by Guy Mollet's government as a call to desertion during the Algerian War; and Communist fellow-traveller Jean Ferrat's often political songs were also unwelcome on state television at times during the late 1960s and 1970s, even though his Communist sympathies were far from unqualified. Censorship was also brought to bear on songs considered salacious, such as Yvette Guilbert's big hit at Le Divan japonais in the 1890s, 'Les Vierges' (The Virgins), and half of Brassens's output between 1952 and 1964.

Beyond this, the absence of anything resembling aid to popular music seemed perfectly natural given that, as entertainment not art, it was assumed to be alive and well in the private sector. By the 1970s, however, these assumptions were looking anachronistic. First, there was the emergence of Morin's 'age-class' of young people, which could no longer be ignored. Certainly the Gaullist government was voluntarist on this front in one sense, taking up the popular-culture movement's concern with disadvantaged young people. Youth and Sport's budget for building new youth facilities was vastly superior to Culture's, from which it was independent and which was struggling to find the funds to set up the *maisons de la culture*. And yet the attraction of the kinds of activities provided under Youth and Sport's auspices, in the hale and hearty tradition of popular education and the Popular Front, was waning among a new, more sophisticated generation raised on international pop.

Much the same was true of Malraux's attempts to democratise high culture, which by 1968 were also being seriously questioned. The measurement of cultural practices by the Ministry's research unit, the SER, revealed that democratisation in this sense was not working. This eventually brought about an alternative policy strategy for cultural democracy known as cultural development, associated more with local than central policy-making. Cultural-development theory drew heavily on May 1968. Malraux's conception of democratisation had translated the republican ideology of universalism into cultural terms: one culture fits all. But May rejected this in the name of particularism and pluralism. Hence a plethora of demands for the right to difference and cultural self-determination, for recognition of regional, popular and gender identities. This call for pluralism was provided with ammunition by the SER's statistical surveys, which demonstrated both the social immobility of demand for high culture and the dynamism of more popular practices, including pop.

Cultural development was also influenced by the social sciences, in particular Bourdieu, Dumazedier and Certeau. In cultural-development theory, the priority given to culture as professionally created works of art or heritage is removed. Today's French citizens, it is argued, have a deep-seated need for the cultural in their lives, but not exclusively for 'works'. The real need is for autonomy, self-expression and communication; the need to participate in society yet stand back from it so as to make one's own choices. What is required, then, is a policy which makes individuals and communities the agents of their own cultural lives. Especially important is amateur creativity, the chance for everyone, individuals and communities, to express themselves, which is a vital dimension of citizenship.

In 1969, de Gaulle and Malraux resigned, and after a short interim, the Centrist Duhamel took over as Minister of Cultural Affairs under a new Gaullist president, Georges Pompidou. Duhamel implemented the cultural-development strategy as best he could, but it was nipped in the bud by the oil crisis, unemployment, and other seismic changes that came in their wake. When Pompidou died in 1974 and was replaced by Giscard d'Estaing, cultural development was effectively sidelined at central-government level. The Landowski Plan continued to be implemented successfully, allowing the Ministry's Music directorate (the DMD) to produce a triumphant balance-sheet of its achievements in the run-up to the 1981 presidentials, which included the setting up of the prestigious IRCAM under Pierre Boulez, an esoteric institute for experimental music at the Pompidou Centre.[20] Meanwhile, the Ministry had paid scant attention to amateur music or the emergence of non-classical musical forms, hiving these off to a separate association, the CENAM (National Centre for Music Animation) in 1976, subsidised by the Ministries of Culture and Education.

The problem with cultural development was that it did not address a number of the issues which were to dominate the coming decades: unemployment and social exclusion; economic liberalism and the globalisation of trade; gender and multiculturalism. Most important of all, perhaps, it only partially took stock of the soaring cultural industries. As the head of the SER, Augustin Girard, pointed out in a seminal policy essay in 1978, the cultural industries were providing unprecedented access to 'culture' – albeit a very different culture from what Malraux had had in mind – via the market and with little assistance from the state. The purpose of Girard's article was to persuade policy-makers to take note of this paradox for, as the 1970s came to a close, it was becoming evident that government neglect of the cultural industries was both undemocratic and damaging.[21] As we saw in Chapter 5, throughout the 1970s and 1980s surveys drew attention to the exponential growth in listening to recorded music, covering all musical genres and all sectors of the population. They also showed that while the liking for classical and opera records was stagnating between 1973 and 1981, enthusiasm for *chanson*, rock, pop and folk was rising. Nevertheless, the late 1970s saw a serious crisis in the French record industry, due to the fact that this taste for pop increasingly meant the Anglo-American variety, especially with the disco craze. The French share of the total turnover of record companies based in France fell alarmingly from 90 per cent in 1968 to only 55 per cent in 1981. In 1975, the balance between international copyright income and outgoings had been in France's favour; by 1978, it no longer was.[22]

Against this complex background, a provocative article appeared in *Le Monde* in August 1979 by the journalist Henri Chapier, entitled 'Plot against French song'.[23] Chapier rounded upon the French accomplices of the Anglo-American invasion: the 'gang of four' radio stations (the public station France-Inter and the three 'peripheral' commercial stations broadcasting in France from outside its borders: RTL, RMC and Europe 1), whose playlists were dominated by English-language pop at the expense of new *chanson* talent. The commercial stations' well-rehearsed defence was that they were market-driven and that this was what audiences wanted to hear. But Chapier pointed up the sophistry in their reasoning, which conveniently put the cart before the horse. How can anyone be sure what audience tastes are when there is only one dish on the menu? Record sales also demonstrated that French-language music sold considerably better than the stations' output implied. Chapier also attacked the inadequacy of television coverage of French music. He was not alone. A study carried out in 1979–80 on the quality of broadcasting said of one music programme, 'Palmarès des chansons' (Hit-Parade of Songs), that it 'offers little originality and too often conforms to the imperatives of show-business [   ] Certainly, the public is very fond of this kind of show, but is it really the role of a public-service channel to encourage a taste for the facile and contrived in this way?'[24] The breaking up of the public broadcasting body, the ORTF, into seven separate companies in 1974 under Giscard had been meant to improve quality by encouraging competition between the public channels, but in the event it encouraged only uniformity. Both of the main channels, TF 1 (at the time a public channel) and Antenne 2, relied heavily on popular-entertainment programmes alongside cheap American imports, because both, well before the debates on privatisation in the late 1980s, were dependent on advertising revenue and therefore ratings.

Such criticisms of the media were all part of the wider debate about the *chanson* 'crisis' and Anglo-American market domination. In 1975, statistics provided by Phonogram showed that fifteen of the new French singers that year had sold more than 200,000 copies of their first record, as against only one non-French newcomer. Three years later, the ratio had switched alarm-ingly: six French as against thirteen non-French.[25] By 1979, however, the year of Chapier's article, the record industry worldwide was in a fix, after almost thirty years of growth estimated at between 10 and 20 per cent. The oil crisis had hit the industry hard, because the production of vinyl, on which some twenty French pressing firms relied, required thermoplastic resins derived from oil. Furthermore, although the French surveys showed that pop and rock were favoured by both the young and the not so young, record production was not reaping the benefit as much as it should. Consumers facing hard times tended to sacrifice non-essentials like records, turning instead to radio stations and individual home-taping, a practice made easier when some stations started playing whole LPs to improve their listening figures.[26] Other forms of competition, from television, video and organised piracy, had also become a threat. In 1979, there was a 15 per cent drop in record sales in most Western countries.[27] By 1983, when the slump was at its worst, vinyl LP sales across the world (CDs had not yet made an impact) had fallen by around 30 per cent since the *annus mirabilis* of 1978; and by around 38 per cent in France.[28] But the reasons for this crisis were more complex than they appeared. This was demonstrated by a study commissioned by the Ministry from the Bureau for Economic Information and Forecasting (BIPE) and published in 1987.[29]

According to the BIPE, the two most commonly identified causes of the crisis – piracy and private copying, on the one hand, competition from broadcasting, on the other – were not the only factors involved, significant though they were. On home-taping, for example, record companies estimated that, with 120 million blank cassettes in circulation and 30 million more being sold each year, the industry was losing 20 per cent of turnover from private copying. Such estimates are questionable in so far as there is no guarantee that those who tape would otherwise buy, but the problem was real enough. When, for example, a new recording of Berg's opera *Lulu* had the misfortune of being released at the same time as a simulcast of it on Antenne 2 and France-Musique, its sales were 30 per cent lower than projected.[30] However, the situation for popular music was less clear-cut, as the BIPE showed. There was, for example, no hard evidence of a surge in sales of blank cassettes in the late 1970s big enough to make home-taping have such an impact on record sales. Indeed, the markets for both records and tapes were stagnating equally by the early 1980s. As for piracy, this mostly affected the home products of Asia, Africa and the Middle East.[31] The report also queried the dangers posed by broadcasting. Inevitably, the increasing amount of time spent in front of a TV screen was having a deleterious effect on music-listening. So too was the growing supply of FM pop stations and constantly upgraded equipment to listen to them on, which of course made home-taping an even more attractive option. But again, the BIPE qualified these assertions because they underestimated the extent to which the new stations *promoted* record sales, and they took no account of the fact that the crisis in the industry was international, affecting countries like Britain and West Germany which had relatively stable numbers of radio stations during this period.[32]

The BIPE therefore identified several additional factors to explain the slump. First, records had become comparatively cheaper since 1960 and in particular since 1975. In the process, they had become less prized, more banal commodities. Second, in the 1960s, huge numbers of people had acquired record-playing equipment and begun vinyl collections from scratch. As a result, by the mid-1970s, many potential buyers had already built up record libraries and were purchasing less. The population was also ageing, so there were fewer young people to start collecting than in the 1960s. Third, the appearance of compact discs so soon after cassettes, and the promise of more new media to come such as videodiscs, were having a complex effect on sales. Those who could afford to pay virtually double for a CD found that the superior sound quality restored some of the music's magic and set about renewing their collections in the new format. Those who could not found record-buying less exciting than ever, since vinyl now looked and sounded old hat. Lastly, basing itself on Yonnet, the study argued that the pop phenomenon of the period from 1955 to 1975 was socio-historically specific, an 'accident' whose economic impact could not go on forever.[33] However, behind the BIPE's sober economics was a deeper sociocultural change. Pop had changed its social meaning by the late 1970s, having ceased to be an exclusively youth-oriented, identity-forming phenomenon. Across the Western world, it had turned from culture into commodity. As the 1960s generation grew older, they took their tastes with them into middle age, sustaining the careers of a number of fading rock stars. But the middle-aged are less prolific record-buyers than the young, who were themselves buying less due to recession but also perhaps because they could no longer recognise themselves as Morin's 'age-class' in a bland commercial product which had segmented into a thousand sub-genres. This evolution was confirmed by disco, which soon fizzled out. As the BIPE asserted, disco was a free-floating product manufactured by the industry, rather than a cultural phenomenon rooted in a social demand capable of sustaining it for any length of time.[34]

As in the 1930s, when the music industry was first threatened by radio, crisis led to concentration. Even a major like the UK's EMI, which had signed the Beatles and helped engineer the 1960s pop revolution, had begun to founder and was bought out by Thorn Electrical Industries in 1979, as was the historic French label Barclay that same year, by Polygram. In France, the state's reluctance to intervene was making things even worse. On home-taping, for example, West Germany had reacted swiftly by taxing the software. But French governments had long been deaf to entreaties from the Syndicat national de l'édition phonographique et audiovisuelle (National Union of Record and Broadcasting Publishers) for a similar tax on tape. Moreover, in 1979 a French record-buyer paying 56 francs for an LP was being charged four times as much as an American and twice as much as a German.[35] One reason for this was that in 1978, the Minister of the Economy, René Monory, chose to free prices in the sector in the name of competition, as he was soon to do more controversially with books. This put an end to the voluntary price restraint which had capped the annual rise in record prices at 3 per cent since 1976. Rather than competition keeping prices low, as liberal dogma would have it, they soared by between 10 and 30 per cent; and this at a time when purchasing power was falling. The FNAC, a national chain of book and record stores, revealed that while its previous year's sales had averaged out at three to four albums per customer, the current figure was now around 1.5 albums.[36] But the critical reason for high record prices in France was a luxury-goods VAT rate of 33.3 per cent, when West Germany's stood at 11 per cent and Britain's at 8 per cent.[37] The tax brought in some 900 million francs, which naturally the government was loath to forgo. Even as the presidential elections of 1981 approached, candidate Giscard spoke up for it and would do no more than promise to review the situation, unlike his three main rivals (Mitterrand, Chirac and the Communist George Marchais), who all guaranteed to reduce it in line with the 7 per cent levied on books.

The hard economics at the root of the crisis were disguised and magnified by disco, whose impact came in two stages. At first, the 'go with the flow' strategy adopted by the French industry (see Chapter 3) made sound business sense. Since the Francophone market was small in comparison to the Anglophone, and the domestic industry could do little to protect itself without government support, the solution was simply to change languages. French record companies duly signed up or manufactured disco acts by the dozen, irrespective of quality. The four radio stations also began pumping out English-language product. This led to the second stage. Inexorably, in France as elsewhere, audiences tired of disco, and in 1979, having invested in it so heavily, the industry felt the pinch of over-exploitation, especially as those who danced to the music could not be relied on to buy the records. Meanwhile, promising new singers in French were being ignored, the risky launch of a first record often being shelved until a more propitious moment. Thus, the record-buyers who no longer appreciated disco, or never had, could find little else in the shops and would often leave without buying.

Chapier's 1979 article in *Le Monde* took stock of this complex economic picture and called for change. It was hardly surprising, he maintained, that the commercial channels played Anglo-American music or plugged their own co-productions, when not even the state-run France-Inter was subject to regulation in this regard. What he demanded was government intervention in the form of a quota of French-language music to be imposed on the four radio stations, as existed already for cinema, which was his constant point of comparison; and the reduction of VAT, at the very least on new releases. At first, his article appeared to have worked. In November of that year, the Culture and Communication Minister, Jean-Philippe Lecat, who by this time was eyeing the flourishing cultural industries as a possible justification for reining back arts funding, asked Chapier to draw up a report on the subject. At the same time, Lecat took several small but symbolic steps towards a *chanson* policy by bailing out the struggling Printemps de Bourges festival and inventing a national prize for *chanson* (awarded to Trenet in 1979). More promising still, he spoke of launching a 'French Song Foundation', announced in the *Journal officiel*. With some optimism, therefore, Chapier and a small commission set to work on the report, defining *chanson* widely enough to include rock but not *variétés*. However, the Ministry's enthusiasm proved short-lived and the funds set aside to finance both report and foundation were derisory. Disillusioned, Chapier submitted a terse mid-term document, 'Action Platform for French Song', in July 1980, which spelt out what was necessary to save French *chanson*. He padded it out with an ample appendix of press cuttings which he left to tell their own story, of a Ministry snatching defeat from the jaws of victory. With barbed formality, he also handed back the remainder of the pittance he had been allocated to carry out his task.[38]

This revealing episode is briefly recalled in Bertin's *Chante toujours, tu m'intéresses*, where he too wants both professional and government intervention to protect an endangered national art-form and improve the employment conditions and status of those struggling to make a living from it, in the absence of adequate professional protection.[39] During the presidential campaign of 1981, such calls became common. Amongst them was that of Mitterrand's Socialist Party and its cultural 'delegation' headed by Jack Lang. But if the Socialists of the 1970s could live with French *chanson*, they had little sympathy with pop, having been educated in the left-wing school of grim disapproval. Both the post-war militants of popular culture and the Leftists who had challenged it in 1968 were hostile to the Americanised entertainment industry and alarmed that pop was becoming the dominant culture that French youth identified with. Like Adorno, the Left still largely condemned the cultural industries for disseminating 'the second-rate products of an imported and imposed culture which aim in fact to make minds conform and sensibilities wither, to impose the same ways of thinking, acting, living'.[40]

But this earnestness was relaxed a little in the course of the 1970s, at least among certain left-wing intellectuals and local politicians. As we saw, some on the extreme Left in the early 1970s had detected a subversive energy in youth music worth exploiting politically, just as the PCF had since the early 1960s. Others broke with revolutionary Leftism altogether and became reconciled with the pleasures of the cultural supermarkets. As Rigby argues, mass culture was becoming indistinguishable from popular culture and in the process going legitimate.[41] Those on the Left who began working for local authorities or launching new cultural associations in the 1970s had themselves grown up with pop and were taking modest steps towards recognising it, such as making it available in municipal libraries and at events organised in the MJCs. It was therefore the PS municipalities above all, especially after Socialist gains in the local elections of 1977, which paved the way for a new music policy. Obliged as they were to be sensitive to local expectations, they discovered an irreducible demand for pop. For some, this was an unpleasant shock. Faithfully peddling post-1968 notions of popular creativity, local party workers found that there was indeed a thirst for creativity in young people (more and more wanted to learn an instrument), but that it was taking the very form which the Party had considered to be inimical to it. As Claude Petit-Castelli wrote at the time in a study of PS municipal policies, '"mass musics" like pop music, rock, folk, *chanson*, have generated an irreversible passion which has to be taken into account. [. . .] Whether it is a consumer product or not, this musical explosion is part of a culture and has become a means of musical expression in its own right.'[42]

PS councils like Grenoble and Rennes thus began exploring ways of implementing a new, more pragmatic policy for cultural democracy which embraced popular-musical forms like jazz, traditional music and pop, all of which, it was argued, needed to be rescued from domination by multinationals and given back to young people and the community. In Grenoble, local officials realised that amateur or semi-pro bands were short of places to rehearse and fitted out a sound-proofed basement studio open to any form of music. Le Printemps de Bourges came about with the help of the city's Maison de la culture, and Rennes created its own festival, Les Transmusicales. Rennes in fact thought of itself as the French Liverpool, having spawned a number of successful bands like Starshooter and Marie et les Garçons. A campaign was therefore launched for a respectable rock venue, which culminated ten years later in the Transbordeur. Councils also became aware of the need for the training available in their own music schools and in state education to be extended to musical forms and norms other than those inherited from the Paris Conservatoire, and to 'sociocultural animation' in underprivileged local communities, though persuading music educators of this need was a different matter. Easier to achieve was the integration of amateur music of all kinds in the various festivities organised by local councils.[43]

Eventually, this shift was reflected at national level, though not entirely comfortably or consistently. As Minister, Lang at first used the ideological rhetoric of the 1970s, as in his controversial Mexico speech given in 1982, where he spoke out against the 'intellectual and financial imperialism' of the USA. Yet this clearly did not define either his own or his party's position. By the 1981 victory, there was in reality widespread agreement on the need for a more pluralist and generous definition of culture and for youth-cultural issues to be addressed. As presidential candidate, Mitterrand ostentatiously took the side of local pirate radio (*radios libres*) in its battle with government, since the issue conveniently combined a youthful mass-medium with the PS's commitment to regional identities and opportunities for popular expression. The PS even set up its own illegal station in Paris, Radio Riposte, prodding the embarrassed regime into pressing charges against a presidential candidate.

Mitterrand also committed himself to major legislation on the continuing problem of music and art education in state education. In 1980, a substantial report by a former trade-unionist, Daniel Moreau, 'Perspectives for Music and Opera in France', spelt out the difficulties. Despite earlier attempts at improvement, the vast majority of the 300,000 primary-school teachers still had no musical training, with the result that most children went on to secondary (high) school with no competence in music at all. Once there, they found that music was considered unimportant in comparison to maths or French by parents and staff alike, and optional in the various types of baccalaureate. Of France's sixty-six universities in 1980, only eighteen offered music degrees, and research was equally limited. The network of specialist national and regional conservatoires and music schools could only remedy this situation patchily, given their uneven national distribution, the excess demand and the deterrent effect of high fees for those on low incomes.[44] Indeed, one further element in the PS's change of mind on pop was the realisation that tolerating young people's cultural preferences was a way of tackling urban and suburban disaffection. It could assist in the 'social insertion' of the young unemployed, strengthen local community identities and generally contribute to what became known in the 1980s as 'the cultural treatment of social problems'.

By the time of the 1981 elections, the future of music policy was tied to at least three competing discourses of cultural democracy: Malraux's conception of democratising high culture; the alternative conception which had evolved from pre-war popular education into 1960s 'sociocultural animation' and thence into the notion of cultural development; and the glimmer of an industrial and economic conception of culture outlined by Girard.[45] These discourses amounted to three different representations of popular culture, and of youth culture particularly. Such a diversity of representations was to make it all the harder to formulate a new, coherent government policy for popular music.

Notes

1. Philippe Teillet, 'Éléments pour une histoire des politiques publiques en faveur des "musiques amplifiées"', in Philippe Poirrier and Vincent Dubois (eds), *Les Collectivités locales et la culture: les formes de l'institutionnalisation, 19ᵉ–20ᵉ siècles* (Documentation Française, 2002), pp. 366–70.
2. For a fuller history of cultural policy more generally, see Looseley, *The Politics of Fun.*
3. Duneton, *Histoire de la chanson française,* vol. II, pp. 399–400.
4. For analysis of the popular culture, popular education, democratisation and youth movements, and of their attitudes to mass and pop culture, see Looseley, *The Politics of Fun,* especially Chapters 1–3; and Rigby, *Popular Culture in Modern France,* especially Chapters 1, 2 and 6.
5. Poulanges, 'La Chanson à Saint-Germain', pp. 189–190.
6. Rioux, *Cinquante Ans de chanson française,* pp. 53–4.
7. Ferré was something of an exception here, with his interest in democratising classical music: see, for example, Hawkins, *Chanson,* on Ferré, p. 117.
8. For a fuller history of French music policy, see Veitl and Duchemin, *Maurice Fleuret,* Introduction; d'Angelo, *Socio-économie de la musique en France,* Chapter 8; and Ministère de la culture, *État et culture: la musique* (Documentation Française, 1992), to all of which I am indebted here.

9. My source here is Jane Fulcher's excellently researched *French Cultural Politics and Music: From the Dreyfus Affair to the First World War* (Oxford University Press, 1999).
10. Ibid, quotations pp. 5 and 6, respectively.
11. Ibid., p. 5; the inner quotes are from David Carroll.
12. Ibid., p. 7.
13. Ibid., pp. 130–2.
14. Malraux quoted in d'Angelo, *Socio-économie de la musique en France*, p. 107, note 13.
15. A version of the Landowski Plan is reproduced as Annex 9 in Comité d'histoire du Ministère de la culture (ed.), *Les Affaires culturelles au temps de Jacques Duhamel 1971–1973: actes des journées d'étude 7 et 8 décembre 1993* (Documentation Française, 1995), pp. 589–95.
16. Pessis and Blamangin (eds), *Génération Mireille*, quotations pp. 17 and 9, respectively.
17. All details from Jackson, 'Making Enemies', pp. 183–4.
18. Quoted in Dillaz, *La Chanson française de contestation*, p. 18.
19. Ibid., pp. 18–19.
20. IRCAM was actually funded directly by the Ministry, not the DMD. On the Landowski Plan and the setting up of IRCAM, see Kim Eling, *The Politics of Cultural Policy in France* (Macmillan, 1999), Chapter 4, 'Contemporary Music Policy'.
21. Augustin Girard, 'Industries culturelles', *Futuribles*, no.17 (September–October 1978), pp. 597–605.
22. Both statistics are from Ory, *L'Entre-deux-mai,* pp. 200 and 202, respectively.
23. Henry Chapier, 'Complot contre la chanson française', *Le Monde*, 26–7 August 1979.
24. Coulomb and Varrod, *1968–1988*, pp. 149–50.
25. Robert Mallat, 'Disque la chute' *Le Point*, 14 January 1980, p. 95.
26. See Chocron, 'Les Enjeux économiques du rock', pp. 117–20 on this and other aspects of the 1979 record-industry crisis.
27. Ibid., p. 118.
28. World sales stood at 942 million units in 1978 but at only 652 million in 1983. In France, the fall was from 78 to 48 million units: Gildas Lefeuvre, *Le Producteur de disques* (Dixit-Irma, 1998), pp. 21 and 31.
29. BIPE (Alain Le Diberder and Sylvie Pflieger), *Crise et mutation du domaine musical* (Documentation Française, 1987).
30. Thomas Herpin, 'Sept Ans de culture: le disque. Taxé, libéré, piraté', *Les Nouvelles Littéraires*, 23 April 1981, p. 37, from which the above statistics also come.
31. BIPE, *Crise et mutation*, pp. 27–8.

32. Ibid., pp. 28–9.
33. Ibid., pp. 30–6.
34. Ibid, pp. 35–6.
35. Chapier, 'Plateforme d'action pour la chanson française', typed report submitted to Minister of Culture, 25 July 1980, p. 13.
36. All figures from Herpin, 'Sept Ans de culture: le disque', p. 37.
37. Louis-Jean Calvet, 'Une Non-Politique', *Les Nouvelles Littéraires*, 23 April 1981, p. 35.
38. Chapier, 'Plateforme d'action pour la chanson française'.
39. Bertin, *Chante toujours*, p. 152.
40. Fédération nationale des élus socialistes et républicains (FNESR), 'La Création artistique dans la cité' (report of the FNESR's 'Rencontre de Rennes', 24–5 October 1980), in *Communes de France*, document no. 16, p. 6.
41. Rigby, *Popular Culture in Modern France*, p. 162.
42. Claude Petit-Castelli, *La Culture à la une, ou l'action culturelle dans les mairies socialistes* (Club Socialiste du Livre, 1981), pp. 109–10.
43. Ibid., pp. 109–12.
44. All details regarding the Moreau report are cited in Veitl and Duchemin, *Maurice Fleuret*, pp. 74–9.
45. For a closer discussion of the history and nature of these discursive strands, see David L. Looseley, 'The Work and the Person: Discourse and Dialogue in the History of the Ministry of Culture', in Maggie E. Allison and Owen N. Heathcote (eds), *The Fifth Republic: Forty Years On* (Peter Lang, 1999), pp. 237–53; and Philippe Urfalino, *L'Invention de la politique culturelle* (Documentation Française, 1996).

– 7 –

Music and Politics 1981–93

Lang's two five-year periods as Minister of Culture are mainly remembered for two things: a doubled budget for 1982 and the pursuit of cultural democracy in the form of support for creative forms hitherto unrecognised. At a sitting of the National Assembly on 17 November 1981 where he announced both innovations, he justified them in terms of a number of higher principles, amongst which was a belief that culture was not the preserve of the subsidised arts and that the state should be ready to work with the private sector to achieve four basic objectives. Two of these had been PS themes since 1968: democratising access and encouraging creativity. The others sounded rather less familiar coming from the post-1968 Left: reconciling creation with the market and preserving national identity. With hindsight, the speech suggests a coming of age, a sense that the time has come for the Left to put away childish things and get real. It was the start of a new era in French cultural policy. Hitherto, the disbursement of public funds to support the arts had been justified, in France as elsewhere, in terms of democratic provision: it was needed if minority arts like theatre or opera were to be preserved from extinction. What was now taking place was a shift from seeing the arts as a luxury, as Farchy puts it, to seeing them as an investment which fosters growth in the form of jobs, spending and overseas income; and this shift only fully made sense if mass culture and the creative industries were welcomed under the umbrella of culture.[1] It is in this new discursive context that the invention of a policy for pop needs to be understood.

As soon as the PS came to power, it was plain that youth culture would be a priority. The government moved swiftly to legalise the private radio stations in November 1981, which, once advertising was authorised in 1984, led to a proliferation of pop stations. During the presidential campaign and shortly afterwards, Lang and others mounted a string of media events which exploited pop: an all-night street party at the Bastille to celebrate Mitterrand's victory, a rock concert in June to mark the achievements of the Popular Front, and so on. Lang himself went to see the rock band Téléphone perform in unappealing conditions at the Porte de Pantin, followed by a more publicised appearance at a Stevie Wonder concert. Such photo opportunities spoke of a new openness, which the Minister went on to spell out the following January at the international record trade fair, the MIDEM. The PS, he declaimed, wanted to support and co-operate with the record industry in an inclusive spirit: 'From now on, there will be no more hierarchy between forms of music: *variétés* belongs to culture just as much as classical, experimentation, and living and popular musics.'[2] He also indicated that the competing policy discourses of democratisation, cultural democracy and the creative industries were not incompatible but could form a coherent agenda. But translating this agenda into outcomes was a different matter, especially when in 1982–3 economic crisis necessitated a humiliating climb-down on many of the government's initial promises. It is not my intention in this chapter to survey all the measures adopted for music or evaluate their effectiveness. The aim is rather to show how pop and policy were conceptualised during the Lang years.

Inventing a Policy

To flesh out these general principles, Lang appointed a new Director of Music and Dance, Maurice Fleuret, in October 1981, who became the principal architect of a radical reorientation of the Directorate (DMD). Left-wing music critic and *animateur* since the 1950s, former student of the Paris Conservatoire, and director of the Lille Music Festival, Fleuret believed in music's ability to transform both individuals and society.[3] His work before and after 1981 hinged on an attempt to reconcile the personal and the political, to disprove the notion that music was of all the cultural forms the most inward, private, incommunicable experience and therefore the least suited to becoming an affair of state. This philosophy made Fleuret the ideal person to apply Lang's commitment to a joined-up policy agenda. Fleuret had an inclusive conception of music and is reported to have told Lang that he would only accept the job if he became 'the director of all musics, from the accordion to the record industry'.[4] He had warmly welcomed the Moreau report the previous year, especially its conclusion that a dynamic music policy was not a luxury but 'a national necessity'. Given the marginal status of both amateur practices and non-classical forms in the Ministry before 1981, Fleuret's new democratic conception – 'recognising all practices as equal in dignity' – promised dramatic change.[5]

At press briefings in February and June 1982, Lang and Fleuret unveiled their new music policy. It was apparent that plans for popular music specifically were still in the making. They included a number of isolated measures, most notably a purpose-built concert hall for popular music to be built at Bagnolet and a strong emphasis on further consultation. Lang announced the imminent creation of a Higher Music Council which would bring together the music professions, broadcasting and other Ministries to help drive and co-ordinate policy-making in a consultative capacity. The Council formally came into existence in November 1982. There would also be national commissions for jazz and improvised musics, *chanson* and *variétés*, and 'traditional musics'.[6] With the benefit of hindsight, this early slant towards consultation invites two remarks. First, all the consultations in the world would make no difference if the Ministry did not obtain the co-operation of other Ministries, essential for real reform in music. Lowering VAT would mean persuading the Ministry of Finance to forgo hundreds of millions of francs a year. Improving the presence of French music in broadcasting would need to be negotiated with the Ministry of Communication, now separate from Culture in the new government. And most important of all – 'keystone of France's musical future', Lang admitted at the February briefing – the reform of creative-arts education in state schools relied entirely on the notoriously slow-moving Ministry of Education.

Second, as Kim Eling points out, consultation with the popular-music milieu was not as straightforward as it sounded. What in reality distinguished the policy-making process for popular music, at least during Lang's first five years, was the element of direct political control he exerted, with relatively little resort to outside bodies. It was from the Ministry, not the industry, that the policy initiative had first come, and the policy continued to be largely Ministry-driven even when selective private-sector involvement did come about. This was partly because, unlike *variétés*, bodies representing the rock end of the spectrum scarcely existed; and partly because the music milieu was wary of state manipulation.[7] This was not altogether unjustified. The consultative structures listed above did have representation from appropriate private-sector professions (though mostly from *variétés*), which worked closely with the DMD in particular. But in *chanson* and pop, the DMD was increasingly marginalised as Lang and his staff became ever more implicated in the policy. This suggested a drive to make use of pop, to derive symbolic benefit from it. Where the state's relationship with its client groups 'remains clearly skewed in favour of the representatives of the state or its component agencies', Eling warns, there is necessarily 'domination, and instrumentalization, of groups by their public patrons'.[8]

To help formulate, enact and co-ordinate the policy, two new Ministry units were set up. While Fleuret created a modest Musical Action Division within the DMD, Lang came up with a wide-ranging new department which would have considerable power in the popular-music arena: the Directorate for Cultural Development (DDC), placed under a former militant of 1968,

Dominique Wallon. As upholders of cultural development had always urged, the DDC was 'transversal', cutting across the various sectoral directorates like the DMD and promoting nation-wide collaboration: between the seventeen ministries having input on cultural matters and with local authorities and voluntary organisations. This was a daring move since the DDC could and did ruffle feathers by intruding on other directorates' turf. Where pop was concerned, policies were conducted by both the DMD and the DDC, but it was the latter which inflected policy more.

Aside from these internecine complexities, the difficulty, for the Ministry as a whole, of operating in this one-sided way should not be underestimated since a policy had to be devised virtually from scratch, assisting genres which had not received national support before, whose contours were not clearly defined, and which in some cases had relatively little in common. This could only mean identifying the specificity of each, then designing policies accordingly. Jazz is a case in point. Although there was no jazz policy to speak of before 1981, its aesthetic legitimation was quite advanced. It was therefore less difficult to invent a policy modelled on existing forms of aid, such as creating an official qualification for those teaching jazz in music schools (1985) or encouraging new work, by means of public commissions. But commissioning actually confirms the importance of made-to-measure action, for, given the improvised, performative nature of jazz, it could no longer be a question of simply commissioning a score, as with contemporary experimental music: 'to me', Fleuret explained, 'jazz seems above all to be action [*(un) geste*] and you can't commission action; by contrast, you can create the context for action, the need for it'.[9] Where newer musics like pop were concerned, some of the same problems and solutions obtained, but the sector was distinguished by a much bigger industrial dimension, which again required a made-to-measure approach.

Lang and his staff initially defined contemporary popular music (aside from jazz) as *chanson* and *variétés*, rather than 'rock' in the narrow sense. Given the status of *chanson* as national patrimonial myth at the beginning of the 1980s, this was the obvious option. It was also the safer one, since both *chanson* and *variétés* could be represented as national or naturalised forms rather than Anglo-American interlopers. *Chanson* was also a personal preference of Lang's *directeur de cabinet*, Jacques Sallois, who successfully lobbied the Minister even though the civil servants of Fleuret's Musical Action Division were unconvinced and were already investigating what a rock policy might look like. Rock attracted serious attention only after it finally dawned on Lang's entourage that *chanson* carried little weight among the young. But evolving a rock policy was no easy task, because of the term's semantic ambivalence. For some, it retained the subversive connotations of rock'n'roll in the late 1950s, or of squats and Leftism in the early 1970s. Remembering the *blousons noirs*, some still viewed it as a crude, disaffected form linked not just with noise pollution but also with drugs, violence and delinquency. Jacques Renard, a member of Lang's staff with responsibility for popular music, cites an unnamed representative of the Paris city council declaring on television as late as May 1986 that rock presented dangers for youth and social order.[10] It was also associated, as we saw in Chapter 3, with a subterranean culture of suburban or provincial groups, amateurs or semi-pros struggling with limited resources and restricted conditions. And for many, of course, it meant music of Anglo-American origin. On the other hand, the term 'rock' was already becoming less specific both musically and sociologically, covering a range of successful French-language forms. Here too, then, like the PS municipalities of the late 1970s, the government had to bow to the evidence of demand, or, as Lang put it in December 1984 at the fashionable Parisian discothèque Le Gibus, 'receive in the name of the national community the immediate and imperious message of its entire youth'. He also maintained that, given the size of the rock phenomenon and the market imperatives within which it functions, state intervention was indispensable.

But what precise form should so unprecedented a policy take? Initially, there was no question of directly subsidising creative output, as happened in other arts sectors. This was because the Ministry was anxious not to create yet another dependent sector or appear to be hijacking a milieu whose self-image was of unfettered recalcitrance. Ministry personnel also feared their own incompetence in such an unknown area of artistic production. As a result, two different representations evolved of what a policy for youth music should be. These were, as Teillet defines them, a social policy and a professional one. In practice, these two concerned, respectively, amateur or semi-professional music-making, and the economics of the music industry and professions.[11] Behind them, however, was a third, more shadowy representation: of pop policy as primarily symbolic. In the remainder of the chapter, I shall outline each of these three representations and how each was implemented.

A Social Policy

From the outset, Fleuret described his policy as distinctively social, in the sense that it was about reducing inequalities in all genres and practices. Closed to the kinds of reception theory exemplified by Hennion, Fleuret took the standard view of listening as passive consumption. Society today, he argues, produces people who can only listen, but this is not enough: 'Everyone has acoustic awareness within them but often it is not developed. [. . .] The transistor destroys this awareness; and everyone is beginning to feel the need to re-establish a balance. We have to be penetrated by vibrations, we need to vibrate.' Clearly, for Fleuret, doing music should above all mean making music. His aim is to end the redundant hierarchy of professional and amateur by unleashing the musical creativity which is 'a natural act' in all children.[12] Hence the creation of the Musical Action Division, working on behalf of all the musical activities hitherto marginalised by previous administrations, irrespective of their amateur or professional status: choirs, *chanson*, *variétés*, rock, jazz, 'popular' and 'traditional' musics (that is, the living folk musics of French regions and ethnicities, but above all world music). The new unit was the symbol of Fleuret's whole philosophy, though a bigger and better one was to follow.

Ideally, the outcome of this conception would be a transformation of music training not only in specialist establishments like the conservatoires but in state education too. But given the size and ponderousness of the Education Ministry, this was likely to be a slow business. So when the latest cultural-practices survey revealed that there were already five million instrumentalists in France and that half were young, a more immediate application of the Fleuret philosophy suggested itself. To draw attention to this abundant activity, Fleuret and two of Lang's staff devised a one-day street festival celebrating music-making of every kind. Only weeks later, the first Fête de la musique took place on 21 June 1982, organised by the Musical Action Division and the CENAM, at which amateur and professional musicians of every genre and every level of talent were invited to take to the streets and other public spaces to mark the summer solstice by making music.

This first event was a modest success, albeit a rather quirky one as government ministers formed combos in the street and the Ensemble intercontemporain created by Boulez played Xenakis outside a Beaubourg supermarket to an audience of puzzled tramps.[13] Derided by the political opposition as a demotic gimmick, the occasion was actually well rooted in the collective and personal mythologies of the Left. Lang and Fleuret had both been organisers of arts festivals in the past and believed in the mobilising power of the festive. The Fête also had echoes of the public music-making improvised during May 1968, of the Popular Front and Albert Doyen's 'people's festivals', and even of the Revolution. Intended primarily to persuade the Ministry of Finance to release more funds for music, at the symbolic level it sent out three easily decipherable messages: it exploded the myth that the French were not musical; it challenged the aesthetic hierarchies which divided music; and it privileged enjoyment, immediacy and do-it-yourself creativity over po-faced theory, apprenticeship and technique. Less explicitly, it emphasised social cohesion and a new experience of nationhood in the sharing of musical creativities. Far from being an unmusical nation, France, it would seem, could actually *become* a nation through music. Lang came close to voicing this notion when he insisted that 'policy for culture is also a policy for rebuilding different relations between us, for establishing between French citizens a different art of living'.[14] The Fête also targeted the creative energy of the young, the government's role being not to direct that energy but to create structures which would stimulate its free deployment.[15] Accordingly, the Fête has become an established annual fixture.

Another source of theory pushing in a comparable direction was a report on cultural action and youth commissioned by Lang from an *animateur*, Jean Hurstel. Submitted in 1984 to the DDC, the report was not published officially because of its controversial critique of existing cultural institutions for youth.[16] Nor did it have very much specific influence on policy practice. But it does shed light on how, via the DDC, youth music came to be harnessed to a welfare policy which went beyond what Fleuret had in mind when he spoke of a social policy for music. Hurstel's concern is with the cultural institutions which should be set up for young people from disadvantaged backgrounds in the big housing estates. His premise is that in the 1950s there was a 'cultural big bang' whose consequences are ongoing. Since the birth of rock'n'roll, an autonomous, international youth culture has grown up whose values and practices differ radically from those of traditional culture. Youth culture, he argues, is locally heterogeneous – even the young of the big urban estates subdivide into those still in school, workers, second-generation immigrants, and so on – but globally homogeneous. Perhaps, then, he postulates, the youth 'problem' (delinquency, marginality, low achievement) reveals not cultural penury but the existence of an alternative culture which simply resists normalisation. And perhaps this resistance should make us ponder 'the obsolescence, the sclerosis of our cultural institutions'.[17]

Where this clash can best be seen at work is in youth facilities. I described earlier how in the late 1950s Johnny Hallyday's gang had appropriated the Square de la Trinité then the Golf Drouot as their turf. This territorialism was still visible twenty-five years later, according to Hurstel, despite a huge increase in the 'official' facilities available to the young. Youth 'foyers', 'houses' and 'centres' abound but infuriatingly the young prefer to invent their own social spaces, like the porches of supermarkets, the cellars of tower-blocks, and local bars. The reason, Hurstel contends, is that, in the standard bricks-and-mortar reflex of institutional planning, youth facilities are erected, then young people are invited to find a use for them. The homely lexis employed – hearth (*foyer*), house, centre – bears witness to their hopeless incongruity, in urban districts which have no centre and council estates and tower-blocks which have no houses or hearths. 'The young do not even reject this model of the happy family inscribed in youth facilities: they are totally indifferent to it. They can no longer understand the values of reference, the codes of conduct, the overall meaning of what people are trying in vain to hand down to them.'[18] Hurstel's way forward is a much more pluralistic, supple institutionalisation of youth culture. The key word is mobility: the young do need places to go but not permanent or inflexible ones; they in fact need spaces rather than places. The locations young people appropriate are specific to a group and a time, born of and tied to a project; and it is the project which counts, the content not the container. Hence his overarching recommendation: 'close the youth centres, open the bistrots'. We have bars in cultural centres, why not cultural centres in bars, where rock or jazz concerts could be organised, local groups find an audience, and well-known touring groups perform? Why not open local radio stations to local groups so they can record their work or experiment with new sounds? Or equip each new apartment block with a sound-proof rehearsal space, convert abandoned industrial buildings, and so on?[19]

Hurstel's recommendations have two salient discursive features. As with Fleuret, one is the blurring of amateur and professional, creation and *animation*. The young themselves, he insists, refuse such cut-and-dried distinctions. For them, happy-clappy amateurism without aesthetic ambition (and even commercial remuneration) is unacceptable; but so too is the art for art's sake narcissism of the professional artist. There is therefore a strong demand by young people for challenging creative activity founded on different aesthetic principles from those which obtain in traditional community-arts institutions. Harking back, as such institutions do, to nineteenth-century models of bourgeois academicism (little girls doing ballet in tutus) or faux-ruralist kitsch (a steel-worker embroidering a fawn in moonlight) will have little appeal to adolescents. Hence Hurstel's prolific suggestions for new initiatives involving music: commissions to rock or jazz bands; grants for professional musicians willing to live and work with local amateurs; the development of world music; poets working with bands to produce better lyrics; rock-operas, and so on. The second discursive feature is the link Hurstel makes between the flexible, short-term project and the festive conception of culture I have just outlined. Why do the young not go to theatres yet flock to the Avignon Theatre Festival, he asks? Because they are attracted by conviviality and sociability. 'We must reinvent our cultural *fêtes*. Less training, access, acquisition, "culturalisation"; and more imagination in organising festive moments, the pleasure of being together and of experiencing an exceptional moment.'[20] Hurstel is very close here to the principle behind the Fête de la musique. It is also striking how, consciously or not, he echoes Certeau and anticipates aspects of Maffesoli's neo-tribalism, which he sees as already a dominant characteristic of youth culture.

By the time the report was submitted, the national policy for popular music was underway, though it had not got very far. On the aesthetic side, the DMD, having declined to aid creation directly, had few alternatives available, and in any case its Musical Action Division had limited funds. As for the sociocultural dimensions of the amateur sector, these were chiefly the responsibility of the Youth and Sport administration and largely decentralised. Even so, the sociocultural was assisted to an extent by the DMD, though more so by the DDC. Socialisation through music has in fact become one of the main forms of youth-oriented cultural development at local level in sensitive inner- and outer-city areas, as Hurstel recommended.

But the Ministry's main social policy during Lang's first term was called a 'policy for places' (*une politique des lieux*). Implemented by the DDC either alone or with the DMD, it occupied a middle ground between the cultural and sociocultural, coinciding at least with the letter of Hurstel's recommendations though scarcely with its spirit. The initial scheme, in keeping with Sallois's preference, was to invent new places for *chanson*. It was announced at the February briefing that four decentralised 'Regional Song Centres' would be set up in Bordeaux, Bourges, Nanterre and Rennes, as the first step towards a national network. Their purpose was to provide training, information and other forms of assistance for would-be performers and songwriters in their respective regions. Each encountered difficulties, though Rennes and Bourges proved successful. But after a while, under pressure from Fleuret and the DMD, who were never very convinced of *chanson*'s viability as a policy option, the programme was abandoned and rock took its place. By the early 1980s, specialist venues like Le Gibus were springing up spontaneously, some of which provided both performance and rehearsal space where the amateur, the semi-professional and the professional could circulate easily. Finding premises to rehearse in without attracting complaints about noise was a particular problem for budding amateur or semi-pro bands. A typical instance was brought to the attention of the press in 1985 when Lang intervened in support of a number of rock groups being evicted by their municipality from a multi-storey car park called Parking 2000 where they had been rehearsing four floors underground. Such conflicts were further politicised when the extreme Right took them up at local level and denounced this 'loutish music', giving the Left all the more reason to take a stand on the issue.[21] The Ministry helped with the high cost of sound-proofing and by funding a publication produced in 1984 by the CENAM and initiated jointly by the DDC and an informal non-governmental organisation called the Réseau Rock (Rock Network), which represented voluntary organisations involved in amateur or semi-professional rock and was one of the few pop organisations ready to work with the Ministry. Entitled *Maxi-rock, mini-bruit*, the publication was a guide to rehearsal facilities, containing advice and information for the supposed 25,000 rock groups in France.[22] This first collaboration then led to the setting up of a semi-official rock information centre, the CIR, in 1986. A joint venture by Culture, the Youth and Sport Ministry and the Réseau Rock, the CIR began by providing inexperienced musicians with the information, training and practical assistance they needed to pursue careers and steadily became an instrument of rock's institutionalisation.[23]

In Lang's second term, institutionalisation was taken further still within an interministerial urban programme. More and more local authorities were adopting social policies for pop, though by this time rap had become the privileged genre, as young ethnic populations were taking it up as their hallmark. In 1989, the Ministry also created a special agency in charge of the places policy, which came up with two new programmes. One, entitled 'New places, new adventures', helped fund a number of medium-sized music facilities, such as Le Confort moderne in Poitiers, which occupies 4,000 square metres and has adjacent rehearsal facilities. Six years on, some 800 groups had performed there and it had acquired a staff of around thirty people.[24] The Agency also took a step in Hurstel's direction with the setting up in February 1991 of 100 *cafés-musiques* in deprived urban districts, small towns and rural areas, another interministerial programme with local-government input. The official description of a *café-musique* conformed closely to what Hurstel had advocated: a place where young people could meet, hear music and express themselves. One aim was to let local youths set up and run the venues, which had to achieve financial independence within two years or close down.[25] Nevertheless, although avoiding a one-size-fits-all approach was deemed important, the project departed from Hurstel's recommendations by stressing that the cafés were permanent structures.

This was equally true of a much more ambitious plan to set up a number of flagship venues across France specifically meant for pop concerts. Pop did not have a major, purpose-built concert hall in the capital, so promoters were still obliged to book sports halls or stadia where acoustics and visibility were often inadequate. The remedy was the Paris Zénith at the Parc de la Villette, opened in January 1984 as a stop-gap after the Bagnolet project fell through. Hurstel had called for youth facilities to be adaptable and ephemeral, such as marquees or big inflatable structures, and the Zénith conformed to both requirements to an extent. Inflatable and lightweight so easily erected, adaptability was built into the Zénith's design since it can house from 3,000 to 6,000 spectators, standing up, seated, or both. Nevertheless, success has made the stop-gap permanent. The Paris facility established itself rapidly and had by the beginning of the new century attracted in excess of 2,000 events and ten million spectators. It has also engendered ten other structures in the regions, all with the same name and governed by the same statutes, all therefore fully institutionalised as a national network.[26]

Although the Zéniths are often cited as a major initiative in the places policy, that policy tended in practice to bifurcate, separating amateur and professional again in a way neither Fleuret nor Hurstel had wanted. The Paris Zénith particularly heralded a drift away from multi-purpose (*polyvalent*) venues to dedicated professional ones. The social policy for pop and the notion of cultural development through youth music were in fact decentred by policies for career musicians, professionalisation and the music industry, in all of which pop was being viewed primarily as an economic activity.

An Economic Policy

A month after coming to office, and several months before Fleuret's appointment, Lang commissioned Pascal Sevran, singer, TV presenter and ex-pupil at Mireille's Petit Conservatoire, to make proposals for a policy for *variétés*. His report addressed a range of practical issues in the music business, paying special attention to the employment conditions of artists and to live performance.[27] Sevran wanted VAT on records lowered, though he sounded slightly lukewarm on the matter; and he shared Chapier's irritation with the broadcasting media's lack of commitment to new French talent. To help resist the Anglo-Saxon invasion of the airwaves, he wanted to see contractual obligations imposed on the newly legalised local FM radio stations, and various other conditions on broadcasting generally, including (again like Chapier) a radio quota system to favour French music. He also called for live music to be given a boost by reducing miming on television, for legislation to ensure that performers (not just songwriters) receive royalties when their music is broadcast, and for the setting up of France's first state-sponsored *variétés* school, to be known as the Studio des variétés, which would provide coaching for singers (an endangered species at the time) much as the Petit Conservatoire had done. Sevran also suggested creating a national theatre for *chanson* and light opera in Paris to function like the Comédie française; a guarantee fund to help independent producers obtain bank-loans; and a 'High Council for *Variétés*' to represent the views and problems of the profession and act in an advisory capacity.

Some of Sevran's recommendations were promptly acted on. The Studio des variétés, already planned by the SACEM before 1981, enrolled its first intake in September 1983 on a two-year course, where the tuition ranged from voice training to the legal issues involved in contracts, copyright, and so on. Other recommendations, like the quotas, came into being much later, and a number of new industry institutions and structures were devised broadly in the spirit of Sevran's report. But by Lang's second term, pop policy was taking a different turn by becoming more institutionalised. As Eling notes, the CIR grew into 'something resembling an implementing agency for the Ministry's "rock policy"', under its President (and former President of the Réseau Rock), Bruno Lion.[28] Then, in 1989, Lang appointed Lion to a Ministry post as his adviser on and co-ordinator of pop policies. Lion became a member neither of Lang's personal staff nor of the DMD but was directly answerable to the Minister himself, intensifying the direct involvement of the Minister in the policy and further politicising it. Civil servants were nudged out of the picture, a process made easier by the fact that Lang's new Director of Music during his second term, Michel Schneider, disagreed with pop policy in its entirety. So, with the Music directorate and the DDF (successor to the DDC) sidelined and an active policy co-ordinator with a direct line to the Minister, not to mention a 50 per cent increase in the budget available to the pop sector in Lion's first year, the policy took another big stride away from the amateur sector, towards the music professions.

Some industrial support had begun in Lang's first term, involving, for example, record and music publishing and the manufacture of musical instruments. In 1984, the Ministries of Industrial Redeployment and Culture introduced the 'Sound Plan', designed to help companies involved in music production to adapt to new technologies like CD pressing, digital recording studios, software production and synthesisers. The object here was to make France more competitive in its domestic market while helping industrialise new products and market them abroad. State help was also given to record producers trying to break into US and UK markets. The Ministry organised the first French rock festival in Britain, 'Fall for France', in which some twenty acts performed in London clubs, though British audiences mostly reacted with the usual indifference. A similar event, 'French Revolution in New York', took place in the USA in 1989, and Lang also fulfilled a promise to set up a music export office in New York with the help of Foreign Affairs; other offices followed over the next few years, including in Germany, Japan and the UK.

Equally important were a number of more general measures which impacted on music in some way, for example the extension of the youth-employment scheme, the TUC, to include young musicians. But the most significant of such measures was the 'Lang law' of 3 July 1985 on copyright and neighbouring rights (*loi sur les droits d'auteurs et droits voisins*), which tackled some of the issues Bertin had raised five years before by giving artists, performers and producers a new legal status. For music in particular, the act entitled both record producers and performers, in addition to songwriters, to royalties when their records were played on the air or in other public spaces, and levied a tax on blank cassettes to compensate the industry for private copying. Similarly, the IFCIC (Institute for the Financing of Cinema and the Cultural Industries), a Ministry-backed agency set up under Lang to encourage finance companies to make loans to small and medium enterprises by guaranteeing up to 50 per cent of the loan, became increasingly involved in music, for example by assisting small independent labels.[29]

Support mechanisms of this kind for the music professions and the industry are not always distinguishable from aid to creation, which the Ministry had initially shied away from but gradually crept back to in a variety of similarly indirect ways. One example is the Fonds de soutien (Aid Fund) pour la chanson, la variété et le jazz, set up just before the March 1986 election. Administered by music professionals, the fund is fed by redirecting an existing tax on live music performance and topped up by Ministry grant. Its aim is to assist music in a variety of areas from training to new live shows. Another instance was Lion's 'Labels Plan', initiated in 1989 to assist struggling independent record companies. By 1992, fifty-four had received eight million francs between them, the condition being that they become properly professional operations. With Bondage, New Rose or the perplexingly named Bollock Productions, the Plan had some success, but it proved ineffective in its other objective, which was to stop French independents having their best acts snatched by the majors, in whose pockets the aid sometimes ended up, as Vogue, New Rose and other French labels signed deals with them.[30] After Lang's departure in March 1993, the Plan was wound up.

Indirect aid to creation also took the form of published technical guidance on the various music sectors, for example the now well-established directory *L'Officiel du rock* produced by the CIR since 1986, containing details of thousands of concert organisers, labels, studios, and so on. Equivalent units to the CIR were also set up for jazz and traditional musics, and today all three are combined under the name IRMA. But Lion's most radical step was the introduction of an 'action and initiatives' fund for rock, the FAIR, a scheme funded by the Ministry, the SACEM and other sources, including sponsorship from the drinks manufacturer Ricard. The FAIR is unequivocally a form of direct aid to creation, each year assisting fifteen new pop acts, selected competitively by industry representatives, to go professional. Over a limited period, the performers and their management receive information, training and a small amount of financial assistance with touring and equipment, the main means of launching a career before other forms of remuneration such as royalties come on-stream. Unmistakably, the FAIR was the ultimate step in the shift from a social to a professional policy for pop. [31]

A Symbolic Policy

This shift brought Lang and Lion face to face with an intractable problem, however, which was the existence of endemic industrial, commercial and legal parameters lying outside a Culture Ministry's control. The situation was not helped by the pop industry's reluctance to get into bed with the state, or by the fact that policy was being elaborated from scratch, on a low budget, and with little interministerial co-operation. These obstacles help explain why, from start to finish, the Lang Ministries resorted to what Jim McGuigan, borrowing from Raymond Williams, calls 'cultural policy as display'.[32] The Fête de la musique is the most obvious instance. Rapidly snowballing to the point where today it is an international event involving some eighty countries, it enabled Lang to develop his own signature. Just one year after the victories of 1981, his Ministry had changed from dour, parsimonious bureaucracy to champion of anything-goes music-making in happy-go-lucky mood. A lifelong believer in the public function of festivity, Lang learnt new lessons from its success. By 1982, *décloisonnement*, the departitioning of culture, was already becoming his core concept, but the Fête demonstrated just how easily it could be achieved – or, more accurately, symbolised – if one simply called on the existing enthusiasms of amateur musicians and encouraged the professionals to let their hair down. Represented as naturally festive, live music became the standard-bearer of a new government discourse. Through it, the discourse implied, French culture's fault-lines – amateur versus professional, high versus popular, creation versus creativity – can be seamlessly resolved, since the carnivalesque enjoyment of music is what connects the amateur rock band in a suburban youth club to Johnny Hallyday, Madonna or, for that matter, the Orchestre de Paris.

With the Fête's success, policy as display began to assume other forms. Lang went out of his way to cultivate pop stars and advertise his closeness to them. In June 1986, when Lang was temporarily out of office, the singer Bernard Lavilliers provided a revealing insight into how things used to be: 'In Lang's time, you'd go to the Ministry a bit like you'd go to a bar. You'd have a quick drink, it was friendly. You'd go and see Monique [Lang's wife], she was like our Mum.'[33] In similarly convivial vein, a new award for popular music was established, Les Victoires de la musique, with its own glittering ceremony. Lang also conferred national honours on established pop stars, both French and otherwise (Bob Dylan, Lou Reed, David Bowie). Then, in the mid-1980s, he latched on to the anti-racist movement, which was attracting youthful support, especially SOS Racisme, whose first 'Hands Off My Mate' concert at the Place de la Concorde in 1985 was carefully stage-managed by Lang.

Against this backcloth, the popularity of world music and later hip-hop proved especially fortuitous. World music could be promoted as a symbol of multiculturalism and inter-ethnic solidarity, which Lang was keen to represent as contemporary expressions of French republicanism. This was a politically painless response to metropolitan France's ethnic conflicts at a time when the

National Front was growing in strength. The Gipsy Kings had become popular internationally by the late 1980s and Lang went to the trouble of flying to Britain to attend their Wembley concert in November 1989, describing them as the very symbol of French culture. Rap lent itself equally well to such symbolism, as we glimpsed in Chapter 3. Justifying his support in the Assembly, Lang described hip-hop as 'a phenomenon of civilisation' which at its best draws unconsciously on the *commedia dell'arte*; while various commentators readily held up some French rap (MC Solaar, IAM) as a form of contemporary, urban poetry. Thus, rap could be represented as being as much a continuation of the French oral tradition as *chanson* and perfectly compatible with a European literary cultural heritage. Mitterrand too was doing his bit. In 1984, having apparently outgrown Sheila, he declared his enjoyment of rock music. He even invited a number of key representatives of youth culture to the Elysée Palace for a spot of lunch and friendly conversation. Among them was the supposedly anarchist youth idol Renaud, who unexpectedly emerged from the summit talks dazzled by the President's charisma. Later, in 1988, Renaud campaigned for him to stand for another seven-year term, helping establish the myth that French youth stood solidly behind the President as 'the Mitterrand generation'. In the bicentenary celebrations the following year, Jean-Paul Goude's choreographed parade down the Champs-Elysées mixed high fashion and ethnic musics from across the globe in a celebration of multicultural chic.

Ultimately, events like the Goude parade and the Fête de la musique were evidence of a serious ambition to change the culture. Just as in post-1997 Britain, where a New Labour government, the mourning of Diana, and the millennium celebrations contributed to the public myth of a nation reborn, at ease with itself and no longer emotionally repressed, so too was the French Socialist victory of 1981 constructed as a liberation of feeling, or, as Mitterrand himself had anticipated shortly before the result, 'a surge of popular joy, an explosion of enthusiasm, the seething and effervescence of imaginations'.[34] Behind all this, there seemed to be an urge to counterbalance France's self-image as the cradle of the written word, of analytical reason and classical elegance enshrined in fine prose, with a new identity as the fount of youth, spontaneity and unfettered self-expression, all of which music, when read as festivity and spontaneous creativity, was deemed to embody. For Lang and the new government, popular music, and pop particularly, was a magic wardrobe into modernity, or, more accurately, *post*-modernity, at a time when the post-1968 Left was considered by reconstructed intellectuals to be locked in a semi-Marxist mindset which had lost the plot.[35] In effect, official discourse was nationalising the new tribalism Maffesoli identifies and the multicultural interpretation of authenticity which pop was evolving. It was proposing an ideal way of experiencing culture, which Hurstel had unwittingly summed up when writing about the young's attachment to the Avignon Festival:

> More than wanting to see any particular show in the programme, it is this atmosphere of festivity that people come to take part in. This is perhaps an interesting reminder of what a cultural event ought to be: it is a special opportunity for an outing (in the sense of 'coming out of'), an opportunity for encounter and festivity between an artist and a public.[36]

And in the process it was proposing a new paradigm of nationhood, as an 'imagined community' of feeling, a national multiculture in which everyone could do their own thing, but together.

What judgements should we make of this symbolic politics? One criticism commonly heard is that it served as an easy placebo for properly funded grass-roots action to bring music directly and permanently into people's lives. As one dissenter put it in 1991: 'It is not enough to increase the number of Zéniths, or to let rappers or tattooed rockers in studded leather jackets into the corridors of power at the rue de Valois, in order to redress the balance in music.'[37] But the question is more complex than it appears. Such criticisms are always underpinned by a 'common-sense' cynicism about how politics is besmirched by packaging and spin. But there is a case for saying that in contemporary Western politics form and content are never fully distinct. As Street, arguing for an organic connection between politics and popular culture, suggests: 'Political communication [. . .] is not just about conveying information or about persuading people through the force of argument. It is about capturing the popular imagination, about giving acts and ideas symbolic importance. [. . .] techniques of political communication derive from the cultural context and assumptions of their practitioners; these are drawn in part from popular culture.' In a culture of spectacle, politics inevitably becomes, as Street puts it, performance.[38]

But there is a second, possibly more important interpretation of this inter-relation. For if politics is spectacle, spectacle may also be politics. Some apologists for the Ministry speak quite unashamedly of the symbolic nature of Socialist cultural policy, as if important change had been effected simply by the adoption of a different institutional rhetoric, just as it might be argued that France's self-image as an unmusical nation had been formed by an institutional indifference to music. This is clearly how Fleuret saw the significance of the Fête de la musique, which he promoted not as a frivolous gimmick but as a serious political act. In 1985, he wrote that the Fête 'has led to mutual recognition, exchange and collaboration, and has given more encouragement to the much needed cultural departitioning of our society than had ever been done before'.[39] For Jacques Renard too, the rhetoric of legitimation was a form of action, not just words: 'Art needs recognition as much as subsidy. Recognition by the state of hitherto neglected forms of artistic expression is an essential symbolic act which means a great deal to the artists themselves. In recognising, the state confers new dignity.'[40]

Certainly, this sounds like a glib pretext for not putting up more money, but Renard's reasoning carries some conviction none the less, in a country where the Ministry of Culture is the only agency of legitimation other than the market for creative industries like pop. The Lang Ministry saw itself as deploying the discursive power of the state to bring about what Mignon calls a 'dynamic of reclassification',[41] to change *perceptions* of popular music both in France and beyond. Clearly, then, what matters from this perspective is not the success or failure of particular measures but the fact of doing anything at all. Even so, whether one finds this perspective convincing or not, it does not justify making popular-music policies simply the icing on the cake rather than addressing the ongoing issues of the music industry; nor does it preclude evaluation of the policies themselves.

Notes

1. Farchy, *La Fin de l'exception culturelle?*, p. 187. For full analysis of this discursive shift, see Looseley, *The Politics of Fun*, and Urfalino, *L'Invention de la politique culturelle.*
2. 'Jack Lang: "Plus de hiérarchie entre les musiques"', *Le Matin de Paris*, 26 January 1982, p. 31.
3. See the Fleuret text included in Veitl and Duchemin, *Maurice Fleuret*, pp. 347–8; and their commentary, pp. 22–5 and 80–1.
4. Fleuret quoted in Mark Hunter, *Les Jours les plus Lang* (Odile Jacob, 1990), p. 144.
5. Fleuret quoted from a 1984 interview in Veitl and Duchemin, *Maurice Fleuret*, p. 152.
6. Typed transcripts of both of Lang's speeches on his new music policy, in February and June 1982, can be found in the unpublished bound volumes of his speeches available in the documentation centre of the Ministry's Département des études et de la prospective (DEP): vol. I, pp. 201–10 (hand-paginated) (3 February 1982) and 213–22 (16 June 1982).
7. Eling, *The Politics of Cultural Policy*, pp. 136–40. I am indebted to Eling's chapter 'Public Funding of Popular Music', pp. 128–48, throughout this chapter.
8. Ibid., p. 129.

9. Quoted in Veitl and Duchemin, *Maurice Fleuret*, p. 163.

10. Jacques Renard, *L'Élan culturel: la France en mouvement* (Presses Universitaires de France, 1987), p. 165.

11. Teillet, 'Éléments pour une histoire', pp. 371–7. In Teillet's analysis, the professional policy (or 'register', as he calls it) actually includes both an economic 'logic' and an artistic 'logic'. But as he rightly points out, the artistic dimension was largely ignored, leaving the economic in pole position.

12. Fleuret quoted in Veitl and Duchemin, *Maurice Fleuret*, pp. 155 and 84.

13. Reported in Hunter, *Les Jours les plus Lang*, p. 149.

14. Lang's speech at press briefing on music policy, 10 June 1982, transcript in unpublished bound vol. I, p. 221.

15. Renard, *L'Élan culturel*, pp. 171–2.

16. Jean Hurstel, 'Rapport: Jeunesse et action culturelle', unpublished and undated typescript. A revised version of the report was subsequently published by a private publisher, as Jean Hurstel, *Jeunes au bistrot: cultures sur macadam* (Syros, 1984). I shall refer to the unpublished typescript, abbreviated as 'Hurstel report'.

17. Hurstel report, p. 2.

18. Ibid., p. 13.

19. Ibid., pp. 14–20 (quotation p. 14).

20. Ibid., p. 40.

21. I am grateful to Pierre Mayol for drawing my attention to this conflict.

22. The figure of 25,000 groups has become virtually iconic among those calling for state support for them, but it is unreliable. Mayol quotes a possible 35,000 (*La Planète rock*, p. 11), while Teillet cites only 3,000: see 'L'État culturel et les musiques d'aujourd'hui', in Darré (ed.), *Musique et politique*, pp. 111–25 (p. 116). Eling explains how the 25,000 figure came to be accepted with no verification (*The Politics of Cultural Policy*, pp. 203–4, note 25).

23. On the CIR, see Eling, *The Politics of Cultural Policy*, pp. 135–40.

24. Anne-Marie Gourdon, 'Le Rock en France: dix ans de politique culturelle (1981–1991)', in Gourdon (ed.), *Le Rock*, pp. 141–50 (p. 146).

25. On the *cafés-musiques*, see *Lettre d'information*, no. 297 (11 February 1991), p. 5, and no. 336 (26 November 1992), pp. 3–4; also Gourdon, 'Le Rock en France', p. 146.

26. *Lettre d'information*, 11 February 1991, p. 5, and *Le Monde*, 3–4 February 1991, p18; and website: *http://www.le-zenith.com/*.

27. Pascal Sevran, 'A propos de la chanson française' (unpublished document, 1981).

28. Eling, *The Politics of Cultural Policy*, p. 138.

29. *Lettre d'information*, no. 407 (13 March 1996), p. 10.
30. Gourdon, 'Le Rock en France', pp. 146–7.
31. On the FAIR, see ibid., p. 145, and Ministère de la culture, *État et culture: la musique*, p. 115.
32. Jim McGuigan, 'New Labour, Cultural Policy Proper and as Display', unpublished paper read to the Tribunal on Cultural Policy, University of Copenhagen, 20–3 April 1999.
33. Lavilliers quoted in *Paris Match*, 27 June 1986.
34. Mitterrand quoted in Looseley, *The Politics of Fun*, p. 64.
35. On Left intellectuals' reactions to the Socialist victory, see ibid., pp. 83–6.
36. Hurstel report, p. 40.
37. Pierre de Gasquet quoted in Gourdon, 'Le Rock en France', p. 147.
38. Street, pp. 45–60 (quotation pp. 57–8).
39. Quoted in Veitl and Duchemin, *Maurice Fleuret*, p. 161.
40. Renard, *L'Élan culturel*, pp. 52–3.
41. Mignon, 'Évolution de la prise en compte', p. 30.

– 8 –

Policy and the Music Industry at the End of the Millennium

Lang's ten years at the rue de Valois, divided equally by an interlude of Centre-Right government between 1986 and 1988, finally came to a close in 1993. From 1981 to the end of the century, four others occupied the post. Three were on the Centre-Right: the Republican François Léotard (1986–8), the Gaullist Jacques Toubon (1993–5) and the Centrist Philippe Douste-Blazy (1995–7). The fourth, Catherine Trautmann (1997–2000), was in a new Socialist government formed after the Gaullist Jacques Chirac, President from 1995 to 2002, called a snap general election in 1997 which backfired on him.[1] Like Lang, Trautmann made popular music a priority, but also prompted new institutional thinking on the subject. To understand how, we need to review the policies she inherited, assess the Ministry's achievements in the pop sphere between 1981 and 1997, and analyse the state of the music industry in the 1990s. We also need to examine how, on the threshold of the new century, the industry and the policy attempted to move forward.

1981–97: The Policy Assessed

Lang's support for popular music was integral to a comprehensive conception of the Ministry's remit from 1981, summarised in the media as 'everything is cultural' and excoriated by his opponents as shameless vote-catching. Even so, the Centre-Right did not seriously undo his accomplishments in this respect and even seemed to have learnt a trick or two about the politics of display. Between 1986 and 1988, Chirac, Prime Minister during that period, evinced a liking for Madonna and was photographed sitting cross-legged on his lawn in walkman and leisure-wear. The more ascetic Léotard, formerly a Benedictine monk, had greater difficulty looking the part and showed little interest in pop, though he did set up a commission to aid music videos chaired by Johnny Hallyday. He also considered terminating the Fête de la musique, before his advisers hastily persuaded him otherwise.[2] Toubon and Douste-Blazy similarly plumped for continuity in the mid-1990s, despite some gestures to the contrary. A common feature of all three Centre-Right Ministers, however, was a return to the more decorous nomenclature of '*chanson*' as part of a restored focus on heritage. In 1988, Léotard commissioned a report on *chanson*'s inheritance, from which sprang Le Hall de la chanson in 1990, a state-of-the-art centre for preserving and promoting French song, today located in Paris's Parc de la Villette. The Gaullist Toubon, also Minister for *Francophonie* and therefore responsible for language matters, similarly took the long, patrimonial view: '*chanson* envisaged as the primary artistic vehicle for the French language'.[3] This was illustrated in a promotional event, the 'Semaine de la chanson' (Song Week), initiated under Léotard in 1980, relaunched by Toubon in 1994, and extended the following year to cover a whole month of events part-financed by the Ministry. In January 1996, Douste-Blazy also announced new measures for *chanson* based on a report from the singer-songwriter Yves Duteil. Steadily, however, the term *musiques actuelles* (present-day musics) was adopted institutionally, embracing everything from jazz to techno. Thus, when Douste-Blazy continued the 'places' policy with a new type of small live venue to counterbalance the Zéniths, they were called *scènes de musiques actuelles* (SMAC), or present-day music theatres. These successive attempts at naming ('today's musics', 'new musics' and 'amplified musics' had also been tried) bear witness to a continuing institutional uncertainty, particularly on the Right, about exactly what French popular music was and what it ought to be.

Such hesitation seemed to end abruptly, however, whenever the music came under attack. After the National Front took control of Marignane, Orange and Toulon in 1995, pop policy was for a time re-mobilised in a tense ideological struggle over freedom of expression and anti-racism. Minister Douste-Blazy, nicknamed the 'cretin of the Pyrenees' by Le Pen, sided with Gérard Paquet in his conflict with the FN the following year, as did his successor Trautmann; he also supported NTM when the group was sentenced to prison.[4] Toubon's war, on the other hand, was about Americanisation. He and Lang stood shoulder to shoulder in the closing stages of the GATT negotiations of 1993, when the US insisted that European measures against free trade be lifted and France refused to accept that 'culture' (the wrangle was chiefly about film and TV) be treated like any commercial product. The outcome was the omission of culture from the final agreement (leaving World Trade Organisation countries free to make their own arrangements regarding liberalisation) and the foregrounding of the 'cultural exception'. The same defensive mindset led to Toubon's controversial bill the following year banning English terms from public discourse. Even so, neither he nor Douste-Blazy could match the financial support culture received under Lang, for both, like Léotard before them, belonged to governments which reintroduced austerity. Thus, when the

Centre-Right was defeated in 1997 and Catherine Trautmann took over in Lionel Jospin's new PS government, she found an impoverished department and a good deal of resentment from its client groups, though in successive budgets the balance was largely restored.

Measured by what was accomplished rather than the boldness of the undertaking, government policy for popular music from 1981 to 1997 is found wanting in a number of ways, either because cross-departmental co-ordination was missing or because insufficient funding was allocated, even under the spendthrift Lang. In the 1985 budget, the sum of nineteen million francs earmarked for jazz, *chanson* and *variétés* together, was still ten million less than the subsidy to IRCAM alone and just over 2 per cent of Ministry spending on opera.[5] While it may be accepted that popular music is not dependent on state aid for its survival in the way the traditional arts are, the music industry also lagged behind the more comparable cinema industry in terms of aid. One missed opportunity here was the promised reduction of VAT on records, which still stood at 33.3 per cent when Lang left office in 1986, even though in the UK, which had the same population but only 15 per cent VAT, sixty-three million more records were being sold.[6] In addition, the higher price of records in France (caused by a tenfold increase in production costs since the early 1970s, on top of the high VAT) made the average buyer chary of experimental purchasing. Reducing VAT would therefore have been a more productive means of support than subsidy because it would have not only boosted sales but also encouraged new work. But under Lang this line of argument failed to move the Finance Ministry. It was Léotard who finally succeeded, almost halving the rate to 18.6 per cent, though he too failed to convince Finance until the FNAC chain forced the government's hand by refusing to levy the higher rate. Following implementation on 1 December 1987, record sales, down 40 per cent since 1980, rose by 30 per cent in a single year.[7]

This difficulty of persuading other ministries to back cultural-policy initiatives accounts for the minimal progress made on other vital issues, particularly education. True, Lang did make some headway regarding music teaching in schools and in the area of specialist music training and accreditation, where the Ministry had greater power, though change was still very slow. But the promised bill on creative-arts education did not materialise until Léotard pushed one through in January 1988, though even then without the commitment of long-term funding that radical change demanded. Then there was the dissemination of French music on radio and television, criticised by Chapier and a host of others since.[8] Here again, progress under Lang was slow. It was not until 1993 that the 'Pelchat amendment' was adopted in the National Assembly, finally requiring all radio stations to comply with a 40 per cent quota of French music content, of which half had to be 'new talent'. Yet again, though, it was Lang's successors who saw through its phased implementation, between 1 February 1994 and 1 January 1996. Trautmann and her Socialist successor, Catherine Tasca (2000–2), continued to support the quota, since by then the benefits for French music had been confirmed: wider radio programming on the private youth-oriented FM stations like NRJ and Fun Radio (demonstrating to foreign majors that the national repertoire is still a force to be reckoned with); encouragement to 'local' talent; and less record revenue leaving the country.[9] As for television, the Socialists authorised a privately funded music channel, TV6, which began broadcasting in February 1986. The aim was to prioritise French music and boost the domestic pop-video industry, a formula which proved popular but short-lived. To loud protests from the SACEM, top music stars and the channel's young viewers, the new government formed by Chirac in 1986 took away the channel's franchise, which in 1987 was reallocated by the then regulatory body for broadcasting, the CNCL (today the CSA), to a consortium proposing yet another generalist channel, M6, whose music output is significant but necessarily more limited.

Where live music was concerned, progress certainly was made. The Paris Zénith was a positive step, though it was monopolised by big names rather than providing an outlet in the capital for younger or lesser known acts, as originally intended. The 'places' policy similarly bore fruit, with initiatives like the SMACs and the *cafés-musiques*, but it too had its weaknesses. Both Toubon and Douste-Blazy saw pop principally as a tool for tackling social exclusion, urban regeneration and regional development (*l'aménagement du territoire*), at the expense of artistic considerations. At a national conference on 'amplified musics' in 1995, there were criticisms of the *cafés-musiques* particularly in this regard, and warnings that the old municipal discourse which foregrounded community action was no longer appropriate because today's public is more demanding. For Serge Arnaud, formerly of the Ministry's DDF, the core of a cultural youth project should be artistic; the social is merely its consequence.[10]

At the core of pre-1997 policies for popular music was a dual inadequacy. On the one hand, there was a discrepancy between theory and practice regarding amateur music. Lang's initial commitment to cultural development was acted upon in so far as cultural development meant recognising marginalised music activities of all kinds, amateur and professional. But the policy steadily drifted towards the latter, as we saw, with pop conceived as what Frith calls 'an expanding service sector with clear youth opportunities', rather than as a form of creative self-expression for its own sake.[11] On the other hand, this drift towards the professional sector also failed to go far enough. Impelled by the Minister and his staff, the policy was designed with little input from its client group in the early stages, little purchase on music's industrial, commercial and juridical parameters, and, as we have seen, little direct engagement with popular music as a form of artistic creation. This is where much of the interest of the Trautmann Ministry lies.

Of Lang's successors before the end of the century, Trautmann was the most committed to going beyond symbolism. Shortly after taking up her post, she convened a 'National Commission on Present-Day Musics' for the purpose, chaired by the head of the Studio des variétés, Alex Dutilh, who submitted a report on the state of French popular music in September 1998. By then, the policy situation had changed considerably. Although, as we saw, the Lang administration had taken the first policy initiatives for pop and rock alone because, as Eling notes, 'no obvious professional or institutional partners existed',[12] over time this solitary voluntarism did help stimulate demand from the sector: demand for more policy and for more participation in making it. Thus, Trautmann found herself confronted with a better organised, more vocal, more self-aware milieu, as the report's own assertiveness indicates. Dutilh therefore provides a valuable snapshot of a number of elements: the state of the French music industry in the late 1990s, the perceived inadequacies of past policies, and an indication of what industry professionals thought should be done next.[13] He also gives an insight into how the French popular-music world today feels about itself, about the music it produces, and about its relationship with the state.

Policy and the Industry: Looking for a Way Forward

By 1998, the need for a root-and-branch review of this kind was pressing, given that music's industrial and technological contexts were changing and a sense of crisis was again abroad, as Dutilh's analysis illustrates. On the surface, the domestic market looked healthy enough. In 1995, record-buying was well ahead of cinema-going as a proportion of leisure spending, and the annual turnover of the pop industry (7 billion francs in 1998) was three times that of the film industry.[14] In the 1973 survey of cultural practices, only 9 per cent of French people over fifteen listened to recorded music every day, but the figure had risen to 27 per cent by 1997 and a massive 62 per cent for 20–24-year-olds. Even so, this rise in consumption was not reflected in a healthy record industry. The slump in global sales of the late 1970s continued until the arrival of CDs. World sales of CDs then overtook vinyl (LPs and singles) in 1990 and cassettes in 1994. In France, combined sales of albums on vinyl, cassette and CD in 1989 had almost climbed back to the 1978 figure for vinyl and cassette alone.[15] CDs were also creating a substantial new market for compilations and re-releases, as music fans renewed their collections. But the renewal process was always going to be finite and the market grew by only

10 per cent in 1990, 4.3 per cent in 1995, and in 1996 even went down a fraction (by 0.14 per cent).[16] Two government initiatives had played their part in the buying boom: the reduction of VAT and the authorisation of TV advertising for records. Both were implemented during the Léotard interlude and followed by immediate rises in sales.[17] In 1988, Pathé-Marconi advertised a new double CD compilation of Piaf favourites on TF1 in forty twenty-second spots spread over a month. The collection sold over 350,000 copies. Barclay followed, selling 600,000 copies of its double compilation album *Jacques Brel, quinze ans d'amour* (Fifteen Years of Love). There was a downside, though. French independent labels could not hope to compete with this level of expenditure, so it was the majors who mostly benefited from the measure, to the detriment of local new talent. By the mid-1990s, VAT had also become an issue again, with industry pressure to have it reduced further to 5.5 per cent, as for books, though this is now a European Union matter which still has not been resolved.

At a global level, concentration stomped implacably on. The capacity of companies with substantial back catalogues to produce virtually limitless CD compilations and re-releases promised ever richer pickings. From the late 1980s to the end of the century, then, a handful of multinational electronics or media groups bought into record production, music publishing and distribution, becoming massive vertically integrated corporations for the twenty-first century. In 1987, Bertelsmann bought out RCA and formed Bertelsmann Music Group (BMG). The following year Sony acquired CBS, and in 1989 the historic independent labels A&M and Island Records went to Polygram, a subsidiary of Philips. EMI then swallowed Virgin Records in 1992, the only new major for decades. This left five majors in the early 1990s, none of them French: BMG, EMI, Polygram, Sony Music and Warner Music, with a sixth, MCA, owned by the Japanese electronics group Matsushita, coming up behind. Worse still for France, its biggest independent label, Carrère, went to Warner in 1990, as did its classical label Erato in 1992, while its last sizeable independent, the historic Vogue, was bought out by BMG that same year. Having failed to make the first division years ago, France was now having its best players cherry-picked by those who had. But the global musical chairs did not stop there. In 1998, Polygram was sold to the Canadian drinks group Seagram, which had already acquired MCA in 1994 and renamed it Universal. In January 2000, Time Warner, after a takeover bid for the EMI Group which later fell through, clinched a deal with the flourishing Internet service provider AOL, making it the first of the majors to gain a stake in the digital downloading of recorded music on audio files. This worldwide practice – 'piracy' for some, 'free exchange' for others – was threatening to eliminate the need for commercial intermediaries altogether, if MP3 technology and maverick websites like Napster were allowed to go unchecked.[18]

Thanks in part to the success of French techno, exports were looking up by the end of the century, as Catherine Tasca announced with some satisfaction at the 2001 MIDEM: in 1999, more than a third of French albums were sold abroad, mostly in Europe, and still only 10 per cent in the USA.[19] In 1996, world sales reached almost forty billion dollars in retail value (over 230 billion francs). As it had for some years, France came a respectable fifth with a 5.7 per cent share of the world market in 1997, after the USA (31 per cent), Japan (17 per cent), Germany (8 per cent) and the UK (7.3 per cent). But it was also one of the countries where the majors had the highest share of the domestic market, as much as 90 per cent, according to Léotard.[20] The majors are keener to promote their international catalogues in Europe (which have usually broken even in the Anglophone market already) than the work of local artists signed to their French subsidiaries. At the start of the 1970s, the French repertoire's share of the domestic market had stood at around 60 per cent; by 1992, it was under 40 per cent.[21]

As for distribution, the most costly part of the record business, France's share of its own market was even worse. The majors' stranglehold on distribution had been increasing everywhere, but in France it was higher than the international average by the mid-1990s. With most independents forced to contract out, 84 per cent of French distribution went to the top four majors in 1995, as opposed to 64 per cent worldwide. Alongside the high VAT and production costs, this too helped explain the high price of records in France.[22] In 1981, Lang moved swiftly to introduce a minimum retail price for books but did not respond when urged to do the same for records, a missed opportunity regretted by the profession ever since. By 1994, non-specialist outlets like hypermarkets and department stores accounted for some 55 per cent of record sales, an unusually high proportion compared to France's neighbours. Hypermarkets, of course, buy records in bulk, viewing them as loss leaders to attract the young. The sizeable reductions they can therefore offer (30 per cent in some cases) are bad news for the old-style record shops, already hit by competition from giant French or international specialist or semi-specialist chains like Virgin Megastore and FNAC, and by the compilations market, which can damage sales of full albums. Unable to buy in sufficient bulk to compete with the hypermarkets, their number plummeted: from around 3,000 in 1972 to 250 in 1994, while Germany, for example, retained some 9,000.[23] In market terms, this may be a fact of life, but culturally the problem is that hypermarkets keep only limited stock: around 5,000 titles as against the 20,000 stocked by specialist independents. New work by young hopefuls on independent labels therefore suffers when record shops vanish since, if a small town with no FNAC or Virgin Megastore loses its local retailer, consumption is necessarily mediated by what the hypermarkets stock: chiefly well-known artists and releases advertised on television. The town also loses access to the specialist knowledge and services of the retailer, who is often active in local cultural life, selling musical instruments, providing disco services, or as a member of the governing board of a cultural centre.

Broadcasting was still a bone of contention by the time the Dutilh report was drafted. The proliferation of local radio stations after deregulation in the early 1980s has caused a number of problems for the music business as the years have gone by. From small beginnings, the majority have formed nationwide commercial networks like NRJ, or been taken over by existing broadcasters. Many supply chiefly pop and news for the under-25s, such as NRJ, SkyRock and Fun Radio. By churning out Anglo-American hits, they mediate taste and consumption as hypermarkets do and have helped consolidate the majors' dominance. Their ubiquity also makes recorded music more available, without the need to buy, and enhances opportunities for home-taping, which has particularly damaged the singles market. By the early 1990s, some networks, like NRJ, had become involved in record production and some record companies, like CBS-France, had moved into radio, threatening once again to reduce the disinterested exposure of new work. There has therefore been mutual suspicion between record companies and stations, both of them mainstays of the music business which have every reason to remain on good terms. Some stations were also refusing to pay the royalties due to performers and producers under Lang's neighbouring-rights legislation, claiming that they were exorbitant and unfair. Equally problematic was a widespread shift to a 'Top 40' format, and to using panels of sample listeners as a means of matching playlists to audience 'preferences'. This has had the effect of decreasing the number of different titles played per day and increasing the rotation of those that are played, some of which might now be heard ten times a day on the same station. Once again, this reduces the opportunities for new or unfamiliar work to get airplay. Ironically, then, a step designed to adapt output to demand ends up restricting listeners' opportunities as well as damaging the prospects of new artists. The same applies to the growing number of stations playing only oldies, such as Chérie, Europe 2 and Nostalgie, though an added danger here is what has been called an 'impoverishment of memory', since only a limited number of the best-known oldies receive regular airplay.[24]

Yet not all was doom and gloom for radio in the Nineties. The quotas began having a positive impact on sales of French-language music once the CD explosion had passed, because majors based in France began renewing their catalogues by signing up new local acts. Thus, from 1993, the national repertoire's sales began to pick up, overtaking the international in 1995.[25] Inevitably, these changes have also had their fair share of what policy observers call *effets pervers* (unwanted side-effects). The quotas appear to have exacerbated the fall in the number of titles receiving airplay, which went from 48,700 in 1996 to 38,000 in 1997, while the number of artists fell more dramatically still, from 25,000 to 11,000. Most of those who do get exposure are established performers: Patricia Kaas, Mylène Farmer, the eternal Hallyday and, most of all, Goldman, whose recordings were heard on radio no fewer than 28,500 times in 1999, making him the most played artist on radio.[26] National legislation of this kind is also increasingly out of step with technology (from peripheral stations to satellite and the Internet), which is opening up nation-states to outside cultural influences they cannot control.

As for television, the number of hours devoted to music generally was going down by the mid-1990s.[27] Referring to *chanson* specifically, *Chorus* thundered in 2000: 'Television? Its concern for ratings, which leads it to apply the most efficient form of censorship, that of selection by fame (the fame of the artists invited to appear), takes away every shred of cultural credibility it had.'[28] This evolution was taking place despite various obligations regarding cultural content written into charters by the national regulatory body, the CSA, and despite public demand. In a Harris poll of May 1996, 80 per cent of those questioned, across the generations, wanted more music on television, especially concerts by singers and groups.[29]

There are limits to what any culture administration can do about the problems I have outlined, given the web of international, legal, industrial and historical factors beyond its control and because aid to the record industry is more equivocal in its effects than for cinema or books because of the presence of foreign majors. Consequently, apart from discrete initiatives like the Sound Plan or the Labels Plan, the Ministry's efforts by the mid-1990s were largely concentrated on live performance and training. Even here, though, there were conflicts and a degree of incoherence. By 1997, the decision to leave the Fonds de soutien and other fund-holding public bodies largely in the hands of music professionals had produced mixed results. It had allowed Lang's successors to wash their hands of popular music, and had at the same time split the professionals in question into two camps: those from the commercial sharp-end, who served on the various commissions Lang had set up, like the Fonds de soutien, and had become a powerful new bureaucracy; and those who were administrators or activists, like the CIR staff, Dutilh at the Studio des variétés or Yves Bigot, former music journalist and now President of the FAIR, who feared that the Fonds de soutien was manœuvring to take over the FAIR. Another difficulty was that responsibility for the performing arts was split between two directorates: Theatre, and Music and Dance. The *maisons de la culture*, for example, now known as '*scènes nationales*' (national stages) and overseen by the Theatre directorate, could have offered a ready-made network for disseminating live popular music. But their remit since Malraux had been to disseminate the high-brow and they were often run by theatre directors, reluctant to open their programming to popular music other than as a bonus to boost season-ticket sales. One may also account for this kind of tunnel vision by the historical primacy of the written word in France. Farchy interprets the limited aid to the record industry as partly due to a dominant assumption that music is less essential culturally and educationally than literature, as the state-school curriculum attests.[30]

The gravity of the economic situation and the deficiencies of existing policies encouraged the Dutilh report not to mince words. Although the Commission considers 1981 a welcome turning point and applauds Lang's and Fleuret's contributions, it nevertheless arraigns popular-music policy over the last fifteen years, claiming to speak in the name of a strong 'protest movement' among those working in the sector, where the abiding sentiment is of being 'orphans' in comparison to what has been achieved for books and films.[31] This metaphor alone measures the distance the sector had travelled since the launch of the policy, when industry interlocutors had been hard to find; but Dutilh also spells it out by warning of the 'expectations from the whole of the sector with regard to the Ministry of Culture'. Over the last fifteen years, he goes on, the Ministry has been largely indifferent to or ignorant about present-day musics. Funding has been patently inadequate: sixty-seven million francs out of a DMD budget for 1997 of almost two billion, or 3.4 per cent.[32] Policy, poised between the social and the symbolic, has neglected direct aid to artistic creation and has had no overarching vision, so that problems have been treated piecemeal. What Ministry interest there has been has extended only to a few of the more fashionable genres like rock and rap. Like the broadcasting media's abdication of responsibility, this is a mediation which prevents French citizens discovering less mainstream, more inventive, more participative types of popular music. The creative amateur is also neglected, as if people are expected only to want the ready-made.

So what is the material agenda behind such indignation? Crucially, of course, more money: a virtual quintupling of the current sixty-seven million to around 250–300 million, coupled with 5.5 per cent VAT. As Dutilh points out, at the current VAT rate (revised upwards in 1995 to 20.6 per cent, one of the highest in Europe), music is the only arts sector which actually pays into the public purse more than it receives: an incoming 2 billion in VAT in 1997, as against the DMD's outgoings of 1.97 billion. Worse, most of this VAT income is generated by young people, yet almost all is ploughed back into classical music.[33] Beyond these immediate priorities, the report makes proposals for a comprehensive policy under four headings: recognition, proximity, pluralism and restoring the balance (*rééquilibrage*).

On the first of these, the Commission contends that currently present-day musics are in a no man's land between the economic legitimacy accorded other cultural industries and the aesthetic legitimacy of classical and contemporary experimental music. Recognition therefore means accepting their artistic and economic significance – not just their welfare role; and it means acknowledging their diversity – not just chart music but non-commercial forms, musics of social and ethnic groups, amateurs. This will require a formal framework of legislation, professional support services and trained staff. Music tuition in both state education and specialist training must be widened to include popular music, as must public music examinations and the qualifications required of teachers, managers and other mediators involved in training. One important issue raised here, a vexed one with artists' unions, is the need to alter existing employment legislation concerning performers who work only intermittently (*les intermittents du spectacle*), to allow them to teach part-time without losing the unemployment benefits associated with intermittent status. However, the report's appetite for recognition is greater than this. As well as a National Music Centre modelled on the CNC for film, it quite simply wants more of everything: more attention from the national regulatory body for broadcasting (the CSA); more scope for popular music in the *scènes nationales*; more French Music Bureaux abroad; and more recognition for France's latest musical demon, techno. In particular, DJs should be recognised as artist-performers in their own right. As the report's repeated comparisons with books and films suggest, what it is really after is parity and all the financial benefits which come with it.

On the question of proximity, Dutilh calls for the 'places' policy to be extended even further by creating a nationwide network of integrated local resource centres for amateur musicians, bringing together facilities for rehearsal, tuition and advice from trained staff, as well as access to patrimonial resources using new technologies. Government must also do what it did for books in 1981: introduce a single record price to save the local record shop. On pluralism, the Commission outlines a number of factors which are jeopardising popular music's diversity. One of these is that live performance is being replaced by recording as the main form of contact with the public, with touring becoming just a means of plugging a new release. This confronts live-music locations like the SMACs with a moral dilemma. If in the name of diversity they programme artists who are not currently having a record promoted in the media, the cost of promoting the concert falls to them and they risk drawing a smaller crowd because the public's preferences are conditioned by those mainstream artists who are in the public eye. Pluralism also means including amateurs, at least to an extent. One of the report's concerns, for example, is that the regulation of live performance be adjusted to allow amateurs to perform without undercutting professional performers. Yet, here and throughout, pluralism for the Commission seems to be more about professionals. Various forms of support for production are recommended:

aid to the independent artists, publishers and producers involved in mail order and e-commerce; more Ministry money for the Fonds de soutien; state commissions of popular and not just classical work; re-energising the existing bank guarantee scheme, the IFCIC; reviving the aid to independent labels; and further aid modelled on the cinema's 'advance on receipts' and automatic aid systems. It is also the state's job to help circulation. This means regulating a market which is currently at the mercy of unbridled market forces. The government should use all the means at its disposal to prevent FM stations becoming involved in record production. It should reassert a public-service mission for broadcasting, for example by creating a public digital music channel (as had already been done for classical music with Mezzo), and by ensuring that the public channels particularly promote the full range of music. It should also rethink the quota system, because of its unwanted side-effects. Dutilh notes that the CSA currently does not have the means to police the quotas effectively where new work is concerned and therefore calls for the creation of a 'Media and Music' group within the CSA to oversee them. Finally on this issue, he comments that the quotas should be made flexible to allow for stations' individual formats.

As for 'restoring the balance', this seems again to mean achieving parity. The report does, however, admit to there being a dilemma here, in so far as parity would mean present-day musics being undesirably normalised, while remaining outside institutional norms would mean their being 'ghettoised'.[34] Perhaps realising it is on the edge of an abyss, the Commission deftly sidesteps this issue by encouraging articulation between the two 'logics', before moving hastily on to more pragmatic proposals. Particularly serious is the situation of live performance, where there is still a chronic shortage of venues, though it is not more headline-grabbing Zéniths which are needed – since their size means they are not suited to the majority of performers. Instead, the report advocates more medium-sized performance venues and more cash for the struggling SMACs.

Underlying this lengthy shopping list, three related principles can be identified. Surprisingly given the suspicion policy-makers encountered in 1982, one of these is the desirability of formalising, institutionalising and professionalising present-day musics as a route to legitimation. The second is a belief that popular music is a direct responsibility of the state, because it is about neither subversive individualism nor private consumption but conviviality and inclusion. The third principle is that, artistically, popular music is not a case apart: the logic of aesthetic standards and cultural heritage applies as much to popular music as to the other arts and deserves to be addressed by the same means, including aid to creation and preservation. I shall explore these principles further in the following chapter. But what of Trautmann's response to them and to the recommendations they underpin?

Certainly, her response was prompt and mostly positive. At a press conference on 19 October 1998, she was clearly accepting the principle of state responsibility when she expressed her determination to make its recognition a firm, coherent reality this time.[35] She also accepted the Commission's view that in the past state policies had been contradictory. In a speech made before the report's submission, she had stressed by way of justification the enormous difficulty of bringing about such a fundamental attitudinal change with regard to forms operating apparently successfully in a free market. But she had also made it plain that she herself would not use this get-out again, since the state's entire mission is to rectify what the market cannot correct alone.[36] As regards hard cash, a new budget would be set aside spread over three years, beginning in 1999 with thirty-five million francs, a 40 per cent increase.

On the principle of institutionalisation and professionalisation, Trautmann had already been taking steps in the report's direction before its submission. By combining the Music and Theatre directorates as she was in the process of doing, she was making the neglect of present-day musics by the *scènes nationales* easier to deal with. And by drawing up a public-service charter for all publicly funded performing-arts institutions, she was formalising the status and inclusion of new, atypical organisations like the SMACs, whose existence had been improvised rather than properly codified. As regards action to come, there would be particular emphasis on opening up training and diffusion structures to popular music. National music schools and conservatoires would (again) be encouraged to recognise it in the training their staff both offered and received. Popular music was also to be written into all the cultural contracts drawn up between the state and local or regional authorities, and residencies for *chanson* and jazz artists would be developed in arts and music establishments.

However, Trautmann's response to the report also included further consultation, which meant putting several of the report's most radical proposals on hold, including the status of DJs, the creation of a National Music Centre, the hypermarkets issue, popular music on television and the important copyright questions raised by digital reproduction. But she made it clear that she was personally in favour of these proposals and that her draft bill on broadcasting, due shortly, was already addressing several of them. The following June (1999), she convened a special 'États-généraux du disque' (Estates-General of the Record Industry) to take discussion forward. Here, she promised to pursue the reduction of VAT at EU level and proposed a modification (later adopted) of the radio quotas as Dutilh had recommended, which would retain the basic 40 per cent of French-language music but adapt the conditions regulating the promotion of new talent to a station's specific profile.[37] Today, youth stations particularly are able to opt for a 50 per cent quota of French-language music or 'musical forms contributing to musical diversity', of which 35 per cent have to be songs and 25 per cent new talents. The purpose here is to make room for the increasingly successful French techno scene, much of which is instrumental. This acknowledgement of techno, to which I shall return, is the most spectacular measure for popular music of the Trautmann era. That era came to end, however, in April 2000, with many of the issues for further consultation still on hold, though the National Music Centre is to go ahead.[38]

How exactly should Trautmann's response to Dutilh be interpreted? Partly, I suggest, as a genuine determination to move the policy up a gear from symbolism to concrete action, while at the same time recognising the difficulty of producing radical political change. And partly, no doubt, as a desire not to be outstripped by her predecessor Lang, who always seemed to be peering over her shoulder. It was under Lang that the radio quotas had first been mooted which she now had to justify and manage, and it was Lang who had come out in support of the demon techno, to which she could only give her blessing post hoc. Trautmann's stance might also be read as an expedient caving in to what is sometimes represented as the corporatism of the culture professions in France. But her postponing of some of the major measures indicates that she would only go so far down this route. Perhaps too, the postponement indicated a residual resistance to taking legitimation quite as far as the Dutilh Commission was demanding. For the report's third underlying principle identified above – recognition that the same aesthetic and patrimonial issues apply to popular music as to the traditional arts and merit attention on equal terms – was a much bigger question, requiring a truly seismic shift in establishment cultural attitudes. In the remainder of the book, I want to analyse more closely how this question of legitimation, and of resistance to it, has been conceptualised and debated.

Notes

1. The appointment of the Jospin government (1997–2002) marked France's third period of 'cohabitation', the term used when the government is of a different political persuasion from the President. See Chronology for more detail.
2. Reported in Hunter, *Les Jours les plus Lang*, pp. 253–4.
3. Dorian Kelberg, *La Chanson française et les pouvoirs publics* (Presses Universitaires d'Aix-Marseille, 1997), 2 vols, vol. II, p. 617. Much the same phrase was used by Léotard at the press conference (11 December 1986) announcing the first Semaine de la chanson: '*Chanson* is also the primary vehicle of our language.'

4. Reported in *Libération*, 22 June 1995, p. 1. On Paquet and NTM, see Chapter 3.

5. Ministère de la culture, 'Musique': one in a collection of booklets composing 'La Politique culturelle 1981–5: bilan de la législature" [1986?], pp. 13, 17 and 23.

6. Figures cited (from 1985) in François Léotard's review of his two years as Minister of Culture, *Culture: les chemins du printemps* (Albin Michel, 1988), p. 105.

7. On the VAT issue, see ibid., pp. 104–7; Hunter, *Les Jours les plus Lang*, pp. 266–7; and Looseley, *The Politics of Fun*, pp. 178–9.

8. A recent instance is a diatribe by Baptiste Vignol, *Cette Chanson que la télé assassine* (Christian Pirot, 2001).

9. For a discussion of the downside of quotas, see later in this chapter; also Chapter 10, and Keith Negus, *Popular Music in Theory: An Introduction* (Polity Press, 1996), pp. 209–15.

10. Arnaud quoted in anonymous summary of workshop discussion entitled 'Musiques amplifiées et aménagement culturel du territoire', in Adem-Florida (ed.), *Politiques publiques et musiques amplifiées*, pp. 41–3, p. 41.

11. Simon Frith, 'Popular Music and the Local State', in Bennett *et al.* (eds), *Rock and Popular Music*, p. 16.

12. Eling, *The Politics of Cultural Policy*, pp. 136–9 (quotation p. 139).

13. Commission nationale des musiques actuelles, 'Rapport de la Commission nationale des musiques actuelles à Catherine Trautmann', September 1998; consisting of an overarching 'general report' and a number of separate booklets on specific topics by working groups. For brevity, the general report will in future be referred to simply as 'Dutilh report' and the other booklets by their specific titles.

14. '33ᵉ MIDEM: les enjeux technologiques', *Le Monde*, 27 January 1999.

15. Lefeuvre, *Le Producteur de disques*, pp. 21 and 31.

16. Ibid., p. 31–2. The negative result in 1996 proved to be something of a blip, with a healthier rise of 7 per cent in 1997: ibid.

17. Ibid., p. 28. Sales were up 35 per cent in 1988 and 29 per cent in 1989.

18. Napster was neutered as an illegal site but others have sprung up in its place. In the first half of 2002, figures showed a drop in world record sales for the second year running, widely interpreted as the result of downloading and CD writers.

19. *Lettre d'information*, 30 January 2001, p. 7.

20. Lefeuvre, *Le Producteur de disques*, p. 22; Léotard, *Culture*, p. 105.

21. Lefeuvre, *Le Producteur de disques*, pp. 42–3.

22. Farchy, *La Fin de l'exception culturelle?*, pp. 59 and 78. These figures tend to vary from source to source but are roughly confirmed by the Dutilh report, p. 144.

23. Farchy, *La Fin de l'exception culturelle?*, pp. 61 and 79.

24. See *Le Monde*, 3 January 1990 and 15 February 1990, p. 14. For closer analysis of private radio, see Raymond Kuhn, *The Media in France* (Routledge, 1995), Chapter 3.

25. In 1999, 54 per cent of the total turnover from music (including 115 million albums and 36 million CD singles) was from French *variétés*, an increase of more than 5 per cent over the previous year, followed by 'international *variétés*' at 39 per cent, down by 9 per cent. All figures are from Lefeuvre, *Le Producteur de disques*, pp. 34 and 42–3; and Véronique Mortaigne 'L'Industrie française du disque en recul en 1999', *Le Monde*, 24 January 2000.

26. Dutilh report, p. 44, and two *Le Monde* articles by Véronique Mortaigne: 'Les Couacs de la chanson française', 2 August 1997, pp. 1 and 10; and 'L'Industrie française du disque en recul'.

27. On M6, music accounted for 42.3 per cent of programming in 1993 but just over 36 per cent by 1997. That same year, the privatised channel TF1's music programming stood at only 8.7 per cent, and even the public channel France 2 had reduced it slightly, from 17 per cent to 15.5 per cent. Dutilh report, group no. 4: 'La Gestion de carrière', p. 146.

28. 'Le Grand Forum de l'an 2000', *Chorus*, p. 73.

29. D'Angelo, *Socio-économie de la musique*, p. 80.

30. Farchy, *La Fin de l'exception culturelle?*, p. 190. My analysis in this paragraph also draws substantially on Mortaigne, 'Les Couacs'.

31. Dutilh report, p. 14.

32. Ibid, pp. 14 and 20 (quotation p. 14).

33. Ibid., pp. 20–1.

34. Ibid., p. 49.

35. 'Action and development plan for present-day musics', transcript downloaded from Ministry of Culture website.

36. 'Des Mesures pour les musiques actuelles', 19e Rencontres des Trans-musicales de Rennes, undated [January 1998] (downloaded).

37. 'Les États-généraux du disque', supplement to *Lettre d'information*, no. 52 (new series) (21 July 1999), p. 9.

38. The new body, called the Centre national de la chanson, des variétés et du jazz, will take over the role of the Fonds de soutien.

– 9 –

Policy and Its Discontents: The Republican Debate

The term 'culture' has been at the heart of intellectual controversy in France since at least the First World War. But since 1959, and especially since 1981, the controversy has acquired a new twist and a new intensity due to the existence of a national cultural policy. Schematically, this policy has been argued over in two ways. On the one hand, it has generated anxieties about aesthetic relativism and the destiny of French culture in a globalised world. On the other, it has given rise to the theoretical conflict underlying policy which I sketched in Chapter 6, between cultural democratisation and cultural democracy.[1] I want to begin by analysing insider representations of Lang's policy agenda, against which other positions can then be situated. Lang's own ministerial discourse was notoriously effusive and polysemous, but a fuller (though still not entirely limpid) theorisation came post hoc in *L'Élan culturel* (Cultural Momentum), a book written at the end of his first term by his close collaborator and virtual amanuensis, Jacques Renard.

Renard describes jazz, *chanson*, *variétés* and rock as 'forms of artistic expression which are popular par excellence and permeate daily life'. It is this everyday quality, he argues, which has excluded them from the pantheon of legitimate arts because of 'a narrow and elitist conception of culture'.[2] There are echoes here of Certeau's 'culture in the plural' and 'the practice of everyday life', but there is also a faintly Bourdieusian argument that prior to 1981 ministerial recognition was a 'distinctive' strategy, classing bourgeois cultural practices as legitimate and others as barbaric. By contrast, the Lang approach, Renard goes on, was to regard *any* type of creative production, including those we encounter every day, like cookery or fashion, comic strips or pop, as qualifying, potentially at least, for admission to the pantheon:

> There is an act of creation in designing a dress as in writing for the theatre, in composing a new recipe as in architecture. Moreover, French creators, in both fashion and cookery, are internationally recognised, contribute to our country's prestige abroad [*rayonnement*], and drive economic activities whose vitality is

undeniable and highly exportable. So it was unfair for them to remain excluded from cultural life.

No fashion style or recipe is created, he goes on, 'without reflecting in some way the state of a society, its currents of opinion, its mode of social organisation. In this sense too, fashion and cuisine are bearers of culture.'[3]

These assertions can be seen as premised upon a system of value that justifies inclusiveness. In the name of democracy, artefacts deserve ministerial assistance if they involve genuine creativity (an 'act of creation' is left undefined but one assumes it means originality), reflect contemporary society, and induce in the public some form of identification or engagement. These three values effectively replace the traditional gold-standard for selective admission to the canon, which was aesthetic worth as defined by the academies, the universities and other teaching establishments, the specialist press; in short, the bourgeoisie. But Renard slips in a fourth value of a quite different kind: the economic. Fashion and cuisine are represented not just as *equally* creative but as having *added* value ('moreover') because they improve the balance of trade and France's standing abroad. This double legitimation begs a number of questions and is misleading to say the least. Ostensibly setting wider parameters for ministerial recognition, in effect it narrows them again by making the arts which are *already* recognised but vulnerable economically (such as theatre) look like freeloaders.

Behind this sleight of hand is a standard problem for any cultural policy in advanced capitalist economies. Rhetoric aside, any commitment of public funds will require some form of palpable return. Economic benefits and popularity are therefore more palatable justifications of expenditure than art for art's sake or the liberal-humanist conviction that the arts contribute to moral progress, both of which look threadbare in an age when anti-elitism is indistinguishable from anti-intellectualism. Rightly or wrongly, the new Ministry discourse illustrated by Renard looked to some like a brash new attempt to justify state intervention in economic and populist terms. It prompted an intellectual backlash against Lang at the centre of which was pop (much more than fashion or cookery, which could at least be thought of as authentically French). The central issue was the nature of cultural democracy, which led broadly to two kinds of polemics. There were those who objected to mass culture being placed on 'equal' terms with high culture by state intervention (even though this was far from the case in budgetary terms); and those, like the Dutilh Commission, who were in favour of legitimation but challenged the Ministry's way of going about it, calling for more intervention, not less. As so often in French cultural affairs, however, the issues went deeper than this, concerning cherished assumptions about the place of culture in contemporary society and national identity. By the late 1980s, youth music, although ostensibly more accepted than in the early 1960s, became the cradle of such debate, implicated once again in a moral panic in which France's cultural traditions and republican identity were at stake.

Lang's main intellectual opponents were the philosopher and scholar Alain Finkielkraut in *The Undoing of Thought* (*La Défaite de la pensée*, 1987), and a respected art historian at the Collège de France, Marc Fumaroli, in a dazzling but opinionated pamphlet *L'État culturel* (The Cultural State, 1991). Both thoroughly disapprove of Lang's anything-goes doctrine and use it as a platform for a tirade against post-modernity in the name of their respective conceptions of culture and its relation to nationhood. Each reveals an aversion to pop, at least in so far as it lays claim to be cultural, for each believes that only a studious grappling with the timeless aesthetic and intellectual values sanctioned by the Western humanist tradition is culture in the true sense. It is true that Fumaroli himself speaks affectionately of France's own popular traditions, of light or comic operas of the *belle époque*, which at least had the advantage of 'serving the national language well and reinforcing its natural function as a common link between French people'; or of the equally authentic *chansons* of Piaf and Chevalier, who, he insists, were as capable of evoking the great 'commonplaces' of the human condition as was Joyce or Proust.[4] By contrast, pop is plainly an alien travesty: 'France, before adopting social and moral stereotypes invented in Greenwich Village, before dressing in jeans and going deaf and dumb by dancing to a torrent of rock sound, had once been capable of dressing to suit its own taste and of understanding and feeling the words of its own songs as it sang them.' French 'rap culture', which Lang is accused of prescribing to schoolchildren, receives an even worse thrashing, for being 'imported from districts of the New World which have returned to the wild' and a product of 'the servile imitation in France of one of the latest showbiz inventions'.[5] Half-submerged in this splenetic nostalgia is a moral theory of authenticity, which seems to count more for Fumaroli, at least where *popular* culture is concerned, than an aesthetic theory. That which is imported and manufactured is fake, while that which filters the universal 'commonplaces' through a national language and tradition is genuine, whether highbrow or low. But it is hard to resist the conclusion that this moral hierarchy rests on an essentialism of taste which in reality *segregates* high culture from the 'medium and popular taste which truly suited the majority'.[6]

Fumaroli defends republican nationhood in the face of undiscriminating Americanisation. This is true of Finkielkraut too, though unlike Fumaroli he appears to have no objection to cultural policy as a vehicle for this defence. On the contrary, his position on mass culture reprises Malraux's Adornian critique, to whose Ministry he alludes sympathetically.[7] Taking issue explicitly with Lipovetsky and Yonnet (see Chapter 5), he deplores the post-modern confusion between culture as 'life with thought' – that which is aesthetically or intellectually demanding and improving – and the anthropological interpretation which treats it as the customs, habits, ways of life, and entertainments of social groups. He is especially worried by youth culture, which he sees as the epitome of the instant, mass-cultural experience. Youth culture, he argues, is in fact at the root of a crisis in contemporary republican education in which the values of post-Enlightenment modernity that underpin state education are being eroded. The problem is that the education system is modern but the pupils in it are post-modern. For them, culture is no longer a way of achieving human emancipation but an obstacle to it: 'Within such a [post-modern] perspective, individuals will have taken a decisive step towards maturity when intellectual activity ceases to be a supreme value and becomes as optional (and is accorded the same legitimacy) as betting or rock'n'roll. To enter the age of autonomy properly, we must transform all the *obligations* of the authoritarian age into *options*.'[8]

One simple 'answer' to the education crisis, then – which Finkielkraut sincerely hopes we will reject – would be to bring education closer to consumption and 'teach youth to the young', as apparently happens in American schools, where pop and computer games are used to help pupils learn. But in his view such techniques infantilise learning rather than educating the young to think. Another illustration of such reductionism is the glib collaboration between pop and humanitarian aid in such events as Live Aid in 1985. Here, Finkielkraut maintains, mounting a televised spectacle showing celebrity hearts bleeding for starving children merely distracted those involved from a more serious assessment of how to stop the money collected being hijacked in Ethiopia for political ends.[9] All the same, young people's regression as a result of pop culture would be harmless, he goes on, if youth had not now become a model for the whole of society, causing a nation-wide 'de-intellectualisation', a dumbing down. By such means is thought defeated.

Especially eloquent is Finkielkraut's recourse to pop when he needs a commonly agreed benchmark of cultural decadence. Bob Marley is evoked alongside Beethoven or Renaud alongside Rimbaud as a provocation, to make us concede at once that equating high and popular cultures, as he accuses post-modernity of doing, is patently absurd. This suggests an unexamined faith in high culture as intellectual emancipation, in the need to *reason* our way to self-realisation. Pop culture, he believes – and he is undoubtedly correct in one sense – is based on the very opposite principle. It implies that emancipation and self-realisation are achieved only by *letting go* of reason, as soon as we release the Dionysian within and start to party. On this issue, Finkielkraut tackles Yonnet head-on by quoting the following passage from *Jeux, modes et masses*:

– 170 –

The best illustration of this is the distinctive communication system, which is highly autonomous and for the most part cryptic, expressed through rock culture, in which *feeling* counts more than words, sensation more than the abstractions of language, atmosphere more than actual meanings or rational discourse. All this is alien to the traditional criteria of Western communication. [. . .] *Guitars are more expressive than words, which are old (they have a history) and not to be trusted.*[10]

Finkielkraut then analyses this quotation:

One thing at least is clear. Founded as it is on words, culture in the classical sense has [for Yonnet] the double drawback that it both *ages* people by giving them a memory which exceeds that of their own biography, and also *isolates* them by forcing them to say 'I', that is, to exist as distinct individuals. By destroying language, rock music gets rid of this double curse. The guitars abolish memory, the unifying warmth [*la chaleur fusionnelle*] replaces conversation, that relationship between separated beings: the 'I' dissolves ecstatically into the Youth [*extatiquement, le 'je' se dissout dans le Jeune*].[11]

The pop experience, then, creates an intellectual meltdown which negates individual consciousness, furnishing the pleasurable sensation of losing oneself in a crowd. What worries Finkielkraut about this is that the element of bookishness, of solitary, intellectual engagement with words, has been excised. Youth culture is an 'anti-school', as he puts it: it is anti-reason and anti-word. Today's cultural crisis is ultimately a conflict between 'higher thought' and 'vibration', that is, between words and dance, reason and frenzy, cerebration and palpitation.

As with *chanson* discourse premised on the same dichotomies, this is where the question of nation arises, which preoccupies Finkielkraut throughout. He defines nationhood in the rationalist terminology of the Revolution (specifically Sièyes), cornerstone of French republicanism. Rather than being the political manifestation of the German Romantic idea of *Volksgeist*, the innate spirit of a people which *determines* nationhood, a nation is a 'free and voluntary association' between consenting individuals who contract to live together under the same laws.[12] French culture and the French education system are expressions of this model and its guarantors since, like the original contract, they deracinate individuals, freeing them from their origins, defining them by their humanity not their birth. Finkielkraut's deepest fear about contemporary youth culture is that it corrupts this free association by restoring a variant of the deterministic *Volksgeist*, though a globalised rather than national one, that of Youth itself. Premised on anti-intellectual frenzy and emotional intensity, on a sense of belonging to Morin's 'age-class' and a commodification generated by the global economy, youth culture is damaging the intellectual and moral autonomy which French culture and education seek to nurture in the young, the autonomy which should allow them to transcend the 'we' of the *copains* and say: 'I'm twenty, that's my age, it's not my being.' The kind of liberation youth culture provides is too easy, too available, and too conformist, whereas for Finkielkraut 'there is no autonomy without thought, and no thought without work on oneself'.[13]

Both Finkielkraut's and Fumaroli's books are polemical essays and as such have weaknesses which undermine their unfashionable but often probing questions about what contemporary culture means and how classical culture will survive in an age of commodified leisure. In attempting to find answers, both books make unchallenged assumptions about nationhood, European civilisation and aesthetic judgement which one critic calls a 'barrage of elitist, ethnocentric and unreconstructed-humanist pronouncements'.[14] Furthermore, both are closed to the analytical models used in reception studies of the kind studied in Chapter 5. But whatever their worth, their arguments are emblematic of an orthodox cultural republicanism as it tries to come to terms with global pop culture. They are late twentieth-century configurations of the difficulty France's print culture has had with the non-verbal, anti-Cartesian, Romantic nature of Anglo-American pop, and of the tendency we have already encountered to construe authenticity in national terms.

One effect of the ideological nature of these debates is that the opportunity for a more rounded intellectual critique of public culture is missed. Neither author addresses the Ministry's own denials of being relativist: for example, Fleuret's insistence that there is a self-evident difference between asserting that all musics are equally deserving of aid and that they are equal aesthetically, a matter not for the Ministry to resolve.[15] Nor is the need for a cultural-development strategy, which Fleuret's view implies, properly tackled, since Fumaroli and Finkielkraut are arguing only on behalf of ready-made high culture. But two other contributors to the debates of the 1980s and 1990s sought not to avoid such questions, having both been cultural administrators themselves: one was Michel Schneider, a successor of Fleuret at the DMD; the other was Jacques Rigaud, chief adviser to Culture Minister Jacques Duhamel in the early 1970s. Neither is the polar opposite of Finkielkraut and Fumaroli, but having been in the thick of policy-making, both recognise the empirical complexities behind the question of cultural democracy.

Director of Music from 1988 until his stormy resignation in 1991, Schneider developed an approach to music policy that was the antithesis of Lang's, and his book on the subject, *La Comédie de la culture* (The Farce of Culture, 1993), oozes rancour. He detests the phoney 'libertarian democratism' of the everything-is-cultural discourse, which effectively allows the educated elite to have high culture all to themselves since nobody bothers to democratise it any more, now that pop culture and light entertainment have been upgraded: 'We mustn't ruin the native creativity of the dominated with our bourgeois culture, which smells a bit of old age', Schneider ironises. 'We'll just call it all "tag revolution" or "youth culture".'[16] He has no objection to rock and rap being used in a welfare policy; and he accepts that hip-hop, like rock, is a form of social expression, though he cannot resist calling it 'that inarticulate violence'. But what he cannot accept is the 'epistemological leap' which allows a form of 'social expression' to become a form of art. That is simply a ploy to justify the Ministry's politically motivated, tokenist interest in youth.[17]

In this part of his analysis, Schneider comes surprisingly close to Finkielkraut and Fumaroli, though he is critical of both. He identifies the real culprit as the Leftist relativism encouraged by intellectuals like Sartre, Foucault and Bourdieu, who persuaded educators that high culture was a way for the dominant class to achieve distinction and reproduce, not a means of universal emancipation. Even so, he is not an absolutist either but holds rather to what he calls a 'relative relativism'. Although pop is not generally as aesthetically rich as jazz or classical, some of it (Jimi Hendrix, for example) can be richer than some jazz or some classical. Again, though, rap seems to try this indulgence severely, for only through gritted teeth can Schneider admit that everyone is free to prefer 'the sexist and anti-Semitic eructations of Public Enemy to a Haydn quartet'.[18] Citing the state's recent aid (through the FAIR scheme) to 'a group of rappers answering to the charming name of Motherfuckers [NTM]', he pities what he evidently sees as such benighted young performers:

> Are not these young people, who are excluded from everything, from the community and civility, from work and leisure, from consumption and production, suffering above all, though they are unable to say it or even think it, from being excluded from knowledge, key to all the other forms of exclusion? [. . .] Is this not a double form of disdain: disdain for culture which is reduced to vulgarity and ugliness, and disdain for these young people who are made to believe that what they are doing is art? This is not what the young of the suburbs, of which they [NTM] are supposed to represent hip-hop's cultural avant-garde, are asking for. Without doubt, they could listen to a different kind of music if there were a different kind of schooling.[19]

This is the book's keynote. The state's job is not casuistically to move goalposts but to tackle social exclusion head-on, via a reassertion of the true values of republican education. A century ago, Schneider reminisces, the Republic said to the children of the excluded: 'there is a great culture and you have a right to it, through schooling'. This aspiration may have failed, he concedes, but we should at least continue to try, by means of a policy of 'reducing the inequalities of access to real culture, and particularly to culture which demands the most effort, that which is not borne by spontaneous market forces but counteracted by them, and which requires apprenticeship and mediation'.[20] Musical democracy can only mean an education in the difficult understanding of high music, not *fêtes de la musique* or state aid for passing fads. For Schneider as for Mayol, assuming that rap is young people's 'natural' language and meets all their musical needs is reductive. Indeed, in a critique of the assumed affinity between rock, rap and France's troubled suburbs which informs much 'social insertion' work with young people, Mayol himself recalls an illuminating incident when a young man of North African descent from the suburb of Les Minguettes near Lyons, on the receiving end of just such an assumption, asked Mayol bluntly: 'So why shouldn't I have a right to Chopin like everyone else?' Mayol comments: 'It's true that we had internalised the connection between rock and the suburbs. These young people were thus confined to a rock aesthetic, in the same way as people are now trying to confine them to a rap aesthetic.'[21]

Inevitably given this critique, Schneider's main recommendation is a reformed and properly funded creative-arts curriculum in schools. This does not mean encouraging artistic creativity in all – which he describes as a flattering myth – but providing an education in understanding existing works. He therefore remains dedicated to Malraux's notion of democratisation, though unlike Malraux he knows this must entail mediation, or 'instruction'. He does not spurn Fleuret's ideal of *making* music; it is just that education is indispensable here too. The conclusion he draws from all this is as dramatic as Fumaroli's. For both, the Ministry of Culture should be demoted or preferably dismantled. The state has no business involving itself in creation in any form, high or popular, and those tasks which do legitimately fall to it – preservation, reducing inequality, regulation – could easily be farmed out to other ministries.[22]

Schneider's position is not dissimilar in some respects to that of Jacques Rigaud, who has written a number of clear-sighted works on cultural policy since the 1970s, notably *Libre Culture* (Free Culture, 1990), *L'Exception culturelle* (The Cultural Exception, 1995) and a report he drafted as Chair of the Commission for the Study of State Cultural Policy, convened at the behest of Douste-Blazy in 1996. With Duhamel, Rigaud was one of the architects of the alternative policies for cultural development sketched in Chapter 6. One difference, therefore, between him and Schneider is that he firmly believes that the Ministry still serves a purpose, even though it needs downsizing. And as his report argues, that purpose is to implement an updated cultural-development strategy. He is also more successful than Schneider at setting aside his own high-cultural tastes in order to make room for youthful alternatives, however disconcerting they may be. Like Schneider, Rigaud has a healthy scepticism about the idea that everything is cultural, which, on its own, is not what he means by cultural development. Yet, he is less willing than Schneider to assume that youth culture is just 'social expression', of little cultural significance. It has crossed national, ethnic and class barriers, representing 'freedom and modernity' for those deprived of them, and expressing 'the sensibility of several generations'. Who are we, as adults, to deny the intensity some young people experience watching Madonna; or that of the young East Germans whose thirst for freedom just before the Berlin Wall came down was translated into a desire to see David Bowie and Genesis on the other side?[23] All the same, Rigaud is not entirely comfortable with youth culture. Like Mayol and Schneider, he will not accept that pop is automatically the authentic culture of the young since, as the young man of Les Minguettes had implied, such a view runs the risk of never allowing them to glimpse alternatives.

In *L'Exception culturelle* and his report, Rigaud works hard to maintain his optimism about contemporary youth, though he has to confess to finding it 'almost an enigma'.[24] He worries that the current generation may already be cut off from adults by the information revolution it has lived through. Since time immemorial, successive generations of French people have been exposed to Christian and republican-humanist values, but this is no longer the case. Today, even the class of 1968, which supposedly repudiated those values, has more in common culturally with its elders than with its children. In saying this, Rigaud is at pains not to condemn or speak of dumbing down, as Finkielkraut does. But he plainly fears that youth taste rests on a wholesale rejection of traditional culture. If so, if the young really have developed their own codes in isolation from the established references and practices of Western civilisation, what will become of those references and practices? Will they not slip quietly into oblivion as new generations come and go? And if so, will we not be responsible for condemning future generations to a single, mass-cultural model of aesthetic experience for ever? Rigaud rather too conveniently leaves this question open. Nevertheless, if one reads between the lines of his writings, an answer does emerge. Cultural democracy means democratisation combined with cultural development and must not mean avoiding judgements of value. Agreed aesthetic standards must be applied to *all* forms of creative activity, popular or high, amateur or professional: 'giving up all distinctions would amount to dissolving culture in entertainment, and would make cultural action lose its ambition by stripping it of references and exacting standards [*exigence*]'.[25] Any form of public intervention, whether it concerns an amateur rock band or a top symphony orchestra, must discriminate aesthetically. If this is done, the young person's engagement in a cultural activity, however crude or unconventional, may lead seamlessly into the appreciation of high culture.[26]

Behind this insistence on aesthetic excellence is an essentially political preoccupation, as indicated in the report's invocation of Renan, whose lecture

– 175 –

'What is a Nation?' ('Qu'est-ce qu'une nation?', 1882) is also one of Finkielkraut's sources. Rigaud writes: 'Renan used to say that the nation originates
in a shared feeling of having done great things together and of wanting to do
still more. Culture, principal repository of the heritage of the past and of the
concrete or poetic imagining of projects for the future, is a decisive factor in
the identity and solidarity which constitute the nation.'[27] Cultural democracy,
then, is not just about the personal right to aesthetic enjoyment, it would seem.
It is about empowering individuals through culture and, thereby, benefiting
the nation. The personal in fact *becomes* political in the notion of citizenship,
for the wholeness, the authenticity which comes when individuals fulfil their
creative potential produces active participants in society:

> Through education and culture, each individual must be given ownership of the
> keys which will allow him [*sic*] to understand the world and act upon it. Which
> implies, in the strongest sense, a **political will**. [. . .] The aim of cultural policy is
> to realise the Republic, that is, to give *everyone*, through genuinely equal access to
> the works of the spirit, the chance to develop an awareness of being a citizen [*une
> conscience citoyenne*] in the fullest sense.[28]

Thus, despite their diverging views on mass culture's worth, Rigaud at least
shares with Finkielkraut and Fumaroli a belief in the relationship between
cultural aspiration and nationhood.

One of the more entertaining aspects of these debates is that they are about
people as well as principle. Fumaroli, Finkielkraut and Schneider denounce
Lang for asserting that everything is cultural. Rigaud satirises Fumaroli for
being a cultural Jansenist, though Fumaroli had already lampooned Rigaud
for being a cultural technocrat. Meanwhile, Schneider castigates both Fumaroli
and Finkielkraut for being reactionary; and all of them deride Bourdieu for
being a sociologist. But a more serious effect of the rough and tumble is to
obscure practical issues about what exactly a policy for pop should look like
once it is accepted that there should be one. As we have seen, it was not until
the Dutilh report that these issues were properly addressed, revealing a different
kind of debate altogether: about whether a policy for popular music should
be social, economic or aesthetic. And yet beneath this much more empirical
issue lie the same core republican values advocated by the other protagonists,
though the report's take on those values is unusual.

From the outset, the report mounts a spirited defence of present-day musics
using the four headings I outlined in the previous chapter: recognition,
proximity, pluralism, and restoring the balance. Of these, recognition is arguably
the most significant because of what it reveals about French music's self-image
with regard to the state at the turn of the twenty-first century. Above all, we

are told, present-day musics are deserving of recognition because they are 'authentic', which for once is defined, albeit rather flatulently. Their authenticity derives from their being of the people – 'popular musics in the most noble sense of the term' – rather than being confined to an elite. But this clearly does not make them closed or static for they are also important educationally or developmentally. They 'speak "of" the world and "to" the world' and in so doing can, as Rigaud also suggests, open the way to an appreciation of 'all the other forms of art'. If this value were properly recognised, the report continues, present-day musics could play a full, catalysing role in the wider community, because they offer 'a civically aware response [*une réponse citoyenne*] to many of the ills which fracture our society'.[29] Economically, they can generate employment and wealth, while culturally, it would seem, authenticity can have a therapeutic effect on an ailing sense of nationhood at home and abroad:

> At a time when our points of reference are dissolving at the speed of sound, our musics also carry meaning and form a collective memory and a heritage in perpetual motion. And with the logic of unstoppable globalisation before us, a whole host of French artists are capable of making the entirely legitimate song of our cultural exception reverberate beyond our expanding borders.[30]

Underlying this conviction is the premise that the chief danger from the global music industry is not standardisation, as Adorno would have us believe, but its opposite: the social fragmentation of taste brought about by market segmentation, new domestic technologies like the Internet, and the drift of post-industrial societies towards what Lipovetsky calls personalisation, a new individualism which the Commission obviously holds to be damaging to French society's collective existence. One conclusion it draws from this is that rolling back taste horizons – 'encouraging the discovery by audiences of musics or forms of artistic expression which are not among their usual references' – is a duty of the state and publicly funded institutions. Why? Because by so doing the state will be 'encouraging social cross-fertilisations, the emergence of new solidarities, and, through musical mediation, the recognition of Alterity'.[31] From this flows the need to free popular music from purely commercial imperatives, just as Malraux attempted to do with high culture. This is again a matter of 'restoring the balance' between public and private sectors.

This points to what is perhaps the cardinal vindication of pop in the report. Present-day musics are painstakingly situated within the perennial value system which has justified public support for the arts generally in France, including direct aid to creation. Although the Commission details at length pop's material benefits, at the deepest level its rhetoric is not economic but appeals to the republican values of disinterestedness and national continuity enshrined in the notion of a national heritage. This rhetoric can be seen at work beneath its terse objections to the term 'present-day musics' imposed upon it. Its complaint is that the term conditions the way the musics concerned are conceptualised and risks perpetuating prejudice about them. It constructs them as rootless commodities in thrall to the ephemeral present of fashion, social trends and the market. Even when recognised by the state, the emphasis, as we saw in Chapter 7, has been on their value as a social phenomenon, of interest chiefly to those working with deprived communities. But such narrow, social and economic representations ignore 'the multiple ties [they] have with the cultural and social history of our country'. This is where the idea of a 'heritage in perpetual motion' comes in, for these musics are not the product of spont-aneous generation. If they are fully of their time, we are told, it is because they also remember: 'from IAM to Louise Attaque or Julien Lourau, what we listen to today comes as much from Jacques Brel and Boris Vian as from Damia or Émile Vacher'. This '"active" memory' permanently updating the past is seen as creating and enriching cultural identity.[32]

These are loaded, encoded references, understood by the insider as a gambit to earn a place at table. Thus rooted in a national popular-musical heritage which itself is constructed as harking back to the troubadours and the mists of time, pop is released from the present so it can join the immortals of classical French culture: 'Independently of their considerable economic and social importance, present-day musics represent a fully fledged sector of the arts. Humanist values are one of their central features: developing sensitivity, creativity and memory, emphasising subjectivity and difference.'[33] If these are not terms the average English speaker might naturally think of to describe pop, it is arguably because they draw on a republican lexicon peculiar to the business of cultural legitimation in France. With consummate skill, the report in fact controverts the negative implications of the word 'actuelles' (present-day) and thereby answers the attacks of high-culturalists like Finkielkraut, for whom guitars abolish memory. Pop is in fact shown to enshrine precisely those values of humanism, universalism and national memory which Finkielkraut and Fumaroli believe that only *real* French culture enshrines and that youth culture undermines.

By far the richest section of the report is the one produced by the 'Publics' group, which in practice was written by one person, Philippe Teillet. Teillet's analysis is of particular interest because of his unusual vantage-point as both a political scientist who has researched pop policy for some years, and a pop activist, President of the Chabada in Angers, a SMAC comprising performance and rehearsal facilities. This enables him to provide a unique perspective on pop and a useful corrective to the polemics of Finkielkraut and Fumaroli. Like Rigaud, one of his main preoccupations is the articulation of democratisation with cultural democracy.

– 178 –

One of the subtexts of the 'Publics' section is that with popular music the conflicting imperatives of cultural democracy and democratisation need to be resolved.[34] Teillet particularly presses the point that where present-day musics are concerned these two must not be seen as mutually exclusive. A specificity of present-day musics is their vitality and diversity. Unlike the other performing arts, they are not produced solely by professional institutions but also emanate from a multitude of more amorphous sources and situations. The title 'pop musician' does not only imply a qualified professional but can also include various types of amateur; and often the same obstacles are encountered by amateurs and professionals alike: access to rehearsal space, cost of instruments, and so on. Nor is there a clear divide between spectators and musicians, Teillet maintains, since the latter make up a comparatively larger number of the former than in other arts. This rich humus of mutual influence and exchange is what makes popular music so distinctive and it needs to be preserved and allowed to grow richer still. For Teillet, this is a cultural-democracy objective, to do with encouraging diversity and creativity. However, this alone is not enough, in his view, for there is also the question of access to the *products* of such creativity. The idea that pop is fully or equally accessible by nature, simply because it is 'popular' in the sense of widely enjoyed, is a myth. He especially takes issue with the implication (in Fumaroli, for example) that tastes are natural rather than socially conditioned. As the Ministry surveys of cultural practices show, access to pop is in reality shaped by social, economic, geographic and gender variables. Those musics which *spontaneously* reach a diverse audience are relatively few, Teillet insists, and they usually do so only in recorded rather than live form. The undesirable segmentation of national taste referred to earlier is particularly prevalent in the less advantaged social groups, while eclecticism is much commoner in the more advantaged. Conversely, the kind of exclusively high-cultural taste (characteristic of the likes of Finkielkraut and Fumaroli) which allows distinctions to be confidently drawn between culture and entertainment is, for Teillet as for Bourdieu, based upon 'forms of social domination and arbitrary aesthetic choices long considered to be natural'.[35]

What Teillet calls for, then, in a deliberate tautology is the popularisation of a popular form. Cultural democracy needs to be complemented by a policy of democratisation, of the kind already common in other arts since Malraux but so far denied to popular music. As Teillet is aware, this will not be an easy task. Malraux's conception of cultural action meant widening access to the great works, consecrated as such by time and the traditional agencies of legitimation: critics, scholars, curators, educationists. In such sectors, there is a recognisable canon to which policy can refer and, in the case of musics other than popular, a hierarchy of training and qualification. Pop enjoys none of these benefits. Legitimation by time, scholarship or training is largely absent, while the judgements of critics do not have the same legitimating power as in, say, the visual arts. It is therefore only public approval, the market in other words, which provides a credible criterion for judgement, and it is largely to this that policy-makers have turned for guidance. But for Teillet the danger of doing so is that those artists who do not reach a large audience are ignored and public access to them is diminished. Hence the need for a democratisation, which can, he believes, make a difference despite these difficulties.[36]

It would seem, then, that despite manifestly different constructions of the cultural, the Dutilh Commission follows both Finkielkraut and Rigaud to the extent that all three are unashamed believers in public intervention, that is, in the state's republican duty to improve national taste; or, as Teillet puts it, to offer audiences 'a musical journey leading them from familar aesthetic worlds towards less well-known ones'.[37] Furthermore, all three (and Fumaroli too in this respect) view culture, whether high or popular, not simply as a process but as a body of significant works made to last and which connect in some way with other works from the past. As a result, all wish to protect culture from the fashion-driven logic of economic liberalism, making a qualitative distinction between 'works' and products. As with *chanson* discourse, this conceptualisation of the cultural, and the ethic of improvement which accompanies it, are quite distinct from the British cultural-studies perspective described by Jim McGuigan as 'cultural populism', which eschews the standard value judgements made by cultural elites and studies everyday cultural consumption (youth culture or television for example) simply as it finds it, ending up with what McGuigan calls 'the uncritical endorsement of popular taste and pleasure'.[38] Teillet, Rigaud and even Schneider are closer – in this respect at least – to Frith (in *Performing Rites*) and to McGuigan himself, who both problematise such relativism and attempt to establish some theoretical basis for critical judgement in popular culture. However, what quite clearly sets French discourse apart here is its recurrent preoccupation with civic, republican and national values. In the report's case, of course, these values may be flagged up for purely tactical reasons, as the best way of appealing to the cultural establishment; but if so this in itself is revealing. Either way, what is striking is that in all the French discourses I have examined the same republican values are deployed both to condemn pop and to vindicate it.

What the Dutilh report and the debates of the preceding twenty years ultimately show is that, despite changes of political regime and reconstructions of the cultural to include new forms of leisure and entertainment, the focus of policy debate today, and the natural resort when legitimacy is sought, remains the civic, republican, identitarian discourse of democratisation and national culture, the Malraux Ministry's founding principle to which the three administrators in the debate, Schneider, Rigaud and Dutilh, all call for a return. At the same time, today's planners and strategists are trying to map on to it notions of cultural democracy, pluralism and difference in order to welcome all tastes into the national community. Pop, it would seem, is being latched on to as a site where this reconciliation might be achieved. It is striking that, like the report she had commissioned, Catherine Trautmann began speaking of present-day musics as a resolution of the democratisation–democracy dichotomy. Equally significant was the fact that her name became particularly attached to techno music, which I shall examine in the next chapter.

Notes

1. Some of what follows reworks earlier drafts of ideas and arguments I have published as the following: 'Cultural Policy in the 21st Century: Issues, Debates and Discourse', *French Cultural Studies*, vol. 10, no. 28 (February 1999), pp. 5–20; 'Facing the Music: French Cultural Policy from a British Perspective', *International Journal of Cultural Policy*, vol. 7, no. 1 (December 2000), pp. 115–29; and 'Naming the Popular: Youth Music, Politics and Nation in Contemporary France', in Marks and McCaffrey (eds), *French Cultural Debates*, pp. 109–20.
2. Renard, *L'Élan culturel*, p. 52.
3. Ibid., p. 53 (both quotations).
4. Marc Fumaroli, *L'État culturel: une religion moderne* (Fallois, 1991), pp. 99–102 (quotation p. 102).
5. Ibid., quotations pp. 223 and 42, respectively.
6. Ibid., pp. 102–3.
7. Alain Finkielkraut, *The Undoing of Thought*, translated by D. O'Keeffe (Claridge Press, 1988), pp. 115–16.
8. Ibid., p. 115.
9. Ibid., p. 129.
10. Yonnet cited by Finkielkraut and translated by O'Keeffe, p. 126. The italics are Finkielkraut's. I have removed O'Keeffe's puzzling quotation marks round the last (italicised) sentence, since they appear neither in Finkielkraut nor in Yonnet.
11. Ibid., pp. 126–7. I have restored Finkielkraut's italics where they have been omitted in translation, and I have indicated the French original where further clarity is required: *La Défaite de la pensée* (Folio, 1987), p. 173.
12. Ibid., pp. 16–18 (quotation p. 18).
13. Both quotations are my own translations from *La Défaite de la pensée*, pp. 176 and 169.

14. Max Silverman, *Facing Postmodernity: Contemporary French Thought on Culture and Society* (Routledge, 1999), p. 99.
15. Veitl and Duchemin, *Maurice Fleuret*, pp. 174–5 and 328–9.
16. Michel Schneider, *La Comédie de la culture* (Seuil, 1993), p. 76.
17. Ibid, pp. 76–7.
18. Ibid., pp. 68–9 and 78.
19. Ibid., pp. 78–9.
20. Ibid., p. 79.
21. Mayol, *La Planète Rock*, p. 22.
22. Schneider, *La Comédie de la culture*, pp. 150–1.
23. Jacques Rigaud, *Libre Culture* (Gallimard, 1990), pp. 403–5.
24. Jacques Rigaud (President of the Commission d'étude de la politique culturelle de l'État), *Rapport au Ministre de la culture. Pour une refondation de la politique culturelle* (Documentation Française, 1996), p. 24. Future references to this text will be abbreviated as 'Rigaud report'.
25. Ibid., p. 42.
26. Ibid., p. 76. See also Rigaud, *L'Exception culturelle: culture et pouvoirs sous la 5ᵉ République* (Grasset, 1995), p. 234.
27. Rigaud report, p. 51.
28. Ibid., p. 50. The use of bold characters is Rigaud's.
29. All quotations from Dutilh report, p. 24.
30. Ibid., p. 24.
31. The two quotations appear respectively in ibid., p. 41 (general report) and the separate 'Les Publics' booklet, pp. 7–8, where they are in fact combined. Unlike the booklets produced by the Commission's other working groups, the 'Publics' group's booklet is separately paginated.
32. Quotation from Dutilh report (general), p. 16. See also 'Préambule de la Commission', p. 66.
33. 'Préambule de la Commission', p. 65.
34. 'Les Publics' booklet, pp. 2–3; and personal correspondence with Teillet.
35. 'Les Publics' booklet, pp. 3, 11 (quotation) and 20.
36. Ibid., p. 11. See also Teillet, 'Éléments pour une histoire'. I analyse Teillet's position in greater detail in 'Naming the Popular', pp. 116–18.
37. 'Les Publics', p. 20.
38. Jim McGuigan, *Cultural Populism* (Routledge, 1992), p. 6.

– 10 –

Techno and the State: The Cultural Debate

Since 1997, techno has become the latest popular-music form, after rock, world music and rap, to gain state support. Its recognition by Trautmann was more than just political opportunism on her part. It was also, I suggest, because techno wrote itself up as an alternative youth culture that was entirely new and fundamentally different from pop. For policy-makers in search of new solutions to the policy debate discussed in the previous chapter, this looked like an opportunity too good to miss. In this chapter, I want to tie together the perspectives of Parts I and II by looking at techno as in a sense the culmination of both the musical and the political histories of French popular music. It is the issues it has raised about words and sounds, and about artistic legitimacy and national authenticity, issues I have traced since the beginning of the book, which make techno an exemplary case with which to end it, though my remarks in the closing section of this chapter ('Techno and the Policy Debate') are inevitably speculative, given the ongoing nature of the techno phenomenon.

Once again, terminology poses an immediate problem. In English, 'techno' usually designates one of a number of styles of 1990s electronic dance music, including house, acid-house, garage, drum'n'bass, and a galaxy of hybrids (trip-hop, deep house, trance core, and so on), which, to the outsider, only a nuance seems to separate. But the French term *la techno*, used more for convenience than accuracy by all but the purists, usually designates a loose meta-genre of electronic music generally, also sometimes called *electronica*, embracing performers such as Air, Alex Gopher, Daft Punk, St Germain, Étienne de Crécy and Laurent Garnier. In theory, it implies instrumentals, possibly with a sung phrase looped or sampled in, as in Daft Punk's UK hit 'One More Time', which has the looped phrase in English 'One more time, we're gonna celebrate'. Another unifying element (again in theory) is an almost caricaturally fast thud, the BPM (beats per minute). This may vary between 110 and 160 beats per minute, depending on style; hardcore can even reach 180. Thus, even in those forms which retain a sung element, it is the rhythm which dominates. The BPM encourages its own frenetic forms of dance which are meant to induce a state of trance or hypnosis, sometimes assisted by Ecstasy or LSD. In practice, though, the French term covers a multitude of styles, from the disco and club sound of Modjo and Daft Punk to Air's more mellow, experimental, ambient 'lounge' music. St Germain is closer to jazz than dance and has recorded for the esteemed jazz label Blue Note, while conversely some jazz artists like the trumpeter Erik Truffaz or the saxophonist Julien Lourau are moving closer to *electronica*.[1] It is in this loose French sense that I shall use the term: as a convenient shorthand for those contemporary electronic musics which are exclusively or primarily instrumental.

The Story So Far

In its original dance form, techno is the polar opposite of *chanson*. Like hip-hop, it makes DJs creative in that the electronic equipment they use (record decks, mixer, computer and MIDI synthesiser) becomes a musical instrument in its own right. The sound-system lets DJs sample, loop and otherwise edit existing vinyl tracks so as to create individualised dance mixes. Techno grew from house music and, further back, from 1970s disco and the gay club scene; it also has roots in black musics, namely reggae, soul, funk and dub, which it shares with rap.[2] Its 'official' birthplace as a style distinct from house music was Detroit in 1988. But techno also has European antecedents in the electro-acoustic experiments of the 1970s German group Kraftwerk, who had trained under Stockhausen. It is also in Europe that electronic music has gained its biggest fan base. House spread to the UK in the late 1980s, generating a new club scene, particularly identified with Manchester's Hacienda. Labelled acid-house, it attracted hostility from the Thatcher government because of its fabled associations with a seedy club life of drink, sex and drugs. The government reacted with legislation banning alcohol from clubs and forcing them to close at 2 a.m. This merely drove the movement underground, leading to the invention of 'raves'. Unlike clubland, these open-air free parties, organised through clandestine networking and held in the early hours in remote locations, often without the owner's consent, are virtually impossible to police, and the clandestine, cat-and-mouse element only adds to the enjoyment. Soon, the techno movement spread to continental Europe, reaching France a little later than Belgium and Germany.

Three contingencies played a role in its naturalisation in Paris. One was the availability of MTV, as cable was progressively installed from 1987. Another was the presence of a sympathetic record shop, Rough Trade, which sold dance imports as well as providing a meeting-place where discoveries could be made and ideas exchanged.[3] The third element was Britain's dance scene, where some

French acts made their name before having an impact in their own country. At Manchester's Hacienda, for example, one of the resident DJs was Laurent Garnier, alias DJ Pedro. Returning to Paris in 1990, Garnier was instrumental in introducing this new club scene to Paris, at Le Rex, Le Palace and Le Queen. However, with the help of virtual technology and the independent sector, techno did not need to remain as centralised as French pop had originally been, and other cities – Avignon, Lille, Montpellier, Toulouse – became alternative sites.

The first French *raves* – also known as *les free-parties, les frees* or *les teufs*, French backslang for *fête* – had begun in the late 1980s, announced at the last minute via telephone networks (*infolines*), flyers distributed in specialist record shops, and announcements by sympathetic FM stations like Radio-FG or Radio Nova. Raves became associated with unrestrained styles of dance, an eclectic, multicultural dress code less regimented than rap's, and a variety of other marginalised arts, including juggling, acrobatics, body-piercing and tattooing. Sub-groups of ravers formed, calling themselves tribes. On the production side, this movement, like others, turned its back on the majors. Some acts opted for self-production in home studios, while others (the Micronauts, Phoenix) signed to English independents. French independents such as Solid, Roadrunner and Laurent Garnier's F Communications (better known as F Com) also sprang up. The majors' French subsidiaries were rejected for their conventional marketing strategies, looking only to Francophone markets to sell French-made records rather than having the confidence to target the 'Anglo-Saxon' world too, without a sense of inferiority. Although radio was a little slow to respond and NRJ even boycotted techno at first because of the drugs connection, established press organs like *Actuel* and *Libération* began taking notice, speaking enthusiastically of a new culture being born. Clearly, something of significance was happening which seemed to be more than a commercial fad. As one sympathetic observer wrote: 'A new utopia, both cultural and social, is appearing in the ferment of the electronic arts.'[4]

Despite its alternative rhetoric, some forms of the new music were also proving commercially successful abroad. Daft Punk signed first to the British independent label Soma, then Virgin. By the beginning of 1998, their first album *Homework* had sold 150,000 copies in the UK and over a million worldwide. In late 2000, 'One More Time' reached the UK Top 10 and their album *Discovery* (2001) was lauded by the UK dance publication *Mixmag* as nothing less than 'the greatest album ever'.[5] Modjo then became the first French techno act to reach number one in the UK with their single 'Lady'. The duo Air was also making a name for itself after enthusiastic promotion by Virgin in Britain, as were club acts like Kid Loco, Dimitri from Paris and DJ Cam. A&R people started scouring France, and the British press used the label 'French Touch' to describe this unexpected invasion. In *Libération*, an unnamed UK critic was quoted as saying 'for the first time with the Paris dance scene, you get the feeling you're not dealing with a carbon copy of what's being done over here or in the United States'; while the British duo Basement Jaxx commented: 'If we were French, we'd already be selling millions of albums.'[6] Given French music's unenviable reputation in the UK, this was a remarkable reversal. It prompted an equally extraordinary rethink of the state's response to techno.

The first real policy initiative relating to it was repression. Classified as 'variety shows' or 'dances' for legal purposes, raves were subject to the 1945 legislation which requires municipal authorisation of any such event. After Chirac became President in 1995, a government circular to local authorities from the Minister of the Interior, the Gaullist Jean-Louis Debré, instructed them to work effectively and without indulgence against raves because of the drugs connection. In January that year, a national-police report entitled 'Rave parties: high-risk situations' had also appeared, giving advice on how to ban raves and warning recalcitrant organisers of the serious legal penalties they would incur, including imprisonment.[7] Countless applications from rave organisers were duly turned down or proceedings taken against those which had not followed the rules. In one case, organisers were fined for employing security staff without paying the required social-security contributions. The unpaid contributions amounted to 2,000 francs, while the penalty for each of the accused was a 15,000–franc fine and an eight-month suspended sentence. At one trial, techno was described as 'this hellish music' and accused of traumatising deer.[8]

Nevertheless, the music's growing commercial popularity made it irresistible to the new PS government of 1997, still keen to appeal to young people after Lang's successes. By then, protests about police repression had begun, legitimate festivals like the Printemps de Bourges and the Transmusicales de Rennes were programming raves without encountering difficulties, and some raves were turning into festivals. It was clear to the new Jospin government that a compromise somehow had to be struck between the health and safety issues behind the Debré circular and the need to demonstrate openness. Achieving this was not easy. Trautmann, who had previously made concessions to raves as Mayor of Strasbourg, began to acknowledge techno's cultural status, declaring that it was time to stop demonising it, though she still sounded hawkish about banning raves if regulations were not observed.[9] Together with the new Interior Minister, Jean-Pierre Chevènement, she replaced the Debré circular with a new one instructing Prefects to cancel measures against raves and calling for an attitude free of 'a priori assumptions' from the police, whose response to raves began to soften from that time. As for the music, she was ready to recognise the artistic status of DJs as the Dutilh report had urged.[10]

The Ministry's objective was to break techno's association with transgression by professionalising techno artists and raves, turning the former into better musicians and the latter into more structured events. Naturally, the music's spiralling export value simplified matters here, helping techno look more on-message and respectable. A techno 'salon' called Mix-Move had begun in the mid-1990s, displaying music and multimedia technology, which attracted 25,000 visitors in 1997, though it was not allowed to hold a rave as planned. Unauthorised raves were in fact still frowned upon, but bigger, commercially sponsored events were springing up, like Happyland in November 1997 at the Arche de la Défense, which charged 170 francs for admission.[11] In 1998, Laurent Garnier won techno's first Victoire de la musique award and even played the Olympia, *chanson*'s temple of legitimacy.

Garnier's consecration came shortly before an even more symbolic one, the capital's first 'Techno Parade'. In 1997, Lang had visited the Berlin Love Parade and come back committed to doing the same in Paris. Trautmann dutifully authorised it, for 19 September 1998, and, together with the Ministry of Youth and Sport, coughed up 15 per cent of its budget. Still smarting from the recent conflicts with government, the organising body, Technopol, an association representing the techno milieu, remained combative, determined to publicise its demand for 'the recognition of a music and a culture which has been demonised for far too long'.[12] A year later, when a second event took place, things had changed. The new circular to Prefects had been issued and techno was now officially a 'present-day music', even figuring in TV advertising. But the honeymoon did not last. In spring 2001, with 'security' (a term variously embracing law and order, street crime and even terrorism) building into an issue which would eventually torpedo Jospin's candidacy in the first round of the 2002 Presidentials and let Le Pen through to the second, a Gaullist deputy, Thierry Mariani, proposed an amendment to a new security bill which would reintroduce measures against unauthorised raves. Socialist ministers and deputies were divided on the amendment but the Interior Minister, Daniel Vaillant, came out broadly in favour, and in the autumn, after some unfortunate incidents at free parties over the summer, the measures were adopted, causing a sense of betrayal in the rave milieu. As Lionel Pourtau of the collective Voodoo'z Cyrkl declared, 'There is a cultural abyss between us. The government doesn't understand that the culture of free-parties is close to a certain form of nihilism.'[13]

Despite its predictable 'respectabilisation',[14] then, techno culture is still regarded ambivalently in France, just as rock'n'roll originally was. Conversely, the state's embrace and the music's commercialisation have had an equally mixed reception from the techno and rave milieux. Today the music can be divided into three basic types. There is an aesthetic avant-garde slipping quietly away from the dance and rave culture of the early days; and a commercial wing which is doing the same, though for different reasons. At the 1997 Nuits Boréalis event in Montpellier, there was a tendency for participants to listen – to the star names like Daft Punk and the Chemical Brothers – in a more conventional concert format, which the organisers said was a deliberate shift away from the purely festive in favour of a new emphasis on musicality and inventiveness.[15] By contrast, there is a third, authenticist wing, determined to stay true to the founding principles, the DIY aesthetic and the free-parties. Within this basic typology, the music has further subdivided and cross-pollinated, which in some manifestations makes it more difficult to distinguish from rap, world music (which also uses electronic sounds) and even rock. A number of rock and folk artists of an earlier generation have also moved into techno, most surprisingly perhaps the Celtic harp player Alain Stivell, as noted earlier.

So how exactly should the techno experience in France be interpreted? At one level, it confirms the steady maturation of French pop identified in Part I. From *yéyé* to rap, it has learnt to appropriate rather than imitate non-French musics and, for the time being, this would seem to be what techno too is doing. Its evolution from underground to mainstream also follows what has become a standard pop trajectory since the 1950s. Beginning life as incomprehensible, radical and foreign, its more accessible forms (Daft Punk, Air) have steadily been professionalised and legitimated by public consent and state recognition. Even so, techno is possibly the most dramatic and potentially disruptive development in French popular music for some years, though this is to make no assumptions about its aesthetic worth. Some might expect to see rap occupying the pole position here, especially given the amount of attention it has received (sometimes obsessively so) in Anglo-Saxon academia of late, which techno has not, as yet. But although it is too early to say for sure, I suspect that rap may prove to have been a less radical form than techno, having been easier to assimilate into the standard cultural and ethical discourse of national authenticity (see Chapters 3 and 7). According to the aesthetic theorist and philosopher Richard Shusterman, MC Solaar 'illustrates perfectly this continuity with canonical culture by the density of traditional cultural – including philosophical – references in his texts [. . .]. References to erudite culture are much more present and knowing in French rap than in American rap, and this difference says a great deal about the differences in education and culture between the two societies.'[16] Techno, by contrast, being pure sound and rhythm with few or no lyrics, has been much more of a shock to the French system, just as rock'n'roll originally was. As well as being another evil intruder sent by the old devil America, techno has sometimes been represented as a form of aesthetic bankruptcy. Initially, many were disturbed by it on the Left as well as the Right. In 1994, the Communist daily *L'Humanité* even likened it to military marches and accused it of having neo-Nazi resonances.[17] Yet there were and continue to be many positive readings of techno, by practitioners, fans, sociologists and supportive journalists, though sometimes these merely gloss over the perceived dangers – drug abuse, noise pollution, even brain damage – in order to concentrate on techno's sociocultural and aesthetic dimensions. Individually, pro-techno discourses are not always coherent or fully formed. Their analysis as a corpus is therefore needed to tease out their underlying preoccupations.

Techno Discourse

One recurrent discourse concerns techno's position in relation to pop. There is a common perception that techno is a profoundly innovative twenty-first-century idiom, a revolution easily as great as that heralded by rock'n'roll. Analogies are sometimes drawn with computer games or the Internet, implying that techno is the musical spin-off of the digital age. Techno, therefore, is not just another style but a parallel universe. Fans, practitioners and critics like in fact to represent it as the apocalyptic end of the grand narrative of pop since the 1950s. DJ Curtis recounts that he switched to techno because he felt that rock 'was coming to the end of a cycle' by becoming too bland and formulaic.[18] At the same time, techno is depicted as following the same trajectory as its forerunner, imposing itself, altering perceptions and segmenting, just as pop did, the first Techno Parade being the equivalent of the 1963 'Nuit de la Nation'. This millennial rhetoric similarly implies that the generation gap has re-formed. The coming of techno, prepared by rap, shows up pop for what it has long been, a middle-aged self-parody. As one commentator puts it in a poignant epitaph for the 1960s: 'Techno is the music of a generation, parents can't make any sense of it, rock is the music of parents.'[19] Techno, then, brought itself into existence by constructing pop as its other, just as *chanson* had done in the early 1960s. Early techno was in fact marked by an aesthetic fundamentalism. Provoked into militancy by police and media harassment, it built its own hermetic universe, rewriting history by claiming never to have been part of pop culture. *Les Inrockuptibles* condemns what it sees as this peculiarly French attitude, preferring the 'polycultural' ecumenicalism of the UK and US. It also accepts that this kind of particularism is no longer so widespread, as many techno artists now happily acknowledge their roots in rock or punk. But this softer position does not weaken techno's basic premise that pop has eaten itself.

This sense of techno's difference may express itself in other ways. Half-concealed by his (more rarely her) headset and regulation baseball cap, the purist DJ is rarely photographed, distancing himself symbolically from 'the business' by cultivating a more anonymous persona than the preening rock star. This is taken to extremes by Daft Punk, whose faces are always invisible behind robotic masks. Or the DJ may deliberately sell fewer records, unwilling to jump on the promotional bandwagon. Techno also seems expressly designed to deter the middle-aged in search of lost youth, by seeking a level of noise, a pace (the BPM) and a format (the clandestine, open-air, all-night rave) which those over thirty-five are unlikely to have the stamina for. As seen in Chapter 5, Olivier Cathus suggests that noise in pop music can be seen as 'federating youth', expressing 'a generational break, based on a different relation to technology'.[20] Given that pop tastes now straddle several generations, techno, like punk and rap before it, may be interpreted as a form of distinctive practice in Bourdieu's sense, a wilful attempt to smash this homely consensus.

However, a quite different way of making sense of techno in France is to insist that it is art. This too has often been the doing of the techno world itself, which as it were applies for admission to national legitimacy by claiming roots in high culture or other respectable forms. Air, for example, see their Frenchness as coming partly from Debussy, Ravel and Satie, as well as from the soundtracks of New Wave cinema. Another instance of art discourse is the attempt to build bridges with the experimental electro-acoustic movement in 'serious' music, in which France has a respectable reputation. French or France-based composers like Pierre Schaeffer, Pierre Henry, Boulez and Xenakis are cited by some techno artists, as are John Cage, Stockhausen, Philip Glass and Steve Reich. Jack Lang and Catherine Trautmann suggested that DJs be allowed to work with IRCAM, where they might benefit from both artistic synergies and access to state-of-the-art music technology. An obvious problem arises, however, in that not all the 'serious' composers cited are happy with the compliment being paid them. According to the sociologist Amparo Lasén, some of them, showing no interest in exploring techno themselves, simply expect interested techno fans to make the intellectual journey into contemporary music, refusing the possibility of two-way exchange. The chief reason for this haughty indifference, Lasén believes, is the Adornian view 'that all dance music is minor music and that these musics do not constitute a genuinely creative process, for they respond only to the immediate needs of suitability for dancing', the mistake here being to confuse the way the music is listened to and interpreted with the way it is created.[21]

A further virtue ascribed to techno (and in fact to rap) is its democratisation of creativity, embodied in the focal shift from musician to DJ. In early pop and rock, whether or not a musician was formally trained, certain musical skills still had to be learnt, if only by an apprenticeship served in the bedroom playing or singing along to records. But the recent sound technologies coming on the market at ever lower prices are changing all this. First, they have empowered the DJ, once disparaged as a nerd or half-wit burbling inanities on radio or the dance-floor while cueing in another record. From disco onwards through reggae and rap, the creative input of the club DJ has grown. In order to enhance existing recorded music for greater excitement, the club DJ has assumed artistic responsibility for a set of sounds which he or she makes to measure for the dance-floor; and the sound-system and vinyl record are his or her musical instruments. Ultimately, both techno and rap aim to 'reappropriate the machine',[22] regaining control of technologies which were once alienating or inaccessible to all but the wealthy and the highly trained.

However, creativity discourse is about more than improving the expressive opportunities of professional DJs. It is about blurring the line between amateur and professional, live and recorded, in short about widening access to creative musical practice by facilitating the passage from fan to artist, listener to creator. Pop had already democratised music-making to an extent, but techno is deemed to take this a big step further by allowing those who cannot play an instrument or even sing to become creators, placing at their disposal a vast palette of pre-recorded or synthesised sounds, to be mixed wherever and in whatever ways their creativity suggests. As with rap, musical creativity is brought out of the traditional studio, where a live performance is handed over to skilled professionals (producer and sound engineer) and turned into a marketable commodity. In contrast to this supposedly standardising process, seen as disempowering the creative artist, the figure of the DJ is symbolic of the ordinary listener being transformed into artist, producer and sound engineer all in one. 'We realised house music was something you could do in your bedroom,' Daft Punk's Thomas Bangalter has said of their beginnings.[23] For the first time in the history of the record industry, commentators rejoice, it is possible to be single-handedly responsible for a work from inception to production, co-ordinating all the various technologies via the computerised home studio and the MIDI system. By such means, DJs can prepare their sequences at home and independent labels can produce technically proficient work without hiring a recording studio. Accordingly, costs can be minimised, especially as it is common for only a few thousand copies of a record to be pressed. There are no session musicians or lyricists to be paid; promotion and even distribution can be carried out via flyers at raves, the Internet and other improvised means. Technology (home studios, Internet) also allows the decentralisation of music production and distribution, letting both artists and labels set up anywhere.[24] Daft Punk are again at the cutting age here with their 'Daft Club', using the Internet to provide anyone buying their CDs with new forms of exclusive access (online tracks not otherwise available), allowing a more flexible, selective relationship with the music.[25]

Both rap and techno, then, are seen as placing creativity back in the hands of ordinary people and redefining the creative 'work' in terms closer to Certeau's conception of creativity as an everyday practice which subverts mass cultural production. In techno in its purest form, the work is made by the DJ on and for the dance-floor or rave. Like a theatrical performance, it is ephemeral, irreproducible, unique. The recording studio is in a sense brought into the club, turning clubbers into both witnesses and collaborators in a unique act of creation, as their enthusiastic dancing inspires the DJ to greater experimentation, rather than being consumers of a pre-packaged product. The listener-dancer is also active in another sense, in that she or he is forced to make sense of a work which does not follow a linear, 'figurative' structure: 'As in an abstract painting, you have to plot your own route without the reassuring guidance of the melody (or of the figurative motif in painting), plunge without prejudice into the heart of the sound and learn to navigate in this deluge of noise.'[26]

This leads to another vital feature of techno applauded by its supporters: the relative absence of lyrics. Researchers interviewing fans and ravers have located a belief that this absence allows a freer, more interpretative, interactive response to the music, a personal reappropriation. This is coupled with a feeling that, unlike pop songs, techno is authentic because it avoids genre-bound clichés. Shusterman even speculates that techno may be a powerful protest against the domination of words in the information society.[27] Others speak of techno's universality, since it crosses language barriers in a way *chanson* has never been able to do and therefore offers opportunities for a new international youth culture to be forged. Shusterman himself is more sceptical here, and with good reason. He recalls having once danced to techno music in a Berlin club, without hearing a single human voice in the music until a DJ looped a simple 'uh huh' into the mix: 'Spontaneously, the whole crowd of dancers reacted with a rush of emotion, in recognition of the meaning of this human verbal intervention. I interpreted this experience as the sign of the persistent power of the word to touch us emotionally.' Shusterman does not try to resolve the two positions he outlines, admitting that he may be taking too nostalgic a view. But he does conclude that rap is more human and humanist than techno.[28]

Another problem lyrics pose is that they invite the kind of content analysis which Anglo-Saxon popular-music studies now reject. With pop, French commentators have often turned a lyric inside out in search of what makes it tick. With techno, this is virtually impossible given the rarity of lyrics, so those who identify a philosophy in it mostly do so by examining the ideas expressed by the fans, not the music. These generally amount to concerns with the environment, love and peace, cosmic energy, or with the idea of a productive relationship between humankind and the machine. But the most consistent interpretations of techno obtained by this means are those which, like Morin's interpretation of *yéyé*, view it as apolitical, ludic and value-free, asserting merely the value of itself: dance, trance, festivity and fun. Nevertheless, implicit within this valorisation is arguably a politics of the body. As the ethnologists Caroline Fontana and Astrid Fontaine point out, it is sometimes argued that there is no communication at a rave, because each individual is wrapped in his or her private trance. Yet their research prompts them to think that the communication is simply of a different order from everyday life. It is non-verbal and comes about through dance, looks and smiles. Ravers similarly experience a different relationship with themselves, and particularly with their bodies after eight hours of continuous dancing and noise:

> Ravers speak of a rehabilitation of the body through dance, the continuity of the sound. [. . .] Dance can therefore be considered as a technique for going into the trance or a means of expressing it. Rave dancing is not codified, it is often very expressive, it is often abstract and expresses an obvious loss of inhibition in the people dancing. The raver forgets about himself [*sic*]. He is a body which responds to a rhythm and to sounds. The dancer coincides with his emotion.[29]

The trance *is* therefore political in its way, because it is always 'a way of escaping a dominant reality and has in this sense a subversive quality in so far as one contests the social as a system of rules and the individual as a personal identity'.[30]

This festive 'rehabilitation of the body' is rather more complex than the kind of communion Mayol identifies. Several commentators look closely at the psychological experience of the rave, which, they argue, is an experience of collective communion and individual solitude simultaneously. Citing Maffesoli's theme of the plenitude of the present in *Le Temps des tribus* (*The Time of the Tribes*), the sociologist Gaëlle Bombereau also turns her attention to 'communication', which she too, like Fontana and Fontaine, sees as non-standard in the rave experience. It is in fact common, she asserts, for rave participants to remain as anonymous as the DJs; even first names are superfluous and conversation is in any case limited. Sharing the festive present is what matters: 'Mingling, merging in a great collective (that is, not being physically alone) and at the same time seeking solitude, even maintaining it in a non-conscious way.' Whether this solitude is achieved by trance, drugs or total absorption in the music, 'the self dominates the other'. This solitude of togetherness, a state we usually try to avoid in everyday life, is all part of an initiation into adulthood, which is the main focus of Bombereau's analysis.[31] Maffesoli himself, in his own reading of raves, identifies the same dualism but does not place so much emphasis on the narcissism of solitude, viewing rave dancing rather as the embodiment of his overarching conviction that contemporary individualism is being replaced by a 'being-together'. Narcissus drowns after contemplating his own image but the pool is a metaphor of the world, not himself. Thus, whereas for Durkheim, 'the social body' was merely a metaphor, today it is a reality: the body is *literally* social. Alongside other rehabilitations of the corporeal like dieting and body-building, dance is a celebration of the body but always under and for the gaze of others. Rave dancing, like all dancing where one has no explicit partner, is still very much a form of social interaction: 'in the dimension of collective dancing, you have someone who apparently is isolated but who can be included in a whole in which there are already no gender distinctions, where he [*sic*] can dance in front of a man, or a woman, or in front of a man then a woman'.[32]

The rave in this reading would appear to be an ideal instance of the dissolution of self, which for Maffesoli is central to the contemporary phenomenon of the neo-tribe. The neo-tribe exists for no other purpose than simply being together in a form of spontaneous communion, ludically, dynamically, creatively. The group may have an objective of some kind, but this is not its main reason for existing, for the ludic is 'that which does not burden itself with purpose, usefulness, "practicity", or with what are called "realities"'.[33] One recognises here not only Certeau's conception of popular creativity in everyday life but Morin's reading of *yéyé* as 'gratuitous frenzy', 'a life structure which justifies itself essentially through a sense of play and the pleasure of the spectacle'. And like Morin with pop, Maffesoli does not see this ludic void as vacuous, inauthentic. On the contrary, as we saw in Chapter 5, he identifies in it a need for a quasi-religious *intensity*, the desire to melt into the present moment in all its plenitude.[34] The techno trance is not merely imitation, then, the empty shell of bygone forms of ritualistic possession. Its intensity makes it a 'contemporary modulation of the sacred' and gives it 'all the characteristics of authenticity'.[35] What in fact underscores all of these readings is an awareness of techno's anti-rationalism. Techno reinstates the body in a culture fixated on the mind, and this is as far as its 'philosophy' goes. This, I suggest, is part of what has made techno, and pop generally, enigmatic and threatening for some in France, brought up on the literate *chanson* in a word-based culture; and always, therefore, expecting from pop an articulated vision, a 'message', and failing to find one. The ultimate absence of one – an absence which techno merely takes to its logical conclusion – also perhaps explains why some early French accounts of pop (such as Torgue's) seem somehow to miss the point, at least to an Anglo-Saxon sensibility.

There is one last issue which French commentators sometimes raise: the 'identity' of techno. French discourse favourable to both techno and rap often reveals an impulse to justify them by finding roots and connections that make them somehow essentially French, or at least European. Irrespective of whether there really is a distinctively French school of techno, as some maintain (a question which would probably require musicological analysis), artists variously lay claim to eclectic roots in French music from classical (as with the references to Ravel and others) to jazz, film music and *chanson*, particularly the musical experiments of Gainsbourg and the arrangers he worked with like Jean-Claude Vannier. The same trope is traceable in observers too, as when the editor of the British *Mixmag* suggested that 'the new French DJs treat disco in a totally different way from their English or American counterparts; they bring to it a touch of kitsch and a bit of Edith Piaf'.[36] This attempted gallicisation is problematic. Contemporary culture in general problematises identity for nation states because increasingly it focuses on either the local or the global, bypassing the national entirely. With techno specifically, this can be seen in a tendency to decentralise production and to sign to non-French labels. But techno culture challenges the idea of national identity in other ways too. The rave is premised upon a fleeting moment of youthful community, or as Shusterman expresses it, 'the feeling of a new and ephemeral group identity which can be formed and disappear in the space of one night of music or even a few minutes of dancing'.[37] This ephemeral identity has nothing to do with nationality. Certainly, there is a sense of place in techno's dedication to a natural setting or to particular clubs with their own character. But these are universal spaces because of techno's nomadism. As *Le Monde*'s popular-music critic Véronique Mortaigne writes: 'In every corner of the world, the DJ discovers tribes brought together by their tastes, house, jungle or hardcore, etc., and not by some national or racial belonging.'[38] This philosophy of nomadism is expressed aesthetically in *métissage*: sampling and mixing genres, references, national styles, and so on. Rap can still be identified to an extent with a community and a place: the American ghetto or the French *banlieue*, ethnic minorities, Africa. Georges Lapassade, for example, traces hip-hop dance styles back to Senegalese ballet and the Brazilian *capoeira*. Techno, however, derives much more from a stateless Western avant-garde.[39] Also, as I have argued, rap lends itself more readily to assimilation in the national heritage by virtue of its use of the French language and of cultural allusion. A comparable historical continuity is much harder to establish with techno because of the absence of words. Techno is anybody's culture.

As well as post-national, techno is also represented as post-industrial, born literally in the urban wastelands of the West: the abandoned warehouses, hangars and factories of Detroit, Manchester, Berlin, which it recycles just as it re-uses forgotten vinyl. In pro-techno discourse, one may often locate an optimistic representation of this ability to reappropriate the artefacts of yesterday's industrial society using today's technologies, thereby creating new languages, new 'transcultural' permutations which transcend notions of genre. However, not all French commentators share this optimism. Aside from the obvious reservations about drugs and other health hazards, negative depictions of techno are as valuable as positive ones, because they offer insights into the sorts of difficulties French cultural discourse has had in adjusting to the techno mindset, revealing their authors' unspoken expectations of popular music and their wider assumptions about culture itself.

Mayol is a revealing instance, since he has long been open to pop music generally as a way of achieving the kind of alternative creativity Certeau believes in. But by 1997, the doubts about the creativity of rap he had already articulated in *Les Enfants de la liberté* had extended to techno. What particularly worries him is the acceleration of musical obsolescence in recent years. Might it not be, he speculates, that youth culture is drifting imperceptibly from pop and rock, which were highly creative, to marginally less creative rap, to techno, which is significantly more industrialised, and thence to the completely standardised products of boy bands? Is techno genuine creation, he muses, or just 'sophisticated cloning'?[40] In *Le Monde diplomatique*, Sylvain Desmille, a historian and anthropologist, is less hesitant. He examines techno astutely and not unsympathetically but ends up drawing attention to the void at its heart, a void which he construes not as a liberation from grand narratives, as Lipovetsky might argue, but simply as vacuousness. Techno is not a culture, he insists. Like television news, it surfs the present with no sense of the future; it lacks its own meanings, a 'project for society'. It is consequently 'reduced' to sampling, picking at the leftovers of past banquets. Words are 'only sounds, images, the surfaces of ideas'. Far from generating exciting new possibilities from consumer waste, techno itself is just another product like television or advertising, another 'musical movement': 'Being techno consists of being at the outpost of modern consumption. Hence the hypnotic and subliminal techno music beneath advertising messages.'[41]

Clearly, Desmille here identifies the making of meanings only with words, just as *chanson* discourse does. For its allies as for its enemies, techno is in fact constructed as everything that *chanson* is not. An interesting instance can be found, once again, in Lucien Rioux's *Cinquante Ans de chanson française*, which I touched on in Chapter 4. Like Desmille and Mayol, Rioux has difficulty with the idea that club DJs are creative. Instead, diametrically opposed to the kind of reading characterised by Maffesoli, he sees club DJs as sinister mechanoids who dehumanise those on the dance-floor: 'Installed behind his console, fingers glued to the sliders of his control panel, eyes fixed on the two decks he uses simultaneously, the disc-jockey, master of the sound, has the dancers in his sights. He dazzles them with flashes, spotlights and laser beams, deafens them, blinds them and holds them spellbound.'[42] Quite clearly, this experience, as Rioux sees it, is the antithesis of the intensity identified by Hennion or Maffesoli. On the contrary, the dancers are alienated by electronic dance music, just as French *chanson* itself is when serious singers are forced by commercial pressures to record dance remixes of their work specially for clubs. Rioux's discourse is not a nostalgia for lost Frenchness, however. In his world, authenticity has nothing to do with ethnic or geographic purity and he is perfectly at home with the hybrid musics of today like zouk, even when they involve American-style rock. House is inauthentic not because of where it comes from but because it is imposed by fashion and because electronic music reduces other genres – funk, blues, rock, which all emerged as the result of 'an imperious need', in Rioux's view – to 'an insipid and noisy mush'.[43]

What lurks largely unnamed beneath the various discourses I have examined is a debate between post-modernity and cultural tradition. The eddying, undirected reflux constantly created by the looped, repetitive structure of techno can be seen as figuring the end of the linear narratives of both industrial progress and musical modernity. Lasén sees the contemporary music of Boulez and others as locked in just such a narrative, a rigid, elitist notion of avant-garde abstraction, grounded in 'an intellectualist conception of music, following a historical logic of breaking with tradition, eliminating repetition, habit and chance [. . .]. One aspires to the total and rational organisation of all the parameters of the world of sound. It is an eminently learned music, the culmination of modernity, of rational abstraction.' This, she argues, is why the contemporary-music world has shown so little interest in reciprocating techno artists' interest in it, despite the 'bastard filiation' which binds them. What she advocates is a transcending of these frontiers, a two-way exchange between the elite and the popular.[44]

Techno and the Policy Debate

Unexpectedly, perhaps, this theoretical dimension sheds some empirical light on the Jospin government's inclusion of techno in its cultural policy, and on the ambiguities it contains. As I discussed earlier (Chapter 6), French cultural policy-making has been split since 1959 on the question of how to achieve cultural democracy: democratisation or cultural development, professional creation or amateur creativity? Ministers on the Left and the Right generally promise to pursue both poles at once but in practice a lack of resources forces them to make a choice, and it is democratisation and creation which usually win, largely because a policy which includes magnificent new buildings and institutions for the professional arts is more spectacular than one which supports amateurs in run-down suburbs. In 1981, however, Lang seemed to be trying out a discursive third way in the form of a festive ecumenicalism. In the Fête de la musique, all forms of music, from opera to rap, from the tentatively amateur to the smoothly professional, are celebrated, Fleuret's 'equality of dignity' being conferred spontaneously by the party mood. Behind this conception there lies an interpretation of national culture which goes back to the Popular Front, Doyen's Fêtes du peuple, and ultimately the Revolution. Before 1981, it was often theatre which seemed to embody this collective spirit best, but since Lang the weight has shifted towards music, especially youth music. This is where techno comes in. Given the positive representations just examined, it is easy to see how techno suggested itself as a way forward for policy. Being both avant-garde and popular, art and DIY expression, it appeared to abolish the distinction between amateur and professional, personal creativity and professional creation. And the rave, if the 'small' matter of drugs is set aside, might just be seen as fostering that good-natured festive spirit which the Socialists saw as a foundation for a national popular culture.

However, the idea that techno is a policy panacea is not as straightforward as it sounds. The fact that the music is largely instrumental may well be an advantage commercially in that it can more easily reach a non-Francophone audience. But in cultural-political terms, it raises a thorny issue. Specialist magazines like *Les Inrockuptibles* speak of the new confidence in French artists, who have lost their sense of inferiority in the international market-place. Yet this does not alter the fact that the Anglo-Saxon world still calls the tune. When French artists begin producing a form of music originating in Detroit and rooted in disco, with few or no French lyrics, adopt English names and in some cases sign to non-French labels, one may wonder in what sense, other than the strictly economic, techno represents the triumph of French popular music abroad, and how far the situation today really differs from the days when Jean-Philippe Smet preferred to call himself Johnny Hallyday. Of course, this issue may not ultimately be important outside a narrowly nationalistic perspective, and certainly it does not seem to vex either the French industry, delighted at its sudden good fortune, or French policy-makers, delighted at theirs. Nevertheless, French cultural policy has always been concerned, in one form or another, with Frenchness (albeit recently in a multicultural guise) and with language. Hence, in part, the low priority originally conferred on music by the Ministry in comparison to theatre and the *maisons de la culture*. Hence too the continuing commitment of the Ministries of Culture and Foreign Affairs to preserving and promoting the French language abroad. So, after standing up for linguistic and cultural diversity for so long, and even imposing the controversial quotas of French-language music on radio stations, the government now finds itself in a position which is paradoxical to say the least: that of recognising as French a music from which 'national' characteristics are virtually absent. Of course, this paradox may be no bad thing, since the notion of national characteristics is musically and morally problematic, as Keith Negus points out in the context of quotas:

> It is important to highlight the fact that music quota policies involve having to identify what should be promoted as 'ours' and then to classify other musical sounds, or the people producing those sounds, according to the soil on which they were born, the language in which they sing or the ethnic category to which they 'belong'. At the same time, foreign music (and its alien producers) are usually demonized as a 'threat' to the cultural life and economic well-being of the nation.[45]

But, bad thing or not, the issue of national identity and otherness is the biggest test that the post-1981 music discourse of openness and *métissage* faces.

It is not the only paradox, however. Techno, like other genres before it, is changing, and has already moved towards the mainstream. Despite the initial stress on anonymity, limited pressings and improvised self-production, techno is today a much smoother commercial product, with its stars, its best-selling albums, its mega-concerts, and its musical conventions which the mainstream is enthusiastically imitating. Its initial radicalism is already fading and policy has played a part in this. Inevitably so, since another irony when governments start embracing youth movements is that the embrace is often fatal. Credibility is easily lost when a top politico like Lang unctuously describes techno as 'a culture of peace and tolerance'.[46] By the same token, the Ministry too has found itself in an invidious position, supporting a music equated by some (Mariani supporters among them) with illegality, health hazards and unacceptable levels of noise, so there have realistically to be limits to any such policy, however ecumenical and generous. Although the Ministry of Culture under Douste-Blazy supported NTM when it was threatened with imprisonment, lines had to be drawn, just as Trautmann, while undoing the Debré circular, had to insist that the law be respected, that raves clean up their act, and so on. Government effusiveness regarding the Techno Parade stands side by side with the 2001 security bill, and it is significant that, with the bill causing so much bad feeling in the techno world, the 2001 Parade did not take place.

This is a problem for all cultural mediators who wish techno well. At a 1997 conference on techno in Poitiers, a variety of participants displayed an admirably open mind and a willingness to learn. But in some contributions, one still glimpses a discourse of improvement, a quasi-parental itch to intervene and organise. One journalist, for example, called for the quality of raves to be 'enriched' and 'decorated' by other arts, also pointing out that DJs have a responsibility to discover young talent which can feed local movements. 'There are things to invent,' he concluded, brimming with enthusiasm. A Ministry of Culture music inspector similarly showed a genuine eagerness to learn:'It's the cultural and musical phenomenon which interests me. How is the music evolving? In what ways is it creative? Who are the creators?'[47] But others at the conference also seemed conscious of the risk of throwing out the baby with the bathwater. For part of what initially made techno so significant a phenomenon was its clandestinity, its active *resistance* to being understood, the wilful *rejection* of adult encouragement, the determination to place techno by its very nature *beyond* the reach of older generations, including those only too happy (or desperate) to recover their youth by hijacking the tastes of a new generation.

The French government's experience with techno is a microcosm of the ambiguities of policy for youth musics generally and perhaps for all contemporary culture. By virtue of its extremism, techno has reawakened the anxieties and confusion which rock'n'roll first generated in the early 1960s. This is not altogether surprising since, despite its belief in its own newness, it may be interpreted, as I have shown, as the latest in a series of attempts to return to the founding spirit of rock'n'roll: dance, collective frenzy, gratuitous play. At the same time, it demonstrates French popular music's remarkable ability to push at the boundaries of acceptability while simultaneously demanding to be accepted. Like the other genres I have examined, techno allows us to observe differing discourses of authenticity at work, from the national to the personal or communal. Even with a music which sets itself up as the nemesis of pop and a new millennial culture, the issue of authenticity still manages to be at the heart of cultural debate.

Notes

1. *Time Out Paris Free Guide,* 'The Music Issue', Autumn 2001, p. 21.
2. See Jean-Luc Terradillos and Marie Martin (eds), *La Fête techno: approche sociologique, médicale et juridique, d'un mouvement musical à un phénomène de société* (Le Confort Moderne, 1997), p. 92, for an attempted though not altogether helpful genealogy.
3. J.D. Beauvallet, 'La 6ᵉ République: dix ans de révolution techno et dance en France', *Les Inrockuptibles,* special issue, pp. 22–6.
4. Guillaume Bara, *La Techno* (EJL, 1999), p. 34.
5. Quoted in Ben Osborne, 'We Are Not Control Freaks. We Are Freedom Freaks' (on Daft Punk), *Guardian* (G2 supplement), 13 March 2001, p. 12.
6. Quotations from, respectively, *Libération,* 20 January 1998 (downloaded) (this is my retranslation from the French since no source is given); and 'La

Déferlante de la "French Touch"', dossier 'La Musique en fête', *Label France*, no. 36 (July 1999), downloaded.

7. Arnaud Frisch, 'Aspects juridiques: interdiction-répression', in Terradillos and Martin (eds), *La Fête techno*, pp. 73–9.

8. Ibid., pp. 83 and 101.

9. Trautmann quoted in 'Paroles de ministre' (interview), *Coda*, October 1997, pp. 25–6; and in Danielle Rouard, 'Une Vie de rave', *Le Monde*, 19 December 1997, p. 15.

10. Circular reproduced in *Lettre d'information*, no. 44 (new series) (3 March 1999), p. 13. Trautmann on DJs in ibid., no. 20 (new series) (17 December 1997), p. 10.

11. Rouard, 'Une Vie de rave', *Le Monde*, p. 15.

12. Technopol quoted in *Le Monde*, 18 September 1999 (downloaded).

13. 'Retour antirave à l'Assemblée', *Libération*, 27–8 October 2001, p. 12. Organisers must now give advance notice of a free-party, or risk having their equipment confiscated. I am grateful to postgraduate student Rachel Jenkins for updating me on this issue.

14. The term '*respectabilisation*' is Pascal Ory's, in *L'Aventure culturelle française, 1945–1989* (Flammarion, 1989), p. 66.

15. Stéphane Davet, 'Le Son techno prend le pas sur la danse aux Nuits Boréalis', *Le Monde*, 12 August 1997, p. 17.

16. Shusterman, 'L'Expérience esthétique du rap', *Cultures en mouvement*, no. 21 (October 1999), pp. 29–32 (quotation p. 32).

17. Reference to *L'Humanité* in Véronique Mortaigne, 'Éloge de la techno, nouvelle écologie', *Le Monde*, 13 August 1998, p. 10.

18. *Les Inrockuptibles*, special issue, p. 26.

19. Discussion of Pierre Mayol, 'Les Mouvements issus de la jeunesse', in Terradillos and Martin (eds), *La Fête techno*, pp. 14–19 (quotation p. 17).

20. Cathus, 'Les Flonflons d'la balle', p. 26.

21. Amparo Lasén, 'Une filiation bâtarde', *Cultures en mouvement*, no. 21 (October 1999), pp. 49–52 (quotation p. 50).

22. Cathus, 'Les Flonflons d'la balle', p. 27.

23. Osborne, 'We Are Not Control Freaks', *Guardian* 13.3.01, p. 12.

24. See Bara, *La Techno*, pp. 15–16; Jérôme Strazzulla, *La Techno*, (Casterman, 1998), p. 33; and *Les Inrockuptibles*, special issue, p. 24.

25. Osborne, 'We Are Not Control Freaks', *Guardian* 13.3.01, p. 13.

26. Bara, *La Techno*, p. 20.

27. Étienne Racine, 'Diversité des fêtes techno', in Terradillos and Martin (eds), *La Fête techno*, pp. 23–9 (see p. 24); Shusterman, 'L'Expérience esthétique du rap', p. 29.

28. Shusterman, 'L'Expérience esthétique du rap', p. 29.

29. Caroline Fontana and Astrid Fontaine, 'Un Environnement propice à la modification de la réalité ordinaire', in Terradillos and Martin (eds), *La Fête techno*, pp. 34–40 (quotation pp. 36–7).

30. Ibid., p. 38.

31. Gaëlle Bombereau, 'Au Rebord du monde, des passagers en marge', *Cultures en mouvement*, no. 21 (October 1999), pp. 46–8 (quotations p. 48).

32. 'Entretien avec Michel Maffesoli', pp. 113–14 (quotation p. 114).

33. Michel Maffesoli, *Le Temps des tribus*, 3rd edition (La Table Ronde, 2000), p. 147; see also section entitled 'Masses et styles', pp. 175–83. I have preferred to use the original French edition here, so the translation is my own.

34. Morin, 'Salut les copains', 7–8 July 1963, p. 12; 'Entretien avec Michel Maffesoli', p. 110.

35. 'Entretien avec Michel Maffesoli', pp. 102 and 103.

36. Quoted in Didier Saltron, 'Américains et Britanniques saluent le "nouveau son français"', Agence France Presse dispatch, 26 March 1998 (downloaded), my retranslation from the French.

37. Shusterman, 'L'Expérience esthétique du rap', p. 29.

38. Mortaigne, 'Éloge de la techno', p. 10.

39. Georges Lapassade, 'Deux manières d'être au monde', *Cultures en mouvement*, no. 21 (October 1999), pp. 44–5.

40. Mayol, 'Les Mouvements issus de la jeunesse', p. 15.

41. Sylvain Desmille, 'La Vague aléatoire de la musique techno', *Le Monde diplomatique*, February 1999, p. 28.

42. Rioux, *Cinquante Ans de chanson française*, p. 407.

43. Ibid, p. 407.

44. Lasén, 'Une filiation bâtarde', pp. 51–2 (quotation p. 52).

45. Negus, *Popular Music in Theory*, p. 214.

46. Lang quoted in 'La Première Techno Parade de Paris réunit 130 000 ravers et curieux', *Le Monde*, 22 September 1998 (downloaded).

47. Discussion of Alexandre Chevalier, 'Évolution historique et géographique du mouvement techno', in Terradillos and Martin (eds), *La Fête techno*, pp. 6–13 (quotations pp. 12 and 13, respectively).

Conclusion

Throughout this book, I have identified a number of preoccupations relating to French popular music that I want to bring together and set against some of the current theoretical issues in popular-music studies and cultural-policy studies.

In tracing the contemporary history of popular music in France, I have been concerned to explore how pop music particularly has over the years been conceptualised and fought over in a variety of milieux: musical, sociological, intellectual and, especially, political, where it has become entangled in issues to do with the French cultural exception and threats to the republican tradition. The story has been of a fundamental shift in both the nature of the music and the way it has been received. The implanting of an international youth culture from the late 1950s represented what Hurstel calls 'a major challenge to the established cultural apparatus as a whole. It was the first time in history that this culture manifested itself in such a radical and autonomous way.'[1] France's cultural establishment found it difficult to digest, reacting over time with a variety of strategies from disapproval to eventual appropriation. The struggle even to name pop is, I believe, a symptom of the fact that the pop debate has been about more than just economic, industrial or even linguistic matters. A discursive artefact itself, pop has acted for almost half a century as a crucible for discourses interrogating the hierarchy of high and popular cultures in the post-modern age, the place of the state in the face of global commodification, and the nature of musical authenticity.

The notion of authenticity has in fact been at the heart of the popular-music debate since 1958, imprecise and constantly renegotiated but always related in some way to the entangled histories of *chanson* and pop. In the early 1960s, as *chanson* was steadily acquiring legitimacy with Brel, Brassens and Ferré, it also began to be threatened commercially by Anglo-Saxon styles of rock'n'roll, then pop. As a result, *chanson* discourse arguably began to harden into a defensive, 'distinctive' stance in which these three gifted singer-songwriters were enlisted as a national gold standard against which the 'authenticity' of other forms of popular-musical production might reliably be gauged.

Conclusion

Although some fairly fluid aesthetic boundaries between the big three and the stars of *variétés* had already been established during the late 1940s and 1950s, they began to take on clearer, firmer contours in the 1960s, as any music that could approximately be classed as 'Anglo-Saxon pop' was conceptualised as inferior and intrusive: a resentment which the spread of English words to identify such musics only confirmed and exacerbated. Hence the importance of naming pop *in French* among those concerned to have it legitimated and naturalised; the dissatisfaction with the result being no doubt a measure of the difficulty involved and the irreducibility of pop's otherness.

Meanwhile, largely oblivious or indifferent to this discursive conflict, the younger French consumer took to pop quite happily, once the first few years of parental disapproval had passed. In the process, authenticity acquired two more faces. First, what the history of the music points to above all is a coming of age of French pop in the 1980s after the early years of imitation, the gradual development of a more complex, more organic, more confident relationship with pop, culminating in techno, which at the end of the century broke a symbolic barrier by triumphing in the Anglo-Saxon arena, which earlier French stars like Françoise Hardy, Richard Anthony or Serge Gainsbourg had achieved only occasionally. Second, where reception is concerned, authenticity is often 'denationalised' by being located in various forms of intensity of response, in feeling, festivity, togetherness or personalised active listening; the opposite in fact of Adornian or Bourdieusian alienation. At face value, this broad conceptualisation seems a reasonably long way away from the 'national' authenticity associated with *chanson*. However, it is here that the part played by the state in the narrative becomes crucial, since definitions of popular-musical authenticity have become entangled with issues of cultural exceptionalism and threats to the republican tradition.

On the question of cultural policy, I share the theoretical tendency of a handful of writers – McGuigan and Street among them – to see cultural studies, whose focus has already shifted once from content analysis to reception and cultural practice, as needing to turn again, this time towards an engagement with the policies and institutions which shape reception and cultural practice. But I suggest that this is all the more necessary where France is concerned, because of the existence since 1959 of a powerful, centralised Ministry of Culture. In nearly forty-five years, the Ministry has become the most powerful agency of legitimation, particularly for those traditionally marginalised forms like pop which are not consecrated by the state education system or other established institutions. As with cultural industries generally, a different kind of consecration is available to pop artists through commercial success. But even in twenty-first century, neo-liberal France, the market does not offer the kind of solemn national consecration the state confers.

The Ministry has therefore attempted to do its democratic duty by observing pop's maturation and diversification and adjusting its cultural hierarchy accordingly. But legitimation comes at a price, for the state has constantly sought ways of harnessing pop to what Herman Lebovics calls 'the unique role of culture in the making of modern France':

> Culturally, national unity took the form of a population assimilated to a common civilisation, which was from the late nineteenth century classical in content and republican in its prescriptions. French republicanism interpreted the logic of the nation-state as requiring that [. . .] to share in the life of the nation one had to be a part of *the* national culture. This imperative of unity, then, required the French state to concern itself deeply with the cultural life of its citizens in the areas of language and aesthetics.[2]

Since 1981, I suggest, the state has looked to pop to help redefine this 'national culture'. This has effectively meant trying to square the circle. The difficulty is that French republicanism is monocultural and universalist, whereas pop has usually been seen as multicultural and particularist, specific to an 'age-class' or subculture. Much of the Ministry's discourse on pop, therefore, has been generated by the need to conceptualise it as an unconventional form of universalism. This conceptualisation has to do with the national status of music. I began by referring to the 'musicalisation' of French society. Politically, I would argue, this musicalisation has taken the form of a shift in the balance of cultural power, the written being steadily supplanted by the musical as a national paradigm. Since the Enlightenment at least, the gatekeepers of the French cultural establishment – intellectuals, the republican education system, the Académie Française, the arts administration – have built the nation's identity on the bedrock of what Lebovics calls 'the classical way of knowing', that is, on print culture: literature, thought and drama (the latter as an essentially literary form).[3] Within this perspective, France's native tongue has been seen as a finely tuned, rational instrument for defining and transmitting the cultural values of the 'one and indivisible Republic': rationality, clarity, civilisation. How far this self-image ever matched the actuality of cultural practices over the centuries, or was merely a false, even repressive representation of them, is too big a question to deal with here. But since the 1960s, the supremacy of the printed word has been challenged by successive generations of young people (the first of which is now in late middle age) who have become ever more attuned to audiovisual culture, as surveys of cultural practices confirm. As a result, an alternative rhetoric has been quietly gaining on the traditional cultural values of republican France: dance over words, sound over sense, communion over cerebration, body over mind, intensity over rationality.

Since 1959, institutional discourse, it would seem, has been running to catch up with this change. One result was the Ministry of Culture's adoption from 1981 of a conception of the cultural as an experience of intensity: Dionysian, physical, ecumenical. This can be seen not only in the Fête de la musique but also in the general tendency to turn the arts, heritage and commemoration into festive occasions: 'Le Printemps des poètes' (the Spring of the Poets), the bicentenary procession, 'La Fête de l'internet' and, most recently, the Techno Parade. As I suggested in the previous chapter, pop – particularly techno and raves – lends itself well to this kind of representation, seemingly offering the Ministry an ideal resolution of its perennial conflict over priorities. This 'musicalisation', I believe, amounts to a seismic change. From the Popular Front of 1936 until the 1980s, the elaboration of policy had been associated with, if not dominated by, theatre. For the great French directors of the first half of the century, Copeau, Dullin, Vilar and others, theatre was an intense, almost mystical experience of collective communion. Malraux, who had been close to the Popular Front, applied this conception to the *maisons de la culture*. Theatre, then, became a paradigm of what a public culture can achieve, its collective nature serving as a model for a unified nation. But with the advent of cinema, radio, TV and other domestic technologies, theatre today no longer has the same status or appeal. For contemporary French policy-makers, it would seem, music generally, but pop especially, offers a more up-to-the-minute replacement, though it is based on a somewhat different rhetoric from the one involving theatre. Where theatre was supposed to help achieve a single national culture, multiculturalism and *métissage* are taken to constitute a new unity-in-*diversity*, a national multiculture. This is evidenced in the literal and metaphorical importance of the festive in a range of public discourses including Hurstel, Fleuret and Lang: culture, defined broadly to include the popular and the amateur, should be a euphoric, carnivalesque experience to which we all bring our own idiosyncratic contributions but which nevertheless binds us together a community of intensity. The Ministry has also had to provide reassurance by appropriating threateningly 'alien' forms like rap and techno as authentically French, though this has recently meant tying itself in the kind of paradoxes I identified with regard to techno.

But beyond this rhetorical transformation of the notion of a national culture, a number of other issues underlie the history of French popular music in the public sphere, which largely remain unresolved or unaddressed. To begin with, it is important not to lose sight of the fact that pop has only partially been recognised by the state. As the Dutilh report makes plain, it is underfunded and under-prioritised in comparison with, say, opera. Furthermore, its status as 'legitimate' art is still ambiguous. In some readings of popular music's place in society, its amateur dimension is vital and should not play second fiddle to the more politically visible professional sector. This criticism is often made of French cultural policy generally, but with popular music it seems to have special currency because recognising amateur music-making is becoming a more common concern. In *Popular Music in Theory*, Keith Negus represents the diverse world of amateur music production and consumption as a possible third way, 'disconnected' from either commercial or national agendas. Citing a number of instances of how 'everyday musical activities' cross national frontiers and forge new alliances, he maintains that despite their variety such activities 'frequently do not correspond to the interests of the entertainment industry or fit in with the agenda of the nation state' and are therefore ignored. And yet, he goes on,

> it is here, in the often hidden world of everyday music making, where sounds can move beyond simply being a form of aesthetic expression or commercial com-
> modity and when music can take on a political significance as a medium of
> transnational knowledge and affective communication which moves across the
> borders of nation states and out from the generic categories of the music business.[4]

This, for Negus, is the real political and cultural importance of amateur music-making. Developing the idea of 'affective communication', he cites Laurence Grossberg's argument that 'music works "at the intersection of the body and emotions", and in so doing can generate "affective alliances" between people, which in turn can create the energy for social change that may have a direct impact on politics and culture'.[5] Implicit in Grossberg's notion is, once again, a more positive take on the shift in French music from words to sound. It suggests that, rather than being a cause for lamentation, a fall from grace into the abyss of irrationality, as Fumaroli or Finkielkraut appear to believe, popular music's affective nature in fact produces what Negus (quoting Paul Gilroy) calls 'forms of "counter-rationality" which in turn have created affiliations, alliances and understanding amongst dispersed and diverse groups of people'.[6] To an extent we are not all that far here from the Lang discourse of festive together-ness. However, Negus is plainly talking about a virtual underground of amateur musics which evade capture by either the state or the music business.

What underlies Negus's argument is the thought that music's potential in society lies in its 'counter-rational' ability not to unite a nation, as Lang implies, but to educate and transform the world. He emphasises 'how music works as a public form of knowledge and mode of understanding which is shared by vast numbers of people across the world'; it has 'knowledge-producing, transformative and communicative potentials'.[7] Negus accepts that this argument has something 'romantic' and 'utopian' about it, and he is no doubt wise to do so since it might otherwise be misinterpreted as merely a theorised version of that mawkish pop universalism which insists that all the world needs is a love train or a great big melting pot. In truth, his intimation that everyday, amateur, local music-making and the 'intercultural conversations' it can spontaneously generate represent an alternative politics is more grounded than that. It has something in common with Hennion's work on amateurism, with some of the recommendations made in the Hurstel report in the 1980s, and most of all with the theory of cultural development.

As we have seen, however, there is a rival discourse in French music policy, issuing from those like Dutilh who feel that there has been too much policy focus on the welfare and economic dimensions of popular music, and not enough on the aesthetic dimension, on the music as a legitimate creative art. But calls for a creation policy highlight another thorny debate for popular music in the public sphere, about how aesthetic judgements in this field are to be made.

The history of French pop and its official validation sheds light on the processes and discourses of legitimation in France, the strategies instinctively deployed by the pioneers and proselytisers of a particular cultural form in order to have that form officially recognised by the state. In order to speak up for pop against the likes of Fumaroli and Finkielkraut, the Dutilh report must attempt to bring it in from the cold, into the warm bosom of eternal high-cultural values, those consecrated by the republican education system, the arts establishment and the Ministry of Culture. This is a standard legitimating rhetoric in France, which has been at work for some years now on rap, whose emphasis on the spoken word has opened the way to its assimilation into a centuries-old oral and literary tradition. Again, nomenclature is fundamental to the legitimation process. Fumaroli, Finkielkraut and Dutilh all share an anxious awareness that naming is the battlefield on which culture wars are lost or won. Fumaroli and Finkielkraut kick furiously against the application to pop of the lexis of the cultural because it awards a patrimonial status which pop does not merit. Conversely, Dutilh argues that the category *musiques actuelles* denies pop a patrimonial meaning which it *does* merit. This is actually the weaker of the two arguments, since it fails to recognise the category's chief advantage, which is to confer a seriousness, a credibility which the standard nomenclature of 'pop' or 'rock' lacks, partly because of that nomenclature's associations with commercial entertainment and partly because of its origin in the English language. Far from severing pop from the past, terms like *musiques actuelles* or *musiques d'aujourd'hui* actually confer a dual legitimacy, both gallicising and dignifying: they strip away the frivolous, 'neo-colonial' implications of '*la pop*' or '*le rock*' and emphasise the music's place in a continuous French history. As Mignon observes, they also bring rock (in the narrow sense) closer to more legitimate forms like jazz and even, by semantic association, the 'contemporary music' of Boulez and company.[8]

However, legitimation strategies of this kind still evade the essential question of aesthetic judgement: what exactly *is* 'quality' in pop, and who decides? They rest on the dubious twin assumptions that what the Ministry recognises automatically acquires value, and that this value can only be measured by reference to traditional high-cultural criteria. Cultural studies has usefully challenged both assumptions, but as I have already pointed out, the results raise problems of their own. In *Performing Rites*, Frith rejects the out-and-out relativism which cultural studies has slipped into, and which makes any aesthetic judgement appear unacceptably hegemonic and conservative, even though, he argues, aesthetic judgements are made by music fans every day. In France, this is especially common with techno, where the websites of avant-garde or purist branches testify to a remarkable energy being expended on distinguishing what one is tempted to call 'high techno' from its commercial, mass-cultural varieties.[9] Frith's purpose then is, as he puts it, to take 'popular discrimination seriously' and to search for the basis upon which such discrimination functions.[10] His conclusion is that evaluation is carried out in relation not to absolute criteria of judgement nor to the relativity of the pure subject, but to the specific conditions of genre, production, reception, and so on. In his study of theoretical issues in cultural policy, *Culture and the Public Sphere*, McGuigan makes an essentially similar point in the context of policy judgements:

> A real danger, certainly from a critical perspective, is to fall silent about questions of value as a result of extreme relativism, typically in negation of conservative and absolutist positions, because such questions are thus thought to be somehow tainted. There are two initial ways out of this trap [. . .]. The first is really rather common-sensical and none the worse for it. This is that a cultural performance may be deemed 'good' or 'bad' of its kind, that is, within its own discursive field. [. . .] The second point, and closely connected to the first, is the assumption that value and quality are also multiple and variable in relation to specific media, forms and socio-cultural contexts. There is no gold standard that applies to all cultural currency: value is various and variously contestable across different positions, though there may be more scope for communicating across different positions than is imagined by extreme relativism.[11]

What both McGuigan and Frith are intimating is that the as it were 'heroic' relativism which first allowed forms like pop to be thought worthy of analysis in the first place now needs to be tempered if we are to continue making any critical judgements at all. This is all the more essential, of course, where government intervention is concerned, for here evaluation and selection are unavoidable and, in the absence of such judgements issuing from elsewhere, are likely to be carried out by committee. Yet how exactly *should* such selective judgements be made in an age characterised by cultural uncertainty? Or as Georgina Born frames the question in her essay 'Music Policy, Aesthetic and Social Difference', 'can there be a postmodern music-cultural policy?'

This question is especially relevant to French music policy since 1981, as Born briefly acknowledges. For her purposes, post-modernism is defined as characterised by 'radical doubts about modernism and about statist cultural institutions, and involving an accommodation to commercial market forces'; and, aesthetically, 'by an absence of historical certainty, by exploration and parody of earlier cultural forms, by the embrace of "other" (ethnic, non-western and popular) cultures, and so greater pluralism and populism'. Post-modernism therefore 'sits uneasily with the question of developing progressive cultural policy, and the problems of the legitimation and judgement of different cultural or musical forms for subsidy which that subsumes'.[12] This is demonstrated by the Thatcher government of the 1980s, which stripped away UK government intervention in the arts to leave them much more exposed to market forces. Born then contrasts this with the French example after 1981, which has been considerably more interventionist and yet still purports to be pluralist, though all this achieves, in Born's estimate, is to show 'the cracks of trying to bridge the contradictions of a statist postmodernism'.[13]

She nevertheless makes a persuasive case for the continued relevance of policy, but in an altered form. Exploring what a workable post-modern cultural policy might look like, she first proposes aesthetic pluralism: supporting previously marginalised forms (such as rock or ethnic or improvised musics), in the way both Lang and Ken Livingstone's Greater London Council attempted to in the 1980s. To this she adds 'support for new social sources and forms of culture' (women, ethnic and sexual minorities, and so on), and 'support to enable musics which have not been effectively mass-produced and distributed, to be industrialised on a small scale – to find some kind of market niche', for example by 'the setting up of popular music centres and alternative circuits of production and distribution'.[14] Again one recognises aspects of Bruno Lion's policies under Lang. But for Born, such policies, while desirable, are problematic in that they elevate 'the social to such an extent that it risks obliterating the specificity of the aesthetic'. This is precisely the weakness identified in the French model by the Dutilh report. As Born argues, no advances 'in the social and institutional forms of cultural production' will be fully satisfactory 'if they are not matched by ' "*good enough music*" '. Thus in the end, musical-aesthetic judgements must be made, and not evaded [. . .].'[15] For Born, then, as for McGuigan, what is needed to produce an effective post-modern music policy is a way of organising critical evaluation which does not lay down supposedly eternal, all-purpose criteria of judgement but which also avoids complete relativism, one which in fact 'models as closely as possible the contemporary aesthetic process itself: a diverse, plural and volatile set of genre-specific panels, made up of elected musical "experts" (organic intellectuals) from those genres; but changing, evolving, and above all *interrelating*, shifting the boundaries'.[16]

This is the aesthetic issue which French music policy is only just beginning to confront, after years of avoiding it by adopting a more manageable social and economic conception of popular music. As we have seen, versions of Born's central notion of a limited relativism leaving room for critical judgement are present in several recent French discourses, particularly in Rigaud, Dutilh and, further back, Fleuret, who, as a music critic, had inevitably to cast judgment but who did not adhere to the view that there is only one definition of aesthetic excellence. But what arguably prevents a more full-blooded adoption of this notion is, I suggest, a fear of particularism, of contravening the dogma of republican universalism. Identifiable not only in backward-looking intellectuals like Finkielkraut and Fumaroli but also in the diverse political arguments of Rigaud, Dutilh or Lang, in *chanson* discourse, and even in some techno discourses is a persistent concern with the national, with the Republic as one and indivisible, or with immutable national-aesthetic values, whether in the form of an unshakeable faith in French high culture, a tendency to separate *chanson* from pop and easy listening, or the promotion of citizenship through cultural empowerment. This is not to suggest that all such positions are glibly nationalistic, since they are part of much more complex discourses of republicanism and cultural pluralism on both the Left and the Right. But it is to suggest that a concern with national authenticity – whether defined as the home-grown *chanson* or more recently as *métissage* – persists in a surprisingly wide range of public or para-public discourses on music and culture, as one criterion among others used to award aesthetic and cultural legitimacy. It is this, I believe, which puts French music policy in the position of having to square the circle, trapping it in the 'contradictions of a state postmodernism' identified by Born and in the similar paradox which underlies government responses to techno.

Whether and how this paradox will be resolved remains to be seen, especially as a number of imponderable changes have already marked the new century or are about to at the time of writing. Musically, techno in the 1990s represented itself as a new sound for a new century, but it is too early to say with confidence what its real significance is or where it will go. As it fuses with jazz or drifts towards easy-listening, some pundits already detect stagnation in its sound experiments, caused by the widespread use of the same software. *Les Inrockuptibles'* Christophe Conte, who believes that *chanson* has never really stopped being the French mainstream (Hallyday and Goldman still sell albums by the million), suspects that some DJs may have reached their creative limits with computers and that there is what he calls (probably ironically) 'a desire to return to the magic of *chanson*' and 'the cult of the musician'.[17] Industrially and commercially, the potential cataclysm of free downloaded music still hovers over the global record industry and concentration marches unstoppably on, taking a momentous turn in December 2000 when the French media company Vivendi and the French pay TV channel Canal Plus merged with Seagram to form yet another multimedia giant, Vivendi Universal. Precisely what this will mean for France at the international level is again hard to say as yet, though Vivendi Universal's managing director Jean-Marie Messier – a highly Americanised Frenchman based in New York – promptly set the cat among the pigeons by announcing that the French cultural exception was dead.[18] On the political front, although Trautmann's replacement in 2000, Catherine Tasca, did not bring about a major rethink of music policy, what will be the impact of a new Centre-Right presidency, overshadowed by accusations of financial irregularities, an obsession with law and order, and the resurgence of Jean-Marie Le Pen? But whatever happens in tomorrow's France, popular music will surely continue to be one of the leading laboratories in which the French cultural exception is tested, reworked and argued over with passion.

Notes

1. Hurstel report, unpaginated summary on first page.
2. Herman Lebovics, *Mona Lisa's Escort: André Malraux and the Reinvention of French Culture* (Cornell University Press, 1999), pp. 29–30 (original emphasis).
3. Ibid., p. xi.
4. Negus, *Popular Music in Theory*, p. 220.
5. Ibid., p. 220.
6. Ibid., p. 222.
7. Ibid., pp. 221–2.
8. Mignon, 'Évolution de la prise en compte', p. 30.
9. I am grateful to my MA student Rachel Jenkins for pointing out these sites, and this distinction.
10. Frith, *Performing Rites*, p. 16.
11. Jim McGuigan, *Culture and The Public Sphere* (Routledge, 1996), p. 45.
12. Georgina Born, 'Afterword: Music Policy, Aesthetic and Social Difference', in Bennett *et al.* (eds), *Rock and Popular Music*, all quotations from pp. 277–8.
13. Ibid, p. 278.

14. Ibid., p. 279.
15. Ibid., quotations from pp. 280–1 (original emphasis).
16. Ibid, p. 281 (original emphasis).
17. 'Touch Down or Lift Off?' (interview with Christophe Conte and Pascal Dauzier), *Time Out Paris Free Guide*, pp. 15–17 (quotation p. 17).
18. As this book was going to press (July 2002), Messier stepped down and left the company.

Chronology

1851	Creation of the SACEM
	Birth of Aristide Bruant
1867	Cafés which feature singers are authorised to hire acts performing in costume and with props
1869	Les Folies-Bergère opens
1870	Third Republic begins
1871	Commune de Paris
1873	Birth of Jeanne Bourgeois (Mistinguett)
1877	The first phonograph is invented by Edison
c.1880	Bobino opens as a *café-concert*.
1880	Birth of Maurice Chevalier
1882	Free, compulsory primary education becomes law
1885	Bruant opens his own cabaret in Montmartre, Le Mirliton (formerly Le Chat noir), where he performs for the next ten years
1893	L'Olympia opens
1894–6	Based on Emile Berliner's invention of the gramophone and flat recording disc in the late 1880s, the record industry begins when Berliner moves from rubber to shellac pressings
1896	Creation of Société Pathé-Frères
1906	Birth of Mireille Hartuch (Mireille)
1915	Birth of Édith Gassion (Piaf)
1916	Birth of Léo Ferré
	Chevalier's career as a star begins in earnest
1918	Birth of Pierre Delanoë
1920	Birth of Boris Vian
1921	Birth of Georges Brassens
1924	Birth of Varenagh Aznavourian (Charles Aznavour)
1925	Death of Bruant
1928	L'Olympia becomes a cinema
	Birth of Lucien Ginzburg (Serge Gainsbourg)
1929	Birth of Jacques Brel in Brussels

1930	Birth of Monique Serf (Barbara)
1933	Trenet begins his singing career in a duo with Johnny Hess
1936	Popular Front government begins
1939	Birth of Claude François
1940	June: German occupation of France begins, ending the Third Republic
1943	Creation of Radio Monte-Carlo (RMC)
	Birth of Jean-Philippe Smet (Johnny Hallyday)
1944	August: liberation of Paris
	Birth of Françoise Hardy
1945	French record labels Blue Star (later renamed Barclay) and Vogue founded.
	Birth of Alain Souchon
1946	Start of the Fourth Republic
	Birth of Annie Chancel (Sheila)
	Birth of Bernard Lavilliers
1947	The microgroove vinyl record is launched; first adopted in France by Eddie Barclay
1948	Fender becomes the first to market a solid electric guitar
1949	Birth of Maxime Le Forestier
1951	Birth of Jean-Jacques Goldman
1952	Birth of Renaud Séchan (Renaud)
	Brassens's recording career begins
1953	Brel's and Bécaud's recording careers begin
	Marlon Brando stars in Laslo Benedek's film *The Wild One* (*L'Équipée sauvage* in France)
	Birth of Francis Cabrel
1954	L'Olympia re-opens as a music hall, under Bruno Coquatrix's management
	April: Bill Haley records 'Rock Around the Clock'
	May: Presley records 'That's All Right Mama' and 'Blue Moon of Kentucky' for Sam Philips's Sun Records
1955	Europe 1 begins broadcasting
	Mireille's Petit Conservatoire de la chanson begins
	Release of Nicholas Ray's film *Rebel Without a Cause* (*La Fureur de vivre* in France), starring James Dean
	Release of Richard Brooks's film *Blackboard Jungle* (*Graine de violence* in France), which turns Haley's 'Rock Around the Clock' into a worldwide hit
1956	Death of Mistinguett
	Henry Cording (alias Henri Salvador) and his Original Rock and

Roll Boys release an EP on Fontana of rock'n'roll parodies, written by Boris Vian and Michel Legrand

1957   Pierre Delanoë does his first adaptations of Elvis into French
        Creation of MPO, first vinyl record-pressing plant in France

1958   De Gaulle returns to power and sets up the Fifth Republic
        Vian publishes *En avant la zizique*
        Danyel Gérard has a hit with Vian's rock'n'roll spoof 'D'où viens-tu Billy Boy?' During the same period (1958–9), Claude Spiron, Richard Anthony and others release early French attempts at rock

1959   Ministry of Cultural Affairs created, under Malraux
        Death of Boris Vian
        School-leaving age raised from fourteen to sixteen
        'Summer of the *blousons noirs*'
        Summer: first broadcast of 'Salut les copains'; from October the programme goes out daily
        December: Hallyday appears at Marcadet Palace

1960   14 March: Hallyday's first 45 rpm is released on Vogue, an EP containing 'T'aimer follement' and three other tracks: 'Laisse les filles', 'J'étais fou' and 'Oh! Oh! Baby'
        18 April: Hallyday's first TV appearance, on 'L'École des vedettes'
        Hallyday's second EP and first major hit, 'Souvenirs, souvenirs' (also including Elvis's 'I Got Stung', adapted as 'Je suis mordu')
        20 September: Hallyday's first big Parisian concert at L'Alhambra, as support act for Raymond Devos

1961   February: first French pop 'festival' at the Palais des sports
        September: Hallyday first performs at L'Olympia

1962   Hallyday popularises the twist in France; his version of 'Let's Twist Again' becomes his first million-seller
        Françoise Hardy releases her first single, 'Tous les garçons et les filles' (originally the B-side)
        Ferré's collected lyrics appear in Seghers's contemporary poetry series
        June: *Salut les copains* magazine launched

1963   Death of Piaf
        Brassens's collected lyrics appear in the Seghers's series
        22 June: 'La Nuit de la Nation'
        July: Morin's articles on the 'Nation' event in *Le Monde*

1964   Brel's collected lyrics appear in the Seghers's series
        January and February: the Beatles play L'Olympia to a mixed reception but begin to make their mark in France, particularly among *lycée* and university students

1965	Hugues Aufray releases his album *Aufray chante Dylan*, which helps Dylan become more widely known in France
	June: the Beatles second season in Paris, at Le Palais des sports, has a better reception
1966	First hippie communes appear in USA, chiefly San Francisco
	Malraux sets up the Ministry of Cultural Affair's 'Music Service', under Landowski
	Rock & Folk magazine launched
	Under influence of Dylan and the American folk movement, a 'beatnik' fashion begins in France
1967	News of US hippie phenomenon becomes widespread in France
	Brel gives up live performance
1968	Music magazine *Best* launched
	Lancelot's *Je veux regarder Dieu en face*
	April: Lancelot's radio programme 'Campus' begins on Europe 1
	May: student and worker protests bring France to a standstill
1969	Woodstock
	First French, Woodstock-style pop festival held in Amougies (Belgium), featuring French and international acts (Pink Floyd, Frank Zappa)
	Gainsbourg and Birkin's 'Je t'aime, moi non plus' becomes an international hit
	Ministry of Cultural Affairs' Music Service becomes Directorate for Music and Dance
	April: de Gaulle resigns as President, replaced by Pompidou
	June: Malraux resigns as Minister of Cultural Affairs
1970	Hallyday's song 'Jésus-Christ est un hippie' banned on almost all French radio stations
1970–1	Folk-club boom throughout France
1971	January: Duhamel becomes Minister of Cultural Affairs
1972	Death of Chevalier
	Le Forestier's first appearance at Bobino, as support act for Brassens
	MPO among the pioneers of cassettes
1973	Dillaz's *La Chanson française de contestation*
	Moustaki's *Questions à la chanson*
	Richard Branson starts Virgin group, the first new music major for years
	April: Duhamel resigns from Ministry of Cultural Affairs
1974	May: Valéry Giscard d'Estaing (Centre-Right) elected President
	Landowski resigns from Directorate for Music and Dance
1976	IRCAM set up

Chronology

1977	Le Printemps de Bourges festival begins
1978	Renaud's first hit single, 'Laisse béton'
	Disco at its height in France
	Accidental death of Claude François
	October: death of Brel
1979	Barclay label taken over by Polygram (owned by Philips)
	First Transmusicales de Rennes
	Crisis in world record industry
	November: Chapier working party on *chanson* holds first meeting
1980	First issue of *Paroles et musique* (by subscription only)
	July: Chapier submits truncated report
1981	Death of Brassens
	Bertin's *Chante toujours, tu m'intéresses*
	May: Mitterrand (Socialist Party) elected President; Lang becomes Minister of Culture
	November: Private local radio stations legalised by Socialist government
	December: Rita Mitsouko's first single, 'Don't Forget the Night', released
1982	Bondage Records launched
	3 February and 16 June: Lang and Fleuret announce a new music policy, including support for popular music
	21 June: first Fête de la musique
1983	Studio des variétés enrols its first students
1984	Paris Zénith inaugurated by Mitterrand
	'Sound Plan' (Plan Son) launched
	SOS Racisme founded
	MPO becomes the first company to manufacture CDs in France
	November: first edition of the Top 50
	December: publication of *Maxi-rock, mini-bruits*
1985	15 June: SOS Racisme's first Touche pas à mon pote concert at the Place de la Concorde in Paris
1986	Bobigny festival is the first to feature raï acts outside Algeria, including Khaled
	Carte de séjour's version of Trenet's 'Douce France'
	Montpellier Zénith opens
	House music begins in USA
	March: Socialists defeated in legislative elections. Lang replaced by Léotard; Mitterrand appoints Chirac Prime Minister, creating first period of Left–Right 'cohabitation'
1987	Finkielkraut's *La Défaite de la pensée*

FNAC says it will no longer charge full VAT on records
Advertising for records authorised
Chirac receives Madonna in the Paris *hôtel de ville*
Mitterrand attends Printemps de Bourges
MTV begins to be available in Paris
1 December: lower VAT rate on records (18.6 per cent) comes into effect

1988   Sony buys CBS
Birth of techno in Detroit
January: bill on creative-arts education becomes law
May: Mitterrand re-elected President, ending cohabitation, Lang returns as Minister of Culture
Summer: first big raves take place in UK

1989   Lang launches Operation French Revolution in New York
Ministry of Culture's 'Labels Plan' launched
Laurent Garnier is one of first DJs to introduce techno in France
First Love Parade in Berlin
May: Bruno Lion appointed 'Monsieur Rock' at Ministry of Culture
14 July: Bicentenary Parade down Champs-Élysées, orchestrated by Jean-Paul Goude

1990   Release of first *Rapattitude* album and of MC Solaar's first single, 'Bouge de là'
France's largest independent label, Carrère, sells out to Warner
Le Hall de la chanson initiated
Rigaud's *Libre Culture*
November: Lang launches French Music Office in New York

1991   Fumaroli's *L'État culturel*
Death of Gainsbourg
Release of MC Solaar's first album, *Qui sème le vent récolte le tempo*
First *cafés-musiques* launched

1992   Vogue, France's last substantial independent label, is bought out by BMG; Richard Branson sells Virgin Music to EMI
Zéniths open in Toulon and Pau
Autumn: first issue of Hidalgo's *Chorus: Les Cahiers de la chanson*

1993   March: Socialists defeated in legislative elections; second period of cohabitation begins (Édouard Balladur Prime Minister); Lang replaced by Jacques Toubon
May: Trenet's eightieth birthday tour ends at Paris's Opéra-Bastille, in the presence of President Mitterrand
July: Death of Ferré: amongst those paying tribute are ex-Minister Lang, Minister Toubon and President Mitterrand

The Pelchat amendment introduces French-song quota for radio
Nancy and Caen Zéniths open
Schneider's *La Comédie de la culture*
December: end of Uruguay Round of GATT negotiations brings
the notion of a French cultural exception to the fore
French Music Export Bureau created

1994   Laurent Garnier starts his own label, F Communications, and
releases his first album, *Shot in the Dark*
1 February: Radio quota law comes progressively into force

1995   May: Chirac elected President, ending second cohabitation (Alain
Juppé Prime Minister); Toubon replaced by Philippe Douste-Blazy
1 August: VAT on record goes up to 20.6 per cent
Publication of police report 'Les Soirées raves: des situations à hauts
risques'
Rigaud's *L'Exception culturelle*
Debré circular instructing local authorities to act against raves

1996   Summer: dispute between FN Mayor of Toulon and Gérard
Paquet's Théâtre national de la danse et de l'image in Châteauvallon
November: NTM receive a prison sentence for outrage against the
police
Rigaud report submitted

1997   January: Daft Punk's album *Homework* released
June: in surprise legislative elections, the PS triumphs: Jospin
becomes Prime Minister and the third period of cohabitation
begins; Douste-Blazy replaced by Catherine Trautmann
July: Lang attends Berlin Love Parade
November: death of Barbara
December: Trautmann announces new measures for techno and
present-day musics generally, and the creation of Dutilh's Commission nationale des musiques actuelles

1998   Air's first album, *Moon Safari*, released
Laurent Garnier wins the first Victoire de la musique for techno
Ministry of Culture's music directorate (DMD) merged with theatre
directorate
Polygram bought up by Canadian drinks giant Seagram
September: Dutilh report submitted
19 September: first Techno Parade
19 October: Trautmann announces new measures for present-day
musics, which will be a priority area in the 1999 Culture budget
December: new instructions from Trautmann to Prefects concerning raves

1999 May: French Music Bureau in London opens
June: Trautmann convenes États-généraux du disque
September: second Techno Parade

2000 French record sales abroad reach 39 million, from only 1.5 million in 1992 (French Music Bureau UK statistics)
March: in a government reshuffle, Trautmann is replaced by Catherine Tasca
16 September: third Techno Parade
December: Vivendi and Universal (Seagram) merge

2001 Deaths of Trenet (February) and Bécaud (December); anniversaries of deaths of Brassens and Gainsbourg marked
Vivendi Universal's managing director Jean-Marie Messier declares the French cultural exception dead

2002 April–June: Jospin ousted in first round of presidential elections by Le Pen; Chirac then defeats Le Pen in second round and is re-elected President (for another five years); after the ensuing legislative elections, the 'presidential majority union' (Centre and Right) dominates government and National Assembly: end of third cohabitation

Bibliography

I list here all the works and documents cited as well as those which have marked the book most. Of the innumerable press articles, press releases and unpublished institutional documents consulted, I have only listed those of some substance, omitting here the shorter or ephemeral pieces I have cited in full in the endnotes. Unpublished ministerial or other official documents are available for consultation at the Centre de documentation of the Ministry of Culture's Département des études et de la prospective, 2 rue Jean-Lantier, 75001 Paris. Within each section, works are in alphabetical order unless otherwise stated.

Books and Chapters in Books

Achard, M., *Souvenirs, souvenirs . . .*, Paris: Flammarion, 1998.

Adem-Florida (ed.), *Politiques publiques et musiques amplifiées*, Groupe d'étude sur les musiques amplifiées, Aquitaine: Adem-Florida, Conseil Régional d'Aquitaine, 1997.

Amont, M., *Une Chanson, qu'y a-t-il à l'intérieur d'une chanson?*, Paris: Seuil, 1994.

Anonymous, 'Musiques amplifiées et aménagement culturel du territoire', summary of workshop discussion, in Adem-Florida (ed.), *Politiques publiques et musiques amplifiées*, Groupe d'étude sur les musiques amplifiées, Aquitaine: Adem-Florida, Conseil Régional d'Aquitaine, 1997, pp. 41–3.

Bakhtin, M., *Rabelais and His World*, translated by H. Iswolsky, Bloomington: Indiana University Press, 1984.

Bara, G., *La Techno*, Collection Librio Musique, Paris: EJL, 1999.

Barrow, T. and Newby, J., *Inside The Music Business*, London and New York: Routledge, 1995.

Becker, H., *Art Worlds*, Los Angeles and London: University of California Press, 1982.

Benetello, A. and Le Goff, Y., 'Historique (aspects politique, économique et social)', in A.-M. Gourdon (ed.), *Le Rock: aspects esthétiques, culturels et sociaux*, Paris: CNRS Éditions, 1994, pp. 11–53.

Bennett, T., Frith, S., Grossberg, L., Shepherd, J. and Turner, G. (eds), *Rock and Popular Music: Politics, Policies, Institutions*, London and New York: Routledge, 1993.

Bertin, J., *Chante toujours, tu m'intéresses*, Paris: Seuil, 1981.

Bigot, P., *Questions pour la chanson*, Paris: IRMA Éditions, 1996.

Born, G., 'Afterword: Music Policy, Aesthetic and Social Difference', in T. Bennett, S. Frith, L. Grossberg, J. Shepherd and G. Turner (eds), *Rock and Popular Music: Politics, Policies, Institutions*, London and New York: Routledge, 1993, pp. 266–92.

Boucher, M., *Rap, expression des lascars: significations et enjeux du rap dans la société française*, Paris: L'Harmattan, 1998.

Bourdieu, P., *Distinction: A Social Critique of the Judgement of Taste*, translated by R. Nice, London: Routledge and Kegan Paul, 1984; first published as *La Distinction: critique sociale du jugement*, Paris: Les Éditions de Minuit, 1979.

—— and Darbel, A., *The Love of Art: European Museums and Their Public*, translated by C. Beattie and N. Merriman, Stanford, Calif.: Stanford University Press, 1990; first published as *L'Amour de l'art: les musées d'art européens et leur public*, Paris: Éditions de Minuit, 1966.

Breatnach, M. and Sterenfeld, E., 'From Messiaen to MC Solaar: Music in France in the Second Half of the Twentieth Century', in W. Kidd and S. Reynolds (eds), *Contemporary French Cultural Studies*, London: Arnold, 2000.

Brunschwig, C., Calvet, L.-J. and Klein, J.-C., *Cent Ans de chanson française*, Paris: Seuil, 1981.

Calvet, L.-J., *La Chanson française aujourd'hui*, Paris: Hachette, 1974.

—— *Chanson et société*, Paris: Payot, 1981.

Castanet, P.-A., 'Les Années 1968: les mouvances d'une révolution socio-culturelle populaire', in A. Hennion (ed.), *1789–1989, Musique, histoire, démocratie*, actes du colloque international, Paris 17–20 July 1989, 3 vols, Paris: Fondation de la Maison des Sciences de l'Homme, 1992, vol. II, pp. 145–52.

Certeau, M. de, *La Culture au pluriel*, new edition by L. Giard, Paris: Seuil, 1993 (first published 1974).

—— *L'Invention du quotidien*, new, revised edition by L. Giard, 2 vols: I. *Arts de faire*, Paris: Gallimard/Folio, 1990 (first published 1980); vol. II: co-authored by Certeau, Giard and P. Mayol, *Habiter, cuisiner*, Paris: Gallimard/Folio, 1994 (first published 1980).

Chambard, L. and Damoiseau, R., *La Chanson d'aujourd'hui: mythes et images du temps present 1960–1980*, Sevrès: CIEP/ ELP, 1984.

Chambers, I., *Urban Rhythms: Pop Music and Popular Culture*, Basingstoke: Macmillan, 1985.

Chocron, C., 'Les Enjeux économiques du rock', in A.-M. Gourdon (ed.), *Le Rock: aspects esthétiques, culturels et sociaux*, Paris: CNRS Éditions, 1994, pp. 109–39.

Clayson, A., *Jacques Brel*, Chessington: Castle Communications, 1996.

Colin, J.-P., *La Beauté du manchot: culture et différence*, Paris: Éditions Publisud, 1986.

Comité d'histoire du Ministère de la culture (ed.), *Les Affaires culturelles au temps de Jacques Duhamel 1971–1973: actes des journées d'étude 7 et 8 décembre 1993*, Paris: Documentation Française, 1995.

—— *Les Affaires culturelles au temps d'André Malraux 1959–1969*, Paris: Documentation Française, 1996.

Coulomb, S. and Varrod, D., *1968–1988: Histoire de chansons: de Maxime Leforestier à Étienne Daho*, Paris: Balland, 1987.

Coulonges, G., *La Chanson en son temps de Béranger au juke-box*, Paris: Les Éditeurs Français Réunis, 1969.

D'Angelo, M., *Socio-économie de la musique en France: diagnostic d'un système vulnérable*, Paris: Documentation Française, 1997.

Darré, A. (ed.), *Musique et politique: les répertoires de l'identité*, Rennes: Presses Universitaires de Rennes, 1996.

Delanoë, P., *La Chanson en colère: entretiens avec Alain-Gilles Minella*, Paris: Mame, 1993.

—— *La Vie en rose: French Popular Songs in the 20th Century*, London: Thames and Hudson, 1997; first published as *La Vie en rose: hymne à la chanson française*, Paris: Plume, 1997.

Dillaz, S., *La Chanson française de contestation: des barricades de la Commune à celles de mai 1968*, Paris: Seghers, 1973.

—— *La Chanson sous la Troisième République, 1870–1940*, Paris: Tallandier, 1991.

Dister, A., *Cultures rock*, Les Essentiels Milan, Toulouse: Éditions Milan, 1996.

Dumazedier, J., *Vers une civilisation du loisir?*, Paris: Seuil, 1962.

Duneton, C., *Histoire de la chanson française: de 1780 à 1860*, Paris: Seuil, 1998, 2 vols.

Dunn, T., 'The Evolution of Cultural Studies', in D. Punter (ed.), *Introduction to Contemporary Cultural Studies*, London: Longman, 1986, pp. 71–91.

Eling, K., *The Politics of Cultural Policy in France*, Basingstoke: Macmillan, 1999.

Farchy, J., *La Fin de l'exception culturelle?*, CNRS Communication, Paris: CNRS Éditions, 1999.

Finkielkraut, A., *The Undoing of Thought*, translated by D. O'Keefe, London and Lexington: Claridge Press, 1988; first published as *La Défaite de la pensée*, Folio Essais, Paris: Gallimard, 1987.

Fléouter, C., *Un Siècle de chansons*, Paris: Presses Universitaires de France, 1988.

—— *Johnny: la dernière des légendes*, Collection J'ai Lu, Paris: Éditions Robert Laffont, 1992.

Fontana, C. and Fontaine, A., 'Un Environnement propice à la modification de la réalité ordinaire', in J.-L. Terradillos and M. Martin (eds), *La Fête techno: approche sociologique, médicale et juridique, d'un mouvement musical à un phénomène de société*, proceedings of colloquium held in Poitiers, 5–6 June 1997, Poitiers: Le Confort Moderne, 1997, pp. 34–40.

Frisch, A., 'Aspects juridiques: interdiction-répression', in J.-L. Terradillos and M. Martin (eds), *La Fête techno: approche sociologique, médicale et juridique, d'un mouvement musical à un phénomène de société*, proceedings of colloquium held in Poitiers, 5–6 June 1997, Poitiers: Le Confort Moderne, 1997, pp. 73–9.

Frith, S., *Sound Effects: Youth, Leisure and the Politics of Rock*, London: Constable, 1983.

—— *Music for Pleasure: Essays in the Sociology of Pop*, Cambridge: Polity Press, 1988.

—— (ed.), *World Music, Politics and Social Change*, Manchester: Manchester University Press, 1989.

—— 'Popular Music and the Local State', in T. Bennett, S. Frith, L. Grossberg, J. Shepherd and G. Turner (eds), *Rock and Popular Music: Politics, Policies, Institutions*, London and New York: Routledge, 1993, pp. 14–24.

—— *Performing Rites: Evaluating Popular Music*, Oxford and New York: Oxford University Press, 1998 (first published 1996).

Fulcher, J. F., *French Cultural Politics and Music: From the Dreyfus Affair to the First World War*, Oxford and New York: Oxford University Press, 1999.

Fumaroli, M., *L'État culturel: une religion moderne*, Paris: Éditions de Fallois, 1991.

Goudeau, M. and Tourne, P., *Sur l'air du temps: trente chansons qui ont changé la France*, Paris: Lattès, 1999.

Gourdon, A.-M., 'Le Rock en France: dix ans de politique culturelle (1981–1991)', in A.-M. Gourdon (ed.), *Le Rock: aspects esthétiques, culturels et sociaux*, Paris: CNRS Éditions, 1994, pp. 141–50.

—— (ed.), *Le Rock: aspects esthétiques, culturels et sociaux*, Paris: CNRS Éditions, 1994.

Gumplowicz, P., 'Au Hot Club de France, on ne faisait pas danser les filles', in P. Gumplowicz and J.-C. Klein (eds), *Paris 1944–1954. Artistes, intellectuels, publics: la culture comme enjeu*, Série Mémoires no. 38, Paris: Éditions Autrement, 1995, pp. 167–82.

Hawkins, P., *Chanson: The French Singer-Songwriter from Aristide Bruant to the Present Day*, Aldershot: Ashgate, 2000.

Hebdige, D., *Subculture: The Meaning of Style*, London and New York: Methuen, 1979.

Hennion, A., *Les Professionnels du disque: une sociologie des variétés*, Paris: Métailié, 1981.

—— 'Scène rock, concert classique', in P. Mignon and A. Hennion (eds), *Rock: de l'histoire au mythe*, Paris: Anthropos, 1991, pp. 101–19.

—— *La Passion musicale: une sociologie de la médiation*, Paris: Métailié, 1993.

—— 'L'Amour de la musique aujourd'hui: une recherche en cours sur les figures de l'amateur', in A. Darré (ed.), *Musique et politique: les répertoires de l'identité*, Rennes: Presses Universitaires de Rennes, 1996, pp. 41–50.

Hoffmann, R. and Leduc, J.-M. *Rock babies: 25 ans de pop music*, 3rd revised and extended edition, Paris: Seuil, 1978.

Hunter, M., *Les Jours les plus Lang*, Paris: Éditions Odile Jacob, 1990.

Kelberg, D., *La Chanson française et les pouvoirs publics*, Aix-en-Provence: Presses Universitaires d'Aix-Marseille, 1997, 2 vols.

Kelly, M., 'Catholic Cultural Policy from 1944 to 1950: "Bande dessinée" and Cinema', in B. Rigby and N. Hewitt (eds), *France and the Mass Media*, Basingstoke: Macmillan, 1991, pp. 20–36.

Klein, J.-C., *Florilège de la chanson française*, Paris: Bordas, 1990.

Kuhn, R., *The Media in France*, London and New York: Routledge, 1995.

Lagrée, J.-C., *Les Jeunes chantent leurs cultures*, Paris: L'Harmattan, 1982.

Lancelot, M., *Je veux regarder Dieu en face: le phénomène hippie*, Paris: Albin Michel, 1968.

Lapassade, G. and Rousselot, P., *Le Rap ou la fureur de dire*, 5th revised edition, Paris: Éditions Loris Talmart, 1996.

Lebovics, H., *Mona Lisa's Escort: André Malraux and the Reinvention of French Culture*, Ithaca and London: Cornell University Press, 1999.

Le Diberder, A. and Pflieger, S., see BIPE under **Reports, Speeches and Other Documents** below.

Lefeuvre, G., *Le Producteur de disques*, Paris: Dixit-Irma, 1998.

Léotard, F., *Culture: les chemins du printemps*, Paris: Albin Michel, 1988.

Lipovetsky, G., *L'Ere du vide: essais sur l'individualisme contemporain*, Paris: Gallimard/ Folio, 1983.

Longhurst, B., *Popular Music and Society*, Cambridge: Polity Press, 1995.

Looseley, D.L., *The Politics of Fun: Cultural Policy and Debate in Contemporary France*, New York and London: Berg, 1995 (paperback 1997).

—— 'The Work and the Person: Discourse and Dialogue in the History of the Ministry of Culture', in M.E. Allison and O.N. Heathcote (eds), *The Fifth Republic: Forty Years On*, Bern: Peter Lang, 1999, pp. 237–53.

—— 'Naming the Popular: Youth Music, Politics and Nation in Contemporary France', in J. Marks and E. McCaffrey (eds), *French Cultural Debates*, Monash Romance Studies, Newark: University of Delaware Press, 2001, pp. 109–20.

McGuigan, J., *Cultural Populism*, London and New York: Routledge, 1992.

—— *Culture and the Public Sphere*, London and New York: Routledge, 1996.

Maffesoli, M., *Le Temps des tribus*, 3rd edition, Paris: La Table Ronde, 2000 (first published 1988); translated as *The Time of the Tribes*, by D. Smith, London: Sage, 1995.

—— 'Entretien avec Michel Maffesoli', in M. Gaillot, *Sens multiple: la techno: un laboratoire artistique et politique du présent*, Paris: Dis voir, 1998, pp. 101–20.

Maison des cultures du monde, *Les Musiques du monde en question*, Internationale de l'imaginaire, new series, no.11, [Paris]: Babel, 1999.

Marwick, A., *The Sixties: Cultural Revolution in Britain, France, Italy and the United States, c.1958–c.1974*, Oxford: Oxford University Press, 1998 (paperback 1999).

Mayol, P., *La Planète Rock: histoire d'une musique métisse, entre contestation et consommation*, Séminaires de Saint-Sabin, dossier des séminaires no. 2 (December 1993), Paris and Lausanne: Fondation pour le Progrès de l'Homme, 1994.

—— *Les Enfants de la liberté: études sur l'autonomie sociale et culturelle des jeunes en France 1970–1996*, Paris: L'Harmattan, 1997.

—— 'Les Mouvements issus de la jeunesse', in J.-L. Terradillos and M. Martin (eds), *La Fête techno: approche sociologique, médicale et juridique, d'un mouvement musical à un phénomène de société*, proceedings of colloquium held in Poitiers, 5–6 June 1997, Poitiers: Le Confort Moderne, 1997, pp. 14–19

Mignon, P., 'Paris/Givors: le rock local', in P. Mignon and A. Hennion (eds), *Rock: de l'histoire au mythe*, Paris: Anthropos, 1991, pp. 197–216.

—— 'Rock et rockers: un peuple du rock?', in A. Darré (ed.), *Musique et politique: les répertoires de l'identité*, Rennes: Presses Universitaires de Rennes, 1996, pp. 73–91.

—— 'Évolution de la prise en compte des musiques amplifiées par les politiques publiques', in Adem-Florida (ed.), *Politiques publiques et musiques amplifiées*, Groupe d'étude sur les musiques amplifiées, Aquitaine: Adem-Florida, Conseil Régional d'Aquitaine, 1997, pp. 23–31.

—— and Hennion, A. (eds), *Rock: de l'histoire au mythe*, Paris: Anthropos, 1991.

Ministère de la culture, *État et culture: la musique*, Paris: Documentation Française, 1992.

Moustaki, G. (with M. Righini), *Questions à la chanson*, Collection 'Questions', Paris: Stock, 1973.

Negus, K., *Popular Music in Theory: An Introduction*, Cambridge: Polity Press, 1996.

Ory, P., *L'Entre-deux-mai: histoire culturelle de la France mai 1968–mai 1981*, Paris: Seuil, 1983.

—— *L'Aventure culturelle française, 1945–1989*, Paris: Flammarion, 1989.

Pessis, J. and Blamangin, J.-P. (eds), *Génération Mireille*, Paris: Édition° 1, 1995.

Peterson, R.A., *Creating Country Music: Fabricating Authenticity*, Chicago and London: University of Chicago Press, 1997.

Petit-Castelli, C., *La Culture à la une, ou l'action culturelle dans les mairies socialistes*, Paris: Club Socialiste du Livre, 1981.

Poulanges, A., 'La Chanson à Saint-Germain et alentour', in P. Gumplowicz and J.-C. Klein (eds), *Paris 1944–1954. Artistes, intellectuels, publics: la culture comme enjeu*, Série Mémoires no. 38, Paris: Éditions Autrement, 1995, pp. 183–93.

Poulet, G., 'Popular Music', in M. Cook (ed.), *French Culture since 1945*, London and New York: Longman, 1993, pp. 192–214.

Racine, E., 'Diversité des fêtes techno', in J.-L. Terradillos and M. Martin (eds), *La Fête techno: approche sociologique, médicale et juridique, d'un mouvement musical à un phénomène de société*, proceedings of colloquium held in Poitiers, 5–6 June 1997, Poitiers: Le Confort Moderne, 1997, pp. 23–9.

Rearick, C., *The French in Love and War: Popular Culture in the Era of the World Wars*, New Haven and London: Yale University Press, 1997.

Renard, J., *L'Élan culturel: la France en mouvement*, Paris: Presses Universitaires de France, 1987.

Rigaud, J., *Libre Culture*, Collection Le Débat, Paris: Gallimard, 1990.

—— *L'Exception culturelle: culture et pouvoirs sous la 5ᵉ République*, Paris: Grasset, 1995.

Rigby, B., *Popular Culture in Modern France: A Study in Cultural Discourse*, London and New York: Routledge, 1991.

—— '*Les Pratiques culturelles des Français 1973–1989*: A Study of Changing Trends in the Presentation and Analysis of Government Statistics on Culture', in R. Chapman and N. Hewitt (eds), *Popular Culture and Mass Communication in Twentieth-Century France*, Lewiston/Queenston/Lampeter: Edwin Mellen Press, 1992, pp. 1–13.

—— and Hewitt, N. (eds), *France and the Mass Media*, Basingstoke: Macmillan, 1991.

Rioux, L., *Cinquante Ans de chanson française*, Paris: L'Archipel, 1994.

Rorem, N., 'The More Things Change: Notes on French Popular Song', in *Settling The Score: Essays on Music*, London: Harcourt Brace Jovanovich, 1988.

Rutten, P., 'Popular Music Policy: A Contested Area – The Dutch Experience', in T. Bennett, S. Frith, L. Grossberg, J. Shepherd and G. Turner (eds), *Rock and Popular Music: Politics, Policies, Institutions*, London and New York: Routledge, 1993, pp. 37–51.

Salachas, G. and Bottet, B., *Le Guide de la chanson française contemporaine*, Collection 'Alternatives', Paris: Syros, 1989.

Schneider, M., *La Comédie de la culture*, Paris: Éditions du Seuil, 1993.

Shuker, R., *Key Concepts in Popular Music*, London and New York: Routledge, 1998.

Silverman, M., *Facing Postmodernity: Contemporary French Thought on Culture and Society*, London and New York: Routledge, 1999.

—— 'The New Democracy: Michel Maffesoli and The Analysis of Everyday Life', in J. Marks and E. McCaffrey (eds), *French Cultural Debates*, Monash Romance Studies, Newark: University of Delaware Press, 2001, pp. 121–33.

Strazzulla, J., *La Techno*, Collection Les Compacts de l'info, Tournai: Casterman, 1998.

Street, J., *Politics and Popular Culture*, Cambridge: Polity Press, 1997.

Strinati, D., *An Introduction to Theories of Popular Culture*, London and New York: Routledge, 1995.

Teillet, P., 'Une Politique culturelle du rock?', in P. Mignon and A. Hennion (eds), *Rock: de l'histoire au mythe*, Paris: Anthropos, 1991, pp. 217–46.

—— 'L'État culturel et les musiques d'aujourd'hui', in A. Darré (ed.), *Musique et politique: les répertoires de l'identité*, Rennes: Presses Universitaires de Rennes, 1996, pp. 111–25.

—— 'Éléments pour une histoire des politiques publiques en faveur des "musiques amplifiées"', in P. Poirrier and V. Dubois (eds), *Les Collectivités locales et la culture: les formes de l'institutionnalisation, 19ᵉ–20ᵉ siècles*, Comité d'histoire du Ministère de la culture/Fondation Maison des sciences de l'homme, Paris: Documentation Française, 2002, pp. 361–93.

Terradillos, J.-L. and Martin, M. (eds), *La Fête techno: approche sociologique, médicale et juridique, d'un mouvement musical à un phénomène de société*, proceedings of colloquium held in Poitiers, 5–6 June 1997, Poitiers: Le Confort Moderne, 1997.

Torgue, H., *La Pop-Music et les musiques rock*, Que Sais-Je?, no. 1601, 4th updated edition, Paris: Presses Universitaires de France, 1997, first published as *La Pop-Music*, 1975.

Urfalino, P., *L'Invention de la politique culturelle*, Comité d'histoire du Ministère de la culture, Travaux et documents no. 3, Paris: Documentation Française, 1996.

Veitl, A. and Duchemin, N., *Maurice Fleuret: une politique démocratique de la musique 1981–1986*, Travaux et Documents, no. 10, Paris: Comité d'histoire du Ministère de la culture/Documentation Française, 2000.

Verlant, G. (ed.), *Le Rock et la plume: une histoire du rock par les meilleurs journalistes français 1960–1975*, Éditions Hors Collection, 2000.

Vernillat, F. and Charpentreau, J., *La Chanson française*, 2nd revised and corrected edition, Que Sais-Je?, no. 1453, Paris: Presses Universitaires de France, 1977.

Vian, B., *En avant la zizique, et par ici les gros sous*, revised and corrected edition, Paris: Pauvert/Livre de Poche, 1997 (first published 1958).

—— *Derrière la zizique*, revised and augmented edition (ed. G. Unglik), Paris: Christian Bourgois/Livre de Poche, 1997.

Victor, C., and Regoli, J., *Vingt Ans de rock français*, Paris: Albin Michel, 1978.

Vignol, B., *Cette Chanson que la télé assassine*, Saint-Cyr-sur-Loire: Christian Pirot, 2001.

Virolle, M., *La Chanson raï: de l'Algérie profonde à la scène internationale*, Paris: Karthala, 1995.

Waresquiel, E. de, *Dictionnaire des politiques culturelles de la France depuis 1959*, Paris: Larousse/CNRS Éditions, 2001.

Warne, C., 'The Impact of World Music in France', in A. Hargreaves and M. McKinney (eds), *Post-Colonial Cultures in France*, New York: Routledge, 1997, 133–49.

Yonnet, P., *Jeux, modes et masses: la société française et le moderne 1945–1985*, Paris: Gallimard, 1985.

Articles in Academic Journals and Conference Papers

Béreaud, J., 'La Chanson française depuis mai 1968', *French Review*, vol. 62, no. 2 (December 1988), pp. 229–41.

Cogneau, D., 'Le Rock existe: les sociologues l'ont rencontré. A' queu c'en est!' (three articles), *Yaourt*, no .5 (July-August 1990); no. 6 (October-November 1990), pp. 34–5; no.7 (December 1990), pp. 32–4.

Girard, A., 'Industries culturelles', *Futuribles*, no. 17, September-October 1978, pp. 597–605.

Gross, J. and Mark, V., 'Regionalist Accents of Global Music: The Occitan Rap of *Les Fabulous Trobadors*', *French Cultural Studies*, vol. 12, no. 34 (February 2001), pp. 77–94.

Hamblin, V.L., 'Le Clip et le look: Popular Music in the 1980s', *French Review*, vol. 64, no. 5 (April 1991), pp. 804–16.

Hennion, A., 'Music Lovers: Taste as Performance', *Theory, Culture and Society*, vol. 18, no. 5 (October 2001), pp. 1–22.

Jackson, J.H., 'Making Enemies: Jazz in Inter-War Paris', *French Cultural Studies*, vol. 10, no. 29 (June 1999), pp. 179–99.

Looseley, D.L., 'Cultural Policy in the 21st century: Issues, Debates and Discourse', *French Cultural Studies*, vol .10, no. 28 (February 1999), pp. 5–20.

—— 'Facing the Music: French Cultural Policy from a British Perspective', *International Journal of Cultural Policy*, vol. 7, no. 1 (December 2000), pp. 115–29.

McGuigan, J., 'New Labour, Cultural Policy Proper and as Display', unpublished paper read to the Tribunal on Cultural Policy, University of Copenhagen, 20–3 April 1999.

Mignon, P., 'Existe-t-il une "culture rock"?', *Esprit*, July 1993, pp. 140–50 (interview with Mignon).

—— 'Y a-t-il une culture jeunes?', *Projet*, no. 251 (Autumn 1997), pp. 65–71 (interview with Mignon).

Nettlebeck, C., 'Jazz at the Théâtre Graslin: A Founding Story', *French Cultural Studies*, vol. 11, no. 32 (June 2000), p. 216.

Peterson, R.A., 'Why 1955? Explaining the Advent of Rock Music', *Popular Music*, vol. 9, no. 1 (January 1990), pp. 97–116.

Touché, M., 'Où suis-je? Qui suis-je? Dans quel état j'erre?', paper presented at Rencontres du Grand Zebrock 1998 (extracted from his book *Mémoire vive*, Annecy: Édition Association Musiques Amplifiées, 1998).

Bibliography

Selected Press Articles

Bollon, P., 'Le Printemps de la chanson française', *L'Express*, 24 April 1987, pp. 51–3.

Bombereau, G., 'Au Rebord du monde, des passagers en marge', *Cultures en mouvement*, no. 21 (October 1999), pp. 46–8.

Bonneau, J.-C., 'La Nouvelle Génération', in 'Le Dossier rocks nationaux', *Écouter Voir* (January 1990), pp. 29–30.

Bonnieux, B., 'Une Certaine Tendance du rock français', in 'Le Dossier rocks nationaux', *Écouter Voir* (January 1990), pp. 26–8.

Cathus, O., 'Les Flonflons d'la balle', *Cultures en mouvement*, no. 21 (October 1999), pp. 26–8.

Calvet, L.-J., 'Une Non-Politique', *Les Nouvelles Littéraires*, 23 April 1981, p. 35.

Chapier, H., 'Complot contre la chanson française', *Le Monde*, 26–7 August 1979.

—— 'Pour en finir avec la chanson française', *Le Monde*, 3 July 1980, p. 17.

Chorus, 'Cabrel, Goldman, Simon et Souchon: Chorus met ses "parrains" sur la sellette' (interview), no. 1 (Autumn 1992), pp. 10–32.

—— '19ᵉ Printemps de Bourges: le rock en baisse, le rap en hausse', no. 12 (Summer 1995), pp. 74–7.

—— 'Le Dossier: Renaud', no. 13 (Autumn 1995), pp. 88–110.

—— 'Le Dossier: Maxime Le Forestier', no. 15 (Spring 1996), pp. 75–98.

—— 'Le Grand Forum de l'an 2000: la chanson de *Chorus*', no. 30 (January-March 2000), pp. 72–132.

Cultures en mouvement, no. 21 (October 1999), issue devoted to 'Hip-hop, techno: rythmes de passages?'

Davet, S., 'Le Son techno prend le pas sur la danse aux Nuits Boréalis', *Le Monde*, 12 August 1997, p. 17.

Delassen, S., 'Saga Mitsouko', *Le Nouvel-Observateur*, 24 February–1 March 2000, pp. 52–4.

Delbourg, P., 'Sept Ans de culture: la chanson. Les rengaines dans l'isoloir', *Les Nouvelles Littéraires*, 23 April 1981, p. 35.

Desmille, Sylvain, 'La Vague aléatoire de la musique techno', *Le Monde Diplomatique*, February 1999, p. 28.

Événement du Jeudi, L', 'Le printemps très politique de Bourges: Rock against Le Pen' (feature), 10–16 April 1997, pp. 70–3.

Express, L', 'Le Rock'n'roll aujourd'hui' (interview with Daniel Filipacchi, Lucien Morisse and Frankie Jordan), 22 June 1961, pp. 44–5.

Fléouter, C., 'Où en est la chanson', booklet (16 pp.), supplement to *Tendances*, no. 73 (October 1971).

—— 'Ouverture du 23ᵉ MIDEM à Cannes. Le marché du disque tourne rond', *Le Monde*, 22–3 January 1989, p. 13.

Gardinier, Alain, '"World music" ou l'air du temps', *Le Courrier de l'UNESCO*, March 1991, pp. 37–9.

Herpin, T., 'Sept Ans de culture: le disque. Taxé, libéré, piraté', *Les Nouvelles Littéraires*, 23 April 1981, p. 37.

Bibliography

Hidalgo, F., 'Un Cri dans le silence', *Paroles et musique*, no. 1 (June-July 1980), p. 3.

Inrockuptibles, Les, special issue 'Made in France', 7–27 July 1999.

Jeangeot, P., 'Génération son', *Sciences et Avenir*, no. 79 (October 1990), pp. 62–3.

Label France, no. 36 (July 1999), dossier 'La Musique en fête' (feature on French music consisting of eleven articles).

Lapassade, G., 'Deux manières d être au monde', *Cultures en mouvement*, no. 21 (October 1999), pp. 44–5.

Lasén, A., 'Une filiation bâtarde', *Cultures en mouvement*, no. 21 (October 1999), pp. 49–52.

Leymarie, I., 'Musiques du monde: le grand métissage', *Le Courrier de l'UNESCO*, March 1991, pp. 9–11.

Mallat, R., 'Disque la chute', *Le Point*, 14 January 1980, pp. 93–0.

Mauriac, F., 'Le Bloc-notes de François Mauriac (samedi 6 juillet)', *Le Figaro Littéraire*, 13 July 1963, p. 18.

Monde, Le, 'Une Politique de la musique pour la France, 1974–1981', 18 February 1981, p. 17.

—— '33e MIDEM: les enjeux technologiques', 27 January 1999 (downloaded).

Morin, E., 'Salut les copains', *Le Monde*, 6 July 1963, pp. 1 and 11; and 7–8 July 1963, p. 12.

Mortaigne, V., 'Les Couacs de la chanson française', *Le Monde*, 2 August 1997, pp. 1 and 10.

—— 'Éloge de la techno, nouvelle écologie', *Le Monde*, 13 August 1998, pp. 1 and 10.

Nouvel-Observateur, Le, 'Le Choc du rock' (feature), 17–23 June 1983, pp. 40–5.

Osborne, B., 'We Are Not Control Freaks. We Are Freedom Freaks', *Guardian* (G2 supplement), 13 March 2001, p. 12.

Paris Match, '1969. Ferré, Brel, Brassens, trois géants se rencontrent', 29 July 1993, pp. 54–5.

Petit, J.-C. and Rockwell, J., 'Chanson française face à la vague américaine', *Le Monde des débats*, June 1994.

Politis, special 'Culture' issue (tenth anniversary of Mitterrand's election), 3–10 January 1991.

Rouard, D., 'Une Vie de rave', *Le Monde*, 19 December 1997, p. 15.

Salut les copains, no. 13 (August 1963).

Shusterman, R., 'L'Expérience esthétique du rap', *Cultures en mouvement*, no. 21 (October 1999), pp. 29–32.

Sweeney, P., 'Le Sound Barrier', *The Sunday Times* ('The Culture' supplement), 11 February 1996, p. 14.

Time Out Paris Free Guide, 'Touch Down or Lift Off?' (interview with Christophe Conte and Pascal Dauzier), 'The Music Issue', Autumn 2001, pp. 15–17; contains various other articles on French popular music.

Trautmann, C., 'Paroles de ministre' (interview), *Coda*, October 1997, pp. 25–6.

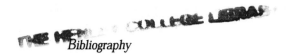

Reports, Speeches and Other Documents

BIPE (A. Le Diberder and S. Pflieger), *Crise et mutation du domaine musical*, Paris: Documentation Française, 1987.

Chapier, H., 'Plateforme d'action pour la chanson française: rapport de mission soumis à M. Jean-Philippe Lecat, Ministre de la culture et de la communication', 25 July 1980, unpublished.

Commission nationale des musiques actuelles (Dutilh report), 'Rapport de la Commission nationale des musiques actuelles à Catherine Trautmann, Ministre de la culture et de la communication', September 1998; unpublished: consists of the 'rapport general' and a number of separate contributions by various working groups, including 'Les Publics' (P. Teillet), separately paginated.

Développement culturel. 'La Musique en amateur', no. 107 (June 1995).

——— 'Le Public des concerts de musiques amplifiées', no. 122 (June 1998).

Donnat, O., *Les Pratiques culturelles des Français: enquête 1997*, Paris: Documentation Française/Ministère de la culture et de la communication, 1998.

——— and Cogneau, D. (Ministry of Culture), *Nouvelle Enquête sur les pratiques culturelles des Français* (statistical volume), Paris: Documentation Française, 1990; accompanied by:

——— and Cogneau, D., *Les Pratiques culturelles des Français 1973–1989* (comparative volume), Paris: La Découverte/Documentation Française, 1990.

Fédération nationale des élus socialistes et républicains (FNESR), 'La Création artistique dans la cité' (report of the FNESR's 'Rencontre de Rennes', 24–5 October 1980), in *Communes de France*, document no. 16.

Hurstel J., 'Rapport. Jeunesse et action culturelle', unpublished and undated; adapted as Jean Hurstel, *Jeunes au bistrot: cultures sur macadam*, Syros, 1984.

Lang, Jack, two unpublished bound volumes of speeches (typed), July 1981–March 1985.

Lettre d'information, no.297 (11 February 1991).

——— no.336 (26 November 1992).

——— no.407 (13 March 1996).

——— 'Les États-généraux du disque', supplement to no.52 (new series) (21 July 1999).

Lion, B. (main author), Comming D., Karezewski, 'Le Rock à la recherche de lieux', Ministère de la culture/SER, 1985.

Ministère de la culture, 'Musique', booklet in the collection of booklets composing 'La Politique culturelle 1981–5: bilan de la législature' [1986?].

——— 'Rock et variétés: conférence de presse de Jack Lang' (press dossier), 25 September 1989.

Rigaud, J. (President of the Commission d'étude de la politique culturelle de l'État), *Rapport au Ministre de la culture. Pour une refondation de la politique culturelle*, Paris: Documentation Française, 1996.

Sevran, P, 'A propos de la chanson française. Mémoire à l'intention de Monsieur Jack Lang Ministre de la culture', unpublished, 1981.

Bibliography

Audiovisual Sources (in date order)

TV Programmes

'Soirée Jacques Brel', ARTE, 24 August 1994.

'Culture rock: spécial Printemps de Bourges' (twentieth anniversary), M6, 14 April 1996.

'Brel' ('Lumières du music-hall' series), La Cinquième, 5 April 1998.

'Soirée Montand', ARTE, 12 April 1998.

'Monsieur Gainsbourg', France 3, 16 June 1998.

'Les Années Barclay', France 3, 14 September 1999.

'Serge Gainsbourg' (twentieth anniversary of his death), TV5, 16 March 2001.

Radio Programmes

'La Culture underground', France Culture, 19 April 1997.

'Le Rock débarque en France' ('Histoire en direct' series), France Culture, 2 June 1997.

Interview Charles Trenet, France Inter, 25 October 1999, repeated on 'Trafic d'influence' (Philippe Bertrand), France Inter, 19 February 2001.

Theses

Harrison, K., 'A Critical Introduction to the Work of the Singer-Songwriter Renaud', MA by research thesis, University of Leeds, UK, 2000.

Teillet, P., 'Le Discours culturel et le rock: l'expérience des limites de la politique culturelle de l'État', doctoral thesis in political science, University of Rennes I, Faculty of Juridical Sciences, 1992.

Interviews

Abélard, Jean-Rémy, 14 April 2000.

Donnat, Olivier, 20 July 2000.

Massé, Monique, 12 April 2000.

Mayol, Pierre, 6 April 1998.

Ménage, André, 11 April 2000.

Mignon, Patrick, 20 July 2000.

Index

Core topics such as 'music', 'popular music', 'pop' or 'rock' are only listed below in relation to other topics. Book, song and album titles are listed under the name of the appropriate author, composer or performer. The reader is also referred to the Chronology, which is not included below.

Index